What's
Holding
You Back?

ALSO BY SAM HORN

Tongue Fu!®
ConZentrate

WHAT'S HOLDING YOU BACK?

30 Days to Having the Courage and Confidence
to Do What You Want, Meet Whom You Want,
and Go Where You Want

SAM HORN

St. Martin's Griffin ☙ New York

Design by Judith Stagnitto Abbate

ISBN 0-312-25440-7

Originally published as *Concrete Confidence: A 30-Day Program for an
Unshakable Foundation of Self-Assurance*

First St. Martin's Griffin Edition: March 2000

10 9 8 7 6 5 4 3 2 1

"A true friend unbosoms freely, advises justly, assists readily, adventures boldly, takes all patiently, defends courageously, and continues a friend unchangeably."

— WILLIAM PENN

*Dedicated to
my sister, Cheri Grimm.
Penn could have added: ". . . laughs frequently,
listens empathetically, and supports constantly."
Thank you, Sis, for continuing to be
one of the great joys in my world.
Life is infinitely better because I get to share it with you.
You are a blessing.*

CONTENTS

INTRODUCTION

I was raised in a small Southern California town (more horses than people) with books, TV, and movie magazines as my constant companions. Until age fourteen, I viewed the "big world out there" from an isolated mountain valley. I pored over articles and photographs that showed in delicious detail the glamorous lifestyles of Hollywood's oh-so-distant celebrities. I envied them their "perfect" lives. I used to think, "Wouldn't it be wonderful to never feel nervous, to never feel uncomfortable or out of place? Wouldn't it be great to always know the right thing to say?" These stars seemed to be sublimely, supremely confident. I hoped that one day I would grow up to be just like them: never at a loss for words, never shy, never a moment's worry.

After I graduated from college, fate conspired to land me on Hilton Head Island in South Carolina, an enclave for affluent homeowners and vacationers. Working at Rod Laver's tennis resort gave me the long-awaited opportunity to rub elbows with the rich and famous I had admired from afar. Much to my surprise, many of these well-known public figures did not have it all together. I discovered that some captains of industry were still terrified at the thought of having to speak in public. The most beautiful woman I'd ever seen (a popular cover model) confessed to being embarrassed about her "skinny" body. A champion athlete obsessed over whether to ask someone for a date. A jet-setter couple lounging on their luxurious yacht looked surprisingly bored and dissatisfied.

I was curious. How could it be that some of these people who had what seemed to be everything going for them didn't particularly like themselves or their lives? How could it be that a sophisticated media personality was plagued with the same insecurities and fears I felt? How could it be that some of these larger-than-life figures were in reality painfully self-conscious and self-deprecating?

At the same time, I had the pleasure of meeting individuals who were as ideally confident as I had always yearned to be. Some of these blissfully contented people were prosperous, some were not. The ones who were consistently confident all shared a common characteristic: they had an amazing ability to put themselves and others at ease, and they seemed devoid of the anxiety that often accompanies a strong need for approval. They appeared to be delightfully at peace with themselves and the world around them.

Those firsthand encounters led me to understand that this thing called confidence is *not* determined by external accolades, acquisitions, or accoutrements. That insight launched me on a lifelong quest to identify exactly what does make us confident or not. Using the questionnaire that you will find on page 11 as a tool, I started asking executives, mothers, lawyers, teachers, kids, salespeople, senior citizens, artists, supervisors, and psychologists what had *contributed* to their confidence and what had *compromised* it.

What I discovered is good news if you've ever wished you could be more confident. You can be. Confidence is not a mysterious characteristic we're born with or not, and it's not a result of extraordinary success, accessible only to an exalted few who achieve superhuman feats. Confidence is a skill *anyone* can acquire. Regardless of your past or present circumstances, you can build a solid self-assurance that is *not* situational. Years of research have allowed me to pinpoint the secrets that can help you develop constant confidence, an ever-present poise that does not depend on where you are or who you're with.

In 1979, I began presenting my findings in public workshops for the Open University of Washington, D.C. I focused on real-life ways participants could be more comfortable in everyday situations. The testimonials began to pour in, and they continue to pour in from the thousands of participants who have attended the corporate and convention presentations I've given across the country. You'll find many of those success stories in these pages, illustrating that people just like you have used these techniques to change their lives for the better.

Virginia Satir said, "I want to get you excited about who you are. . . what can still be for you. I want to inspire you to see that you can go far beyond where you are right now." That's the objective of *What's Holding You Back?*: to give you practical tools to help you become the person you've always wanted to be.

Yogi Berra said (as only he could), "Baseball is ninety percent mental and the other half is physical." In this book you'll learn attitudes and behaviors that can help you feel and act confident anytime, anywhere, and with anyone. I promise not to waste time on theories or platitudes. My dad used to tell me, "Many people want to improve themselves; not many want to work at it." *What's Holding You Back?* is designed to make the work to better yourself easier.

The book is divided into thirty brief chapter/steps. Every chapter ends with a Starting Today Assignment to help you transform what you've just read into real-world results. "Vigor is contagious," noted Ralph Waldo Emerson, "and whatever makes us either think or feel strongly adds to our power." Confidence is also contagious. You will "catch" confidence as you take these steps because they cause you to think and act strong. Better yet, you'll accumulate a growing sense of power ("I can") instead of feeling powerless ("I can't").

You've probably heard Lao-Tzu's famous observation that "The journey of a thousand miles begins with a single step." Vow to yourself right now that you're going to begin your journey to confidence by doing at least one step per day. Each chapter can be read in less than fifteen minutes, so even if you're busy, you can still keep your commitment to complete an assignment a day. Just ask yourself if improving your relationships, performance, and morale is worth fifteen minutes of your time. If it is, turn those intentions into action and you'll be well on your way to acting and feeeling more confident, day in and day out.

PART I

How'd I Get
So Messed Up, Anyway?

"Self-reflection is the school of wisdom."

- B A L T A S A R   B R A C I A N

Understand the Six Cs of Confidence

"Scientists have found the gene for shyness. They would have found it years ago, but it was hiding behind a couple of other genes."
- JONATHAN KATZ

Have you ever wondered why sometimes you're confident and other times you're not? Have you ever wondered why some people can be completely comfortable in almost any situation, and others are barely able to get out the door? You're not the only one who has puzzled over this. This question has been asked in every workshop I've ever offered. One woman asked plaintively, "How can my sister be the picture of confidence, and I'm just the opposite? She loves the spotlight. I run from it. She can talk with anybody about anything. I trip over my tongue just trying to say hello. She doesn't care what people think; I worry about it all the time."

This woman had asked the quintessential question. What determines whether we're confident? Contrary to what Jonathan Katz said, it's not a shyness gene. In this first chapter, I briefly identify the six factors that create confidence and explain how each influences us. The rest of the book is then dedicated to how to put these factors to work *for* us rather than *against* us.

Give Me Six CCCCCCs of Confidence

"Whatever you cannot understand, you cannot possess."
—JOHANN WOLFGANG VON GOETHE

Understanding what constitutes confidence can help you possess it. As you read each of these criteria, ask yourself whether it has helped your confidence or hindered it.

1. Communication skills. Lee Iacocca has said, "If you can't get along with people, you don't belong in this business, because that's all we have around here." Face it. If we can't get along with people, we may feel we don't belong *anywhere*. Are your interpersonal skills an asset or an albatross? Can you communicate in a way that commands the positive interest, cooperation, and respect of the people you deal with?

The word *popular* is rarely used outside of high school, yet it still factors into whether we feel confident. Popular is defined as "to be liked or esteemed." Do you feel liked and esteemed by others, or do you feel isolated and estranged? The quality of our relationships is directly proportionate to the quality of our communication. The ability to educate, entertain, enlighten, and inspire through words is power (the ability to get things done). Can you express your ideas, insights, wishes, rights, and needs in a way that actualizes them? The ability to express our needs and desires to others determines whether we feel connected or disconnected. Are you able to say what you want when you want to whom you want in the way you want? Or are you frequently tongue-tied and unable to articulate how you feel?

2. Concept. How would you describe yourself? What kind of person are you? What adjectives would you use to paint a verbal picture of what you're like? Louis Auchincloss said, "The only thing that keeps a man going is energy. And what is energy but liking life?" What is confidence but liking yourself? Do you view yourself negatively or positively? Do you have flattering or unflattering nicknames (smart vs. stupid) for yourself? Have you locked onto a limiting label ("I'm such a klutz"), or have you given yourself limitless labels ("I'm a capable person"). Do you have a healthy regard for yourself and your powers (the definition of confidence)?

Now describe your *ideal* self. What would you *like* to be like? What adjectives would you select to describe the person you want to be? What are some of the attributes and characteristics of your ultimate you?

The question is, How much of a gap is there between the person you are now and the person you'd *like* to be? If your actual self is almost the same as your ideal self, then you have a healthy self-concept. You probably feel confident because you are the way you want to be.

On the other hand, if you are nothing like your ideal self, then you probably don't feel confident because you're not who you want to be. You don't measure up to your own expectations.

There's an important caveat. Is your image of your actual self accurate? Many of us have an undeservedly negative impression of ourselves because we are our own worst critic. We focus only on what we do wrong and never give ourselves credit for what we do well. We literally and figuratively can't do anything right in our own eyes. It's *impossible* to have confidence if we are habitually hard on ourselves.

There's another important question to ask. Is your ideal self achievable? Some of us doom ourselves to fail, by trying to measure up to unattainable standards. Are you a perfectionist? Perfectionists stack the self-esteem deck against themselves.

Finally, how do you talk to yourself? Does that little voice inside your head that observes and second-guesses everything you do support or sabotage you? Does it build you up or tear you down, empower or immobilize you?

3. Competence. What are you good at? Have you mastered a vocation, sport, or hobby? Do you have current, tangible evidence of your talents, or do you have a case of the "I used to's"? Competence is almost synonymous with confidence. Yet many of us have abandoned the activities that gave us opportunities to excel. Anne Brontë said, "All talents increase in the using." If we haven't been using our talents, our confidence has probably taken a nosedive because we no longer have frequent proof that we're capable. The same is true if you're between jobs. If your identity comes from your career, it may be tough to feel capable if you're unemployed and can't find work.

4. Contribution. We can have all the other factors going for us, but if we don't feel we are contributing, we'll still be asking ourselves, "Is this all there is?"

Leo Rosten believed that "The purpose of life is not to be happy, it's to matter, to feel that it's made some difference that we have lived at all." Rosten wasn't saying it's not important to be happy; it is. We want to celebrate life, have fun, enjoy ourselves. That's just not why we're here. We're here to in some way make the world a better place, to feel that somehow, someone is a little better off because of what we did for him or her.

Do you feel you matter? Are you making a difference? Knowing that you are a contributing member of society gives you a sense of worth that is unconditional. If in your soul you know you count, you have a solid core of confidence you carry with you wherever you go.

5. Control. Are you spending time the way you want? Are you living where you want, with whom you want? Are you making the kind of money you'd like, involved in satisfying activities? Are you comfortable standing up for your rights and asserting your needs? Or is your life "not your own"? If you're unhappy with your career, relationships, hometown, and/or social life, it's hard to have a healthy regard for yourself and your powers. If you feel like you're a victim because other people are taking advantage of you, it will be difficult to like yourself or your life.

Self-respect and control are like the chicken and the egg. The more in charge you are of your life, the more respect you have for yourself. The more you respect yourself, the more confidently you assert yourself and make sure you're getting what you want, need, and deserve out of life.

There's good news. It's unrealistic to think we can be in complete control of our lives. No one has the perfect existence. What I've found after talking with thousands of people is that 90 percent of our lives can be unsatisfactory and we can *still* have self-respect if we are actively involved in or pursuing *one* personally significant goal or dream.

You may be in a "golden handcuffs" situation where you dread going to work, but you stick with this position because it provides for your family and pays the mortgage. If on Saturday, though, you head out to the glider field and take off in a sailplane for a few precious hours of soaring—that one morning can compensate for the rest of the week that's not to your liking.

Are you actively engaged in some meaningful activity that makes up for otherwise miserable circumstances? We can maintain a healthy regard for ourselves if we know intolerable situations are temporary and/or that we're choosing to accept them because they're part of a larger plan.

6. Courage. When comedian Steven Wright was asked, "How do you feel?" he answered, "Well, you know, when you're sitting on a chair and you lean back so you're just on two legs, and you lean too far and you almost fall over, and you catch yourself? I feel like that all the time."

Do you find yourself feeling like this when trying something new or tackling something challenging? We *all* do! It's not that confident people don't have fears, they just choose to act in spite of them. It's normal to feel anxious when putting ourselves on the line—whether it's taking a test, going on a blind date, asking for a raise, or walking into a job interview. If we give in to our anxieties, we end up retreating and withdrawing, reluctant to venture outside what's familiar, comfortable, and safe.

Jean Anouilh said, "To say yes, you have to sweat and roll up your sleeves and plunge both hands into life up to the elbows." Confident people say *yes* to life by refusing to be paralyzed by their doubts. They know that personal growth is a result of taking wise risks. Confident people know action is the antidote to fear.

Are you a courageous person? Have you resolved to work through your issues instead of running from them? As Sir Winston Churchill said, "Courage is rightly esteemed the first of human qualities because it is the quality which guarantees all the others." Do you have the courage to do what you *want* and *need* to do, despite your fears and anxieties?

Tally It Up
— ◉ —

"Ninety percent of the world's woes comes from people not knowing themselves, their abilities, their frailties, and even their real virtues. Most of us go almost all the way though life as complete strangers to ourselves."

—SYDNEY J. HARRIS

So how do you rate . . . in your own eyes? *Do* take it personally! What matters is how you feel about yourself, not what other people tell you. Confucius suggested, "Study the past if you would divine the future." Once and for all, look back over your life and figure out how you rate with the six Cs (or as a student once put it, the Cliffs Notes of Confidence).

Communication: Are you able to express yourself in a way that helps you get what you want, need, and deserve?

Concept: Do you have a healthy regard for yourself and your powers?

Competence: Are you actively involved in activities that give you a sense of capability and mastery?

Contribution: Do you feel that you matter, that you're making a difference?

| **Control:** | Do you feel like you're in charge of your-self and your life? |
| **Courage:** | Are you able to overcome your fears and take wise risks? |

From This Day Forward . . .
━━━━━━━━━━◉━━━━━━━━━━

"Is there ever any particular spot where one can put one's finger and say, 'It all began that day, at such a time and such a place, with such an incident?'"

—AGATHA CHRISTIE

The answer to Agatha Christie's question is yes! At the end of this and every chapter is a sample Starting Today Assignment followed by a sample Action Plan. The Action Plan gives you a concrete example of how someone else put these ideas into practice. The sample Starting Today Assignment suggests one way you could take action; however, you may have a better way. Please use your own words to create a personally meaningful assignment. The more senses we use to imprint information, the more likely we are to remember and use it. If you read, write, and say out loud how you intend to follow up, you're much more likely to actually do it. Or as Samuel Goldwyn expressed it, "A verbal agreement isn't worth the paper it's written on." Please fill out, sign, and date your first Starting Today Assignment so in the weeks, months, and years ahead, you can look back and say, "My new life of confidence began this day."

Sample Starting Today Assignment

"What is important is to begin."
—HORACE

PLEASE TAKE THE TIME TO fill out the questionnaire on page 11. Reflect upon what has helped you to be confident and what hasn't, and then be done with it! To *look* back is one thing, to *stay* back is another. A Spanish proverb states that "self-knowledge is the beginning of self-improvement." Once you have thoroughly thought through your "confidence history," turn your attention to how you can improve your confidence from this day forward. ◎

Action Plan for Understanding the Six Cs of Confidence

Pam was shy as a child and always hoped she'd outgrow it. She now realizes that confidence doesn't automatically come with adulthood. Her first task is to identify what has helped her confidence and what has hurt it. Her next step is to adopt the attitudes and behaviors that build her self-esteem rather than block it.

BLOCKERS	BUILDERS
Poor communication skills *"I'm so shy. I don't know what to say to these people."*	Good communication skills *"I'm going to go over and introduce myself."*
Critical self-concept *"I can never do anything right."*	Healthy self-concept *"I'm doing the best I can."*
Feel incompetent *"I'm not talented at anything."*	Feel competent *"I'm a good musician."*

Life is out of control	Life is in control
"I hate my life. I feel like I've souled out."	*"I'm glad I started saving evenings for my family and myself."*

Not making a contribution	Making a contribution
"Nothing I do matters. Nobody cares whether I live or die."	*"I try to do something that makes a difference for someone daily."*

Has no courage, avoids risks	Has courage, takes risks
"I'm just not comfortable going places by myself."	*"I'm going to overcome my nervousness and go anyway."*

MY PERSONAL STARTING TODAY ASSIGNMENT

Starting today I'm going to _____

_____

_____

Signed _____ Date _____

Confidence Questionnaire
————◉————

1. To me, confidence means _____
_____.

2. A confident person I know is _____.
What makes them confident is _____.

3. Do you consider yourself a confident person? Why or why
not? _____
_____
_____.

4. Someone or something that's helped me to be confident is
_____
_____.

5. Someone or something that's hurt my confidence is _____
_____
_____.

6. I am most confident when _____
_____
_____.

7. I lose my confidence when _____
_____
_____.

8. The most important lesson I've learned about confidence is
_____
_____
_____.

9. The best advice I could give someone about how to be more
confident is _____
_____
_____.

PART II

Communication: The Keys to Connecting

"Once a human being has arrived on this earth, communication is the largest single factor determining what kinds of relationships he makes with others and what happens to him."

— VIRGINIA SATIR

Don't Wait, Initiate

*"Life is to be fortified with many friendships. To love and be loved
is the greatest happiness of existence."*
- SYDNEY SMITH

Remember the three Rs we were supposed to learn in school? Reading, (W)Riting, and (A)Rithmetic? What happened to the fourth R . . . Relationships?

We're taught about the French and Indian War, but we're not taught how to get along with people. We're taught how to figure out the cube root of 27, but we're never taught how to use words constructively. We're taught the leading export of Brazil, but we're not taught how to develop meaningful relationships

Wouldn't you agree that learning how to communicate confidently and effectively is more important than being able to regurgitate statistics about Brazil's coffee crop? Yet most of us pass through grade after grade without one course on how to interact successfully with other people. Somehow we're just supposed to know how to get over the nervousness that goes along with meeting someone new. We're supposed to find out for ourselves how to strike up conversations and keep them going. We're supposed to discover on our own how to, as Dale Carnegie put it, make friends and influence people.

Some of us have never learned. We're in our twenties, thirties, forties, fifties, and sixties still saying the wrong thing at the wrong time to the wrong person.

Getting to Know You

"All real living is meeting."
-MARTIN BUBER

It's time we learned the factor that, as Virginia Satir points out, largely determines what happens to us on this earth. The next seven chapters explain how we can get good at communicating with people. Because if you knew, *really* knew, that you had the ability to draw someone out and interact with him in a way that allowed both of you to relax and enjoy yourselves, wouldn't that give you the ability to go anywhere, anytime, and meet anyone . . . with confidence?

You may be thinking, "This is easy for people who are born extroverts. The problem is, I'm a born introvert." The good news is you can nurture a shy nature if you so choose. Even if you're predisposed to being a "social coward," as one of my students put it, you can acquire the ability to be more socially confident. That's what being a grown-up is all about—evaluating your behavior to see if it is helping or hindering you. If your current interpersonal skills are contributing to your confidence, great. If they're compromising it, you have the power to change.

Alone Together

"Speech is civilization itself . . . it is silence which isolates."
-THOMAS MANN

One evening after I wrapped up a public seminar in Los Angeles on the topic of conversation, *no one left*. I repeated my concluding statements. Everyone stayed put. I thought maybe I hadn't made it clear that the workshop was over, so I reiterated that the course was finished and they were free to go. At that point several people got up and started talking to each other. Within a couple of minutes, everyone was happily involved in animated conversations. A half hour later, after it was clear no one intended to leave anytime soon, I suggested we retire to the hotel lounge to continue the party, which everyone promptly did.

A participant approached me as I gathered my materials and offered an interesting insight into what had just taken place. He said, "Sam, everyone here is surrounded by people from the moment they wake up to the moment they go to bed. We live in a city with over two million people, and the ironic thing is, we're all *lonely*. Many of us work elbow to elbow with dozens of co-workers all day every day, yet we don't feel connected. For many of us in this room, this is the first time in a long time we've been in a relaxed group of people where everyone is genuinely enjoying themselves."

Face-to-Face Communication in a Computer-to-Computer World

◎

"The newest computer can merely compound, at speed, the oldest problem in relations between human beings, and in the end, the communicator will be confronted with the old problem of what to say and how to say it."
–EDWARD R. MURROW

This experience opened my eyes to a disturbing phenomenon. It seems the more advanced our electronic communication is, the more our personal relationships suffer. Some people would rather e-mail their co-worker in the next cubicle than walk five steps and speak to him or her person to person. Internet junkies talk with people halfway around the world, but don't know their neighbors.

There are certainly exceptions to the generalization that our interpersonal skills are regressing while our high-tech skills are progressing. Many people have found e-mail and web sites a fascinating source of information and a low-cost, convenient way to keep in touch. I've heard stories of college students who hardly exchanged a word with their parents throughout their entire adolescence, who are now regularly swapping on-line messages. I've read articles about physically isolated individuals (GICs—geographically inconvenients) who belong to numerous chat rooms so they can "talk story" with people who share similar interests.

So there are certainly advantages to our advances in technology. There are also downsides. As futurist John Naisbitt observed, "We're drowning in information and starved for knowledge." If the consensus from my workshops means anything, we're drowning in people and starved for friendship. Or, as the case may be, we're surrounded by people and don't have the confidence to approach them.

Delightful Opportunities or Dreaded Obligations?
———◉———

"My friend thought he'd never get a date. I told him to think positive. Now he's positive he's never going to get a date."
—BROTHER SAMMY SHORE

Would you like to know the first secret to developing fulfilling relationships? It's easy. All you have to do is approach people *positively*.

You may scoff, "Don't insult my intelligence, I know that." You're right. Both you and I know it. The question is, do we do it? To approach others positively might seem an obvious suggestion, yet many of us do just the opposite. We walk into a party thinking, "This is going to be a waste of time." We register for a business mixer thinking, "No one's going to be interested in me." We continue to harbor our doubts until something negative happens, which we immediately use as evidence to prove our misgivings were justified.

From now on, our goal is to use the mantra "Give it a chance" whenever we're about to talk ourselves out of something we want to do. In *Tongue Fu!*, I suggest we give people a chance by not forming opinions about them until *after* we've met. We need to do the same with events. Decide whether a get-together is worthwhile after we've experienced it, not when we haven't set foot in the door.

Give It a Chance
————————◉————————

"Success often comes to those who dare and act; it seldom goes to the timid who are ever afraid of consequences."
—JAWAHARLAL NEHRU

A friend of mine had always dreamed of having her own restaurant. After years of planning and saving, she opened up a deli in a small town. Patty offered an enticing array of food and gave gracious service to everyone who walked through the door. Unfortunately, not enough people walked through the door. Her deli was tucked away on a side street and didn't get much walkby or drive-by traffic. She didn't have the three requirements of a successful retail outlet . . . location, location, location.

After six months, Patty hadn't begun to turn a profit and her bills mounted ever higher. She called one day in tears, and we talked about possible remedies. I suggested, "Why not get involved with your local chamber of commerce? Perhaps you could cater their monthly meetings and deliver meals to members who are working through their lunch hour on special projects."

Patty demurred, "I'm not a joiner. I've never been comfortable in groups." I countered, "Patty, support from the local community could determine whether you make it through this first tough year. Your shop's survival could depend on whether you establish visibility in your neighborhood." She reluctantly admitted this was true and agreed to attend the next meeting, scheduled for the following Wednesday.

The big day arrived and Patty started driving to the program. Guess what was going through her mind? "I'm not looking forward to this. This is the *last* place I want to go. These people don't know me. I'm going to feel so out of place." Her dread kept growing until in a moment of self-induced panic she gave in to her fears and turned around and drove back to her shop.

By the end of the year, Patty was forced to close her deli. She had to find a job to start paying off all her accumulated debts. She joined a bookkeeping company, and a week after she was hired, her boss volunteered Patty to be the treasurer of the chamber of commerce. She didn't even ask Patty's permission. This firm traditionally provided the accounting services for the chamber, and her boss knew Patty would do a good job.

Would you believe, within a few months, Patty's social life revolved around the chamber of commerce? By the end of the year Patty had made dozens of new friends through her chamber activities. Patty is now *president* of the chamber of commerce! The sad part of this story is that every once in a while, Patty wonders if she had talked herself into attending that luncheon instead of out of it, she'd be a successful entrepreneur today.

Turn Strangers into Friends
─────────◎─────────

"Fears make strangers out of people who could be friends."
–SHIRLEY MACLAINE

Have you ever talked yourself out of something you wanted to do? Have you ever considered going somewhere new, and decided not to because you focused on your fears? How many times have you seen an event advertised in the paper and thought, "I'd like to go to that," but doubts crept in and you put the paper (and your good intentions) aside?

From now on, don't let apprehensions rob you of what you might achieve by attempting. Amy Tan said, "If you can't change your fate, change your attitude." I believe it's the other way around. By changing our attitude about meeting people, we can change our fate. We can turn strangers into friends if we choose to take the initiative instead of allowing ourselves to be intimidated.

Speak Up
━━ ◉ ━━

"Many a friendship is lost for lack of speaking."
─ ARISTOTLE

Have you lost potential friends over the years because you were afraid to speak up or because you were waiting for other people to extend themselves first? Instead of simply hoping other people will make the first move, understand that good things come to those who . . . initiate.

In the seventies I worked for an organization called Open University in Washington, D.C. We sponsored a Halloween party and invited everyone to come in costume. Only a handful of the several hundred attendees chose to do so. I was collecting tickets in the foyer of the hotel ballroom when a woman got off the elevator, took one look around, and stopped dead in her tracks. She had dressed up as Pippi Longstocking, complete with gingham dress, flouncy petticoat, and oxford shoes. To top it all off, she had braided her red hair into pigtails and wired them up Pippi-style. She scanned the crowd again, confirmed that she was the only one dressed up, and dashed into the rest room.

After checking everyone in, I went into the ladies' room to see what I could do. "Pippi" was sitting there, sobbing. I asked what was wrong and she sniffed, "I'm so embarrassed. No one else is wearing a costume. As soon as the lobby is clear, I'm getting out of here and going home. I'm sorry I ever came."

I asked if she had seen the movie *Cabaret*. Puzzled, she nodded yes. I asked, "Do you remember Liza Minnelli singing, 'What good is sitting alone in your room?' What good will it do to go home and sit in your room? Do you like to dance?" She looked at me, still puzzled, and nodded again. "Why don't you go out there and ask someone to dance?" She gazed at me aghast and exclaimed, "I couldn't do that!" "Why not?" I countered. "If you don't like it, you can go home like you planned." She decided she didn't have anything to lose.

Pippi walked into the ballroom, approached a nice-looking young man, and a half hour later had danced every dance and was the life of the party. I looked around the room and saw people looking at her with envy in their eyes. I could tell they were thinking, "I wish I was having fun like her." The irony was, they didn't know that she'd been crying her eyes out in the bathroom thirty minutes earlier. Pippi had discovered that the difference between having a great time and wishing you had never gone . . . is taking the first step.

Take the First Step
◎

"Action may not always bring happiness; but there is no happiness without action."
−BENJAMIN DISRAELI

Initiating may not always result in new friendships, but few friendships result without initiating. Another homework assignment for the multiple-session class I teach in confidence is for participants to introduce themselves to an individual they want to meet and to report the outcome at the next class session. That assignment has yielded dozens of success stories over the years. One of my favorites came from a man named Glenn who kept running into the woman he wanted to meet.

"Every day after work, I drive to a local park, change clothes, and go for a run. I always jog around the park twice, clockwise, a distance of about five miles. For the last couple of months, there's been a very attractive young lady who runs at the same time, except she runs around the park *counter*clockwise. Every time I saw her I thought how much I wanted to meet her. Then that mental critic who second-guesses everything I do would say, 'Nah, if she wanted to run with somebody she already would be.' I never had the courage to speak up because I had convinced myself that she wouldn't be interested.

"Last week I had an excuse to say something to her because of your homework assignment. So on Monday I'm halfway through my first lap and there she is. I said hi. She said hi back.

Tuesday afternoon, here she comes again. I said, 'Nice evening, isn't it?' She said, 'Sure is.' Wednesday, here she comes. I said, 'Do you mind if I run with you?' Guess what she said? 'I thought you'd never ask!' The next day we agreed to meet and run together. Do you know what I realized? If I hadn't initiated, I'd still be running one way and she'd still be running the other."

Forward Ho
———◉———

"There is no advancement to him who stands trembling because he cannot see the end from the beginning."
—E. J. KLEMME

Are you thinking, "But what if the chamber of commerce *had* turned out to be a clique and everyone there snubbed Patty? What if Pippi had asked several people to dance, and they had all said no? What if Glenn had given the female jogger a friendly greeting, and she had told him to get lost?"

You're right to wonder what we can do if we extend ourselves and get rejected. That's why I've dedicated a whole chapter in this Part 2 of the book that explains exactly what to do when things go wrong. If you can't wait, turn to page 134, and you'll discover how to self-diagnose instead of self-destruct when things don't turn out the way you want.

Or perhaps you're thinking, "This is easy to say but tough to do." Maybe you're worrying, "What if people aren't interested in me?" "There is no terror in a bang," noted Alfred Hitchcock. "Only in the anticipation of it." That's why the next seven chapters are devoted to specific social skills so you know exactly what to say after you say hello. Instead of being terrified at the prospect of having to meet people, you will look forward to it because you'll know how to strike up conversations and keep them going. Instead of standing there trembling, you'll learn how to overcome your timidity so you *won't* make a fool of yourself. You'll learn strategies to put yourself and others at ease so your every interaction reaches a successful and satisfactory end.

Sample Starting Today Assignment

"The sure way to miss success is to miss the opportunity."
—PHILARETE CHARLES

MY DAD USED TO TELL me that opportunity knocks; it doesn't break the darn door down. From now on, you're not going to wait for opportunity to knock; you're going to go out and meet it halfway. Instead of expecting friends to come to you, you're going to go to them. As hockey great Wayne Gretzky is fond of saying, "You miss 100 percent of the shots you never take." You're going to take your best shot by taking the first step. Instead of using poor communication skills or lack of confidence as an excuse for not having meaningful relationships, you're going to change your attitude (and your fate) by vowing to think positive. Today's assignment is for you to state specifically who you would like to reach out to, and how and when you're going to initiate with that person. Samuel Johnson said, "The future is purchased with the present." You are going to give yourself a wonderful present by filling your future with friends, one by one, starting today. ◎

Action Plan for Don't Wait, Initiate

Sandra has registered for a course she needs to keep her teaching certification current. She's usually timid around new people, but she has decided to turn over a new leaf. Although she has told herself that she won't have trouble making friends because she'll have a lot in common with her fellow students, she's still scared.

BLOCKERS	BUILDERS
Withdraw	Reach out
"I'm so intimidated by large groups. I'm going to cancel."	*"I'll never get over this fear by staying home. What good is sitting alone in my room?"*

Don't show
"I'm so uncomfortable walking into a place where I don't know anyone. I'll wait until next term and see if I can get someone to sign up with me."

Go
"I'm going to try it out. There's probably a lot of people there like me. I may even find some teachers from nearby schools to swap materials with."

Pessimistic
"These people aren't going to be interested in me. They're probably just going to be a bunch of cliques, anyway."

Positive
"I've always wanted to network with my peers. I can't wait to find out how school-based management is working for them."

Wait for someone else to initiate
"I'll wait to see if they have some kind of icebreaker activity."

You initiate
"I'm going to sit next to someone I'd like to meet and introduce myself."

Too afraid to speak up
"I feel so self-conscious. I'll just read the newspaper and wait to see if anyone talks to me."

Take the first step and speak up
"Hi, my name's Sandra. I teach at Russell Elementary. What school are you with?"

MY PERSONAL STARTING TODAY ASSIGNMENT

Starting today I'm going to _____
_____
_____

Signed _____ Date _____

SMILE to Form Favorable First Impressions

"There are few times in your life when it isn't too melodramatic to say that your destiny hangs on the impression you make."
— BARBARA WALTERS

ow. Our *destiny* depends on our ability to make a favorable impression? Talk about pressure! We often tense up when meeting people as a result of our desperate desire to prove ourselves worthy of the other person's time, interest, and attention. This pressure to please produces a strained atmosphere that is the antithesis of relaxed relations.

Are you at ease when meeting others? Very few of us are. Why is that? Because anxiety is defined as "not knowing." When we meet new people, we feel anxious because we *don't know* them. We don't know if they're going to like us; we don't know if we're going to be able to speak in complete sentences.

You've probably heard the cliché that we don't get a second chance to make a good first impression. How we behave in those first few minutes determines whether people want to spend more time with us. Would you like to know how to introduce yourself in a way that almost guarantees people will be interested in you? Would you like to know how to put yourself and others at ease in that important first five minutes of an interaction? You can if you just SMILE. SMILE is the acronym for the five steps to forming favorable first impressions and to being welcome wherever you go.

S = Smile

———◉———

"A smile is the universal welcome."

−**MAX EASTMAN**

You may be thinking to yourself, "Come on, I know it's important to smile." Once again, we may know it. Do we do it? When I work with people who are preparing to give an important speech, I sometimes videotape them so they can review their performance. I tell them to walk tall to the platform (instead of slinking onstage) and to stand and slowly sweep the audience with their eyes and a big, warm smile. I mention that we can't expect a group to be glad to see us if we don't look like we're glad to see them.

First-time speakers rarely do this. They're so preoccupied with their fears that they often mount the stage with a stern look and never even glance at the audience before launching straight into their presentation. As a result, they miss a golden opportunity to connect with the audience, to bond with the attendees. When students look at their video clips, they're often shocked to see how unfriendly they look. Appearing harsh wasn't their intent; it was just a by-product of wanting to get it over with.

They vow that on their second try they will gift the entire audience with a big, warm smile. The difference is striking. This time when they evaluate their tape, they see a friendly person on the stage establishing immediate rapport with everyone in the room. They see for themselves how a smile can raise the mood and increase the receptivity of those within its perimeter. Simply said, it's hard to dislike someone who smiles at you. A smile sets up a reciprocal reaction. Recipients almost involuntarily smile back.

If it works for professional speakers, it can work for us when we speak socially. The very first step to establishing a positive response in another person is to flash them a genuine, heartfelt smile. If you send it out, chances are you'll get one back, and you'll be well on your way to a positive interaction. It's been said, "A smile is a light on your face to let someone know you are home." Brighten people's days with a smile and you will feel more at home wherever you go.

Years ago I had the privilege of being a guest lecturer on the luxury liner *Royal Viking Sun* during the Los Angeles to Honolulu leg of its around-the-world cruise. During my presentation in their theater, a passenger shared her "smile" success story. She said, "What you're saying about a smile being a universal greeting is so true. At many of our ports of call, I've chosen to spend the day exploring the towns by myself instead of going with an interpreter or tour group. Most places, the local people don't speak English and that's the only language I know. It hasn't stopped me for a minute. Everywhere I've been, people have gone out of their way to help me, and I think a lot of it is because we were able to communicate with a smile even when we couldn't understand a word of what each other is saying."

This woman had found, as my friend and author Allen Klein says, "There are no language barriers when you are smiling."

M = Make the Shake
————— ◎ —————
"Attention is silent flattery."
-ANONYMOUS

To shake hands or not? That is the question. What's protocol these days? Are men supposed to shake hands with a lady? Is a woman supposed to initiate a handshake with a man? Many people don't know what's appropriate, so they suffer through false starts: one person puts out his hand only to withdraw it just as the other person extends his, and back and forth they go. I suggest we *always* shake hands for these four reasons.

1. Shaking hands eliminates that dreaded awkwardness. Instead of hesitating to see what the other person does, set a positive precedent by confidently extending your hand to get the introduction off to a good start.

2. A handshake literally and figuratively connects us. Touching creates a physical bond that cements our meeting in a way that talking at each other never could. It's a tangible way of linking ourselves.

3. Clasping hands helps us look the person in the eye so he knows we're sincere. If we're not looking straight at the person when he says his name, we'll never remember it because it's not linked to his face. Furthermore, if our eyes are moving around, the other person will think we're shifty-eyed and may not trust us. He'll never believe we're truly glad to meet him.

4. Shaking hands causes us to literally and figuratively reach out to the other person. Leaning forward is our body's way of saying, "I'm focusing on you. You have my undivided attention."

You may be thinking, "Aren't there exceptions to this? What if I'm dealing with someone from another country?" You're right. It's smart to be sensitive to cultural norms. For example, if you're dealing with a senior Japanese businessman, it might be more appropriate to give a slight bow than to offer your hand. If you deal with international clients and travel abroad, check the local customs first. Reading up on your hosts' customs will enable you to socialize with confidence, knowing you'll be able to interact in a way that honors the traditions of the people with whom you're dealing.

You may also be wondering, "What if I get one of those dead-fish handshakes?" If you miss and clasp a few limp fingers, say, "Hey, let's do that again," and extend your hand once more for a better grip. This may seem petty, but we don't get an impression of strength from someone who gives a weak handshake. Start over so you can get off on firm footing. Not too firm, though. Shaking hands is *not* meant to be a competition. One pump, instead of an everlasting death grip, is the way to go.

I = Intriguing Introduction
◎

*"Language is the voice of thought. Every time we speak,
our mind is on parade."*
– ANONYMOUS

Every time we introduce ourselves, our personality is on parade.
What do *you* say when you're asked, "What do you do?" Does
your answer lead to interest or apathy? Does your response rep-
resent you fairly, even favorably? Does your description of yourself lead to a delightful discussion or a dead end?

In a seminar on SOCIALSAVVY, I asked participants to introduce themselves so we could see whether their introductions
produced an "I want to know more" response. One woman said
apologetically, "I'm just a secretary." I asked, "If you're not excited about what you do, how can you expect anyone else to
be?" The word *just* diminishes us. Instead of saying, "I'm just a
housewife," say, "I'm raising our children" or "I'm a full-time
mom." Instead of saying, "I'm just a receptionist," say, "I work
for the bank that says yes." If you take pride in what you do,
others will, too.

One man said, "I work for Textron." The collective response
was "Huh?" If people don't understand what your company
does, they won't pursue it. They're embarrassed to say, "I'm
not familiar with that organization," which means they'll feel
uncomfortable because they're confused about what it is you
actually do. It's the equivalent of a conversational black hole.
That's why you should explain (briefly) what your company
does, instead of just supplying its name. Now that man says,
"I'm a scientist for the company that operates the observatory
on top of Haleakala, a dormant volcano." That *always* gets a
follow-up question!

John Oliver Hobbs believed that "the essential charm of good
talking rests upon sincerity, spontaneity, and the willing revelation of character." The charm of a good introduction lies in a
compelling revelation of character. Over the years, I've collected

dozens of innovative intros. A woman now answers the "What do you do?" question with "I'm a massage therapist. I rub people the right way." A refrigerator repairman gives his job title and then says, "We aim to freeze." A tree surgeon says, "I work out on a limb." One of my all-time favorites is the dentist who describes himself this way: "I believe in the tooth, the whole tooth, and nothing but the tooth." These sound-bite bios invariably lead to an interested *"Aaahh"* instead of an apathetic "oh."

L = Learn the Name
———— ◉ ————

"I remember your name, but can't think of your face."

— GRAFFITI

The next step to a successful first few moments is to remember the person's name. Are you saying to yourself, "But I'm terrible at remembering names?" Well, as Henry Ford observed, "If we think we can or can't, we're right." You CCAN remember names if you put your mind to it, and if you use these four steps.

C = Commit. Remembering doesn't just happen. We have to give our mind what's called a determining tendency. In other words, if we want to recall information, we need to make a deliberate decision to imprint it. When we can't remember someone's name, it's because we either *didn't* give the mind a determining tendency or gave it a *destructive* determining tendency. Have you ever walked into a huge room, taken one look at the large crowd, and thought to yourself, "I'll *never* be able to remember everyone's name!" That's called failure forecasting. You just ordered your mind to do what you didn't want it to. From now on, give your mind a *constructive* determining tendency: "I will do my best to remember everyone's name." Put limiting labels in the past by saying, "I used to not be very good at remembering names. Now I realize how important it is, so I make a conscious commitment to imprint people's names."

C = Concentrate. When we can't remember someone's name, it's often because we were distracted when we were introduced. From now on, commit to making the other person the most important thing in your world for those few seconds. Ignore the friend who's waving at you from across the room. Forget the UPOs (unidentified piled objects) stacked up on your desk. For the time it takes to complete the introduction, give this person your full focus.

A = Attention on the face. Preclude preoccupation and physically focus your attention by looking the person straight in the face. If you're gazing over his shoulder or looking elsewhere when he says his name, you won't connect it with his face. Study the face for a couple of seconds so you'll recognize it next time you see it.

N = Numerous repetitions. Repeat the name out loud as soon as you hear it, and then silently repeat it to yourself at least three times in spaced intervals. Repetition, the mother of memory, is important for several reasons. First, you want to make sure you've heard the name correctly (e.g., Rob, not Bob; Betty as opposed to Betsy). Second, physiologists believe our ability to recall information depends on whether or not it has been reviewed at different times with "wait" periods in between (thereby signaling the brain that the incoming data is a keeper and important enough to store in long-term memory). Third, the more senses you use when imprinting information, the more likely you are to recall it. If you *hear* the name and *say* the name while *looking* at his face, you give yourself several hooks on which to hang a memory. Obviously, writing down the names of the people you've met (and a word or two on the back of their business card to remind you of your conversation) will enhance your recollection even more. The next time you see that person, his name should pop into your mind.

A woman in one of my seminars said, "We were at our office Christmas party, and I was introducing one of our board members to several of my co-workers and their spouses. I don't know whether it was the eggnog or what, but I forgot the director's name! I was so embarrassed. What can you do when you forget someone's name?"

Finesse it or confess it! If you're with people you know, you can sometimes finesse the situation by introducing them first: "This is Rhonda, our accounts manager, and her husband, Ron, and this is Bill, our marketing director, and his wife, Jan." Rhonda, Ron, Bill, and Jan will extend their hands and the person whose name you've "misplaced" will probably put his hand out and introduce himself.

If that's not possible, admit you've forgotten his name, but soften this by referring to some information you know about him (for example, "I know we met at the board retreat earlier this year, and your name again is . . ."). Don't exacerbate the situation by apologizing profusely and drawing even more attention to your faux pas ("Oh, I can't believe I forgot your name. This is so embarrassing. How could I do this?"). Just calmly find out what it is and then move the conversation on without belaboring what's happened.

Don't try to bluff your way through this awkward situation. Not knowing someone's name when we're supposed to produces anxiety other people can feel. Even though it's uncomfortable, have the confidence to 'fess up. It's infinitely preferable to pretending to listen while you rack your brain wondering, "What is her name? I *know* I know it."

Shirley Crowe, wife of former Joint Chiefs of Staff Admiral Crowe, contributed her thoughts about remembering names in a workshop years ago: "I meet hundreds of people a week. Sometimes I go to two or three official functions a day. I've realized I'll never be able to recall *everyone's* name. With this system, I CCAN remember more of them." Isn't that the point?

Would you like to know how to make yourself memorable? You can help people remember your name by (1) always looking the person in the eye and speaking clearly when you say your name; (2) pausing for several beats between your first and last name; (3) giving your surname equal vocal emphasis instead of trailing off; and (4) providing a brief association so people link you with something easy to recall. A lady pilot I know introduces herself this way. She says, "My name's easy to remember. It's Tweet. Just picture a bird and think of Tweet. That's me." I doubt anyone ever forgets her name. My friend Maggie Bedrosian says, "Just think of a bed of roses." What could you say to make your name easy to remember?

What if you run into someone you haven't seen in a long time and you see the hesitancy in their eyes? Supply your name and save them the embarrassment of having to scramble for it. Simply walk toward the person with your hand out, say his or her name, and then give your name and how you know each other: "Hello, Joe. I'm Loretta Harvey. We met at Tammy's wedding last year." The other person will probably nod in recognition and the conversation can continue from there.

E = Eye Contact

"One of the most wonderful things in nature is a glance of the eye; it transcends speech; it is the bodily symbol of identity."

-RALPH WALDO EMERSON

In my workshops, I demonstrate how vital it is to look someone in the eye when talking to them. I'll point to a student in the first row and start talking to her. "Carole, I am speaking directly to you. These remarks are not meant for anyone else in the room. Honestly, I am speaking only to you." The entire time I'm saying this, I'm *not* looking at Carole. My eyes are wandering around the audience as I say earnestly, "Really, Carole, everything I'm saying is for your ears only." Then I turn to Carole and ask, "Do you believe me?" Of course not. It's an amazing demonstration of the fact that words are meaningless unless they're backed up by eye contact.

Painfully shy people sometimes find it difficult to look people in the eye. From now on, even if you can hold people's gaze for only a fraction of a second, be sure to look them in the eye at the moment you shake their hand and greet them. That way, they'll still believe you're genuinely pleased to meet them. Ralph Waldo Emerson also said, "An eye . . . by beams of kindness, can make the heart dance for joy." A split second of eye contact can transmit your kind nature, if you'll put your heart in your eyes.

Put It All Together
◎

"People are lonely because they build walls instead of bridges."
-JOSEPH FORT NEWTON

A self-confessed charm-school dropout realized her prickly personality was alienating everyone she met. "I've been single for a long time. I used to come home from parties thinking, 'What a boring evening. There wasn't one interesting person there.' Then I realized *I'd* been there, which meant those uninteresting people included me. I took a long look at myself and didn't much like what I saw. Snobbish was the first word that came to mind. I'd gone overboard in trying to be cool and had turned cold. If I were someone else, *I* wouldn't want to approach me either.

"As you said, we can be icebergs or we can be icebreakers. I can wait for Prince Charming to magically show up, or *I* can be charming and magically show up. It seemed simplistic, but it really was as simple as making more of an effort to be friendly. Instead of trying to come across like I was above it all, I started extending myself and letting people know I was interested in meeting them. Since I've changed my attitude, I've enjoyed every 'single' evening out."

Joseph Addison said, "What sunshine is to flowers, smiles are to humanity." From this day forward, commit to warming humanity with a SMILE.

Sample Starting Today Assignment

"I have found that if you love life, life will love you back."
—ARTHUR RUBINSTEIN

How are you going to introduce yourself from now on? How are you going to make sure your first few minutes form a favorable *first* and *lasting* impression? Today's assignment is (1) to create your own sound-bite bio—a twenty-second intro that builds a bridge to a fascinating conversation; and (2) to commit to getting good at remembering names. From now on, you're going to shake hands, look people in the eye, and repeat and imprint their name so you can do them the honor of remembering and using it. If you forget someone's name, you're going to finesse or confess it. You're going to make yourself more memorable by giving people a hook on which to hang a memory. If you are friendly to people in the first few minutes, they will be friendly back. ◎

Action Plan for Forming Favorable First Impressions

This is Marcia's first day on the job. She's eager to make a good first impression with her co-workers. She has a choice of how to handle these first meetings with her fellow employees.

BLOCKERS	BUILDERS
Awkward, anxious	At ease
"What if they don't like me? I don't know if I'm going to fit in."	*"I'm going to extend myself to my co-workers and let them know I'm glad to be working with them."*

Stern and preoccupied
"I don't belong here. I just want to get this over with."

S = Smile
"I'm going to send out a big, warm smile to anyone who looks my way."

To shake or not to shake hands?
"Oh no, what shall I do? I'll wait to see if she extends her hand."

M = Make that shake!
"I'll put out my hand to get our relationship off to a good start."

Intro that leads to apathy
"Hi. I'm Marcia."

I = Intro that leads to intrigue
"Hello. I'm Marcia from Mississippi, home of the world's most delicious pralines. Want one?"

Forget their name
"Oh no, what was her name again? I didn't hear it."

L = Learn their name
"I'm sorry, I didn't hear your name. Was it Alyssa or Melissa?"

Shifty-eyed
"I'm so nervous. I'm just going to keep my head down and hope no one notices me."

E = Eye contact
"I'm going to look at them when they say their name so I'll be sure to get it straight."

MY PERSONAL STARTING TODAY ASSIGNMENT

Starting today I'm going to _____
_____
_____

Signed _____ Date _____

Converse with Comfort

"For good or ill, your conversation is your advertisement. Every time you open your mouth, you let me look into your mind."
— BRUCE BARTON

When you open your mouth, what does your conversation say about your mind? Does your "advertisement" motivate people to buy more time with you?

Unfortunately, as Margaret Millar observed, "Most conversations are simply monologues delivered in the presence of witnesses." Or, as I sometimes describe them in workshops, "Most conversations are I-to-I combat." In this chapter, you'll learn a variety of discussion do's and don'ts. You'll find out how to start and stop conversations and how to make a friend of everyone you meet. You'll discover why a good conversationalist is rare and welcome everywhere, and how you can overcome self-consciousness once and for all.

Talk to Me
—⊙—

"There are two kinds of people in the world—those who walk into a room and say, 'There you are,' and those who say, 'Here I am!' "
— ABIGAIL VAN BUREN

Which kind of person are you? The first step to making people like us is to like them. Instead of wondering, "What can I say?" ask yourself, "What would *they* like to say?" Bertrand Russell said, "Fundamental happiness depends more than anything else upon what may be called a friendly interest in persons and things." Our happiness depends on our decision to stop trying to get people interested in us and to start becoming interested in other people. You may agree with this in theory, but you're wondering, "How do I put it in practice?" One way is to ask questions instead of making statements.

Balance the Conversational Ball
—————— ◉ ——————

"To seduce most anyone, ask for and listen to his opinion."
-MALCOLM FORBES

Most people talk about themselves when they're nervous. The second there is silence, they rush to fill the void, usually with a comment about themselves. As Fran Lebowitz observed, "Spilling your guts is just exactly as charming as it sounds."

The next time you're not sure what to say, don't say anything—*ask*. Imagine a "conversational ball." Talking about yourself keeps the ball in your court. That may be interesting to you, but it is interesting to other people only in small doses. The goal is to have a *balanced* conversation. A fun conversation is one in which the ball goes back and forth between the two people. It ceases being fun when one person hogs the ball.

Will, a participant in one of my workshops, said, "This makes sense, but how do you do it? I took a potential client to lunch last week. I asked about a hundred questions and all I got back were grunts. It was hard work getting anything from that guy. I said, 'Do you like living in San Jose?' He said, 'It's okay.' I asked, 'Do you have any children?' He said, 'Three.' I asked, 'Have you been with Comtrex long?' He said, 'About five years.' In desperation I asked, 'Did you go to that conference last month?' He said, 'Yeah.' That lunch took forever. It was like pulling teeth to get him to reveal anything."

Will had the right idea, but the wrong questions. "Do you?" "Are you?" "Have you?" and "Did you?" are all *closed* questions. A closed question is anything that can be answered in a few words. "Have you ever been to Washington, D.C.?" "Uh-huh." "Did you try that restaurant I told you about?" "Yup." "Are you going to take Friday off?" "Planning on it."

Closed questions are also often leading questions. Leading questions have the answer already in them. "Did you have a good day at school?" "Did you have fun on your vacation?" These types of questions bring conversations to a screeching halt because you're doing the other person's thinking and talking for them. It's a one-sided way of *holding* a conversation. All you're doing is asking the other person to agree with or deny what you've just said.

Open Conversations, Don't Close Them
◉

"There is no such thing as conversation. It is an illusion. There are intersecting monologues. That is all."
-REBECCA WEST

Sounds like Rebecca West did not have the good fortune of meeting a skilled and genuinely interesting conversationalist. She's right, though; some conversations do resemble "I-to-I combat" more than they do sincere communication. From now on, prevent the "intersecting monologue" syndrome by asking open-ended questions that can't be answered in a couple of words. "What?" and "How?" questions lead to interesting discussions because they ask for information, not an answer. "What's Washington, D.C., like?" "How did you feel about that restaurant?" "What are you going to do this Friday?" "What?" and "How?" questions can't be answered with a yes or no. They seek more in-depth responses that reveal *feelings*, not just facts. The beauty of them is that they lead to multiple topics, which provide fodder for even more questions.

Remember Will, who had a hard time drawing out his client? Will took another workshop and reported his success: "A few days after your class, I took that client out to lunch again, and it was night-and-day difference. The first time I fired questions at him and he grunted answers at me. This time I asked a few open-ended questions ('How did you get into the computer business?' 'What could we do that would be helpful for you?') We had a far-ranging discussion. We never really connected that first time because we were talking *at* each other. This time we were friends by the end of the meal. The difference was in the questions I asked."

Advice Is Nice

————◉————

"If you want to make a friend, let someone do you a favor."
—BEN FRANKLIN

As Malcolm Forbes and Ben Franklin noted, the way to a man's heart is through his opinion. If you want to make a friend, let the person give you advice. A good conversational rule of thumb is to stop spouting your own opinions and start seeking others.

Art, an association president, said he learned this secret early in his career. "When I first started in this business, I was eager to impress everyone with my ideas and intelligence. I was quick to offer my opinion whether people wanted to hear it or not. The founding father of our association observed this compulsion to show off and took me aside after a meeting. He suggested I'd get further in this industry if I started *asking* for advice instead of giving it.

"His wise words have shaped my dealings with people ever since. I used to try to impress the owners and CEOs with my knowledge of the construction industry. That mentor helped me realize that instead of trying to impress people with what *I* knew, it was smarter to find out what *they* knew. Instead of sharing my experience, I should give them an opportunity to share theirs. This isn't empty flattery, either. Many of these men have been in business a lot longer than I have. It just makes sense to find out more about their expertise instead of flaunting mine."

Absorb and Express Ideas
————————⊙————————

"The only listening that counts is that of the talker who alternately absorbs and expresses ideas."
—AGNES REPPLIER

Art had discovered that a key to conversing with people so they like us is to make sure the conversational ball is in their court more than ours. I'm not suggesting we keep it in their court *all* the time. That would be an interrogation, not a conversation. The goal is to give and take, to absorb and express.

Would you like to learn two simple words that are the key to kicking off conversations? They are the simple words "Tell me." As already mentioned, most people ask closed questions, those that already contain the answer. This relegates the other person to confirming or denying what you just said. After a few of these, the conversation winds down because it has no place to go.

"Did you have fun at the dance?" "Yeah."

"Did you enjoy the ball game?" "It was okay."

"Did you get that project finished on time?" "Uh-huh."

End of conversation. This is hard work!

From now, start questions with the words "Tell me." Say, "Tell me about the dance." "Tell me what the ball game was like." "Tell me what it was like to finish that project." See the difference? "Tell me" gives people a hook on which to hang a conversation.

Tongue-Tied? Try Cues and Ws
—————————————⊙—————————————

*"I keep six honest serving men
(They taught me all I knew);
Their names are What and Why and When
And How and Where and Who."*
—RUDYARD KIPLING

Do you ever find yourself in a superficial conversation where meaningless platitudes seem to be the only things being exchanged? You can move past chitchat and engage in a meaningful conversation by using Cues and Ws. When journalists interview someone, they never have to wonder what to say. They simply ask one good open question and then follow up with who, what, when, where, why, and how. You can do the same.

A cue is the key word in what the other person just said. Imagine you've just run into someone you haven't seen for a while. You say, "It's good to see you. What have you been up to?" and she says, "I just got back from vacation." Vacation is the cue word; it's the central theme of what was just said. Now, follow up with Kipling's servants: "Where did you go for vacation?" "When did you get back?" "What was your favorite part?" "Who did you go with?" As long as you ask one good "Tell me" question and follow it up with Cues and Ws, you'll never run out of things to talk about.

The great thing about Cues and Ws is that they give you an insight into the other person's personality, so you get the whole story instead of shallow dialogue. It's one thing to ask, "Do you like swimming with the Masters club?" And it's another thing to ask, "Why did you get involved with the Masters swim club?" Instead of asking, "Are you glad you went with Mac instead of IBM?" ask, "Why did you decide to go with Mac instead of IBM?" Instead of "Are you happy you finally got a dog?" ask, "What made you decide to get a Dalmatian?"

A skeptic spoke up. "I'm not comfortable using these kinds

of tactics. They sound contrived to me." I was glad he voiced his opinion because it gave me the opportunity to introduce a very important point. Abraham Lincoln once said, "Flattery comes from the teeth; compliments come from the heart." These suggestions are not meant to be manipulative gambits that come from the teeth. They are "talk tools" grounded in compassion that can aid us in our heartfelt efforts to connect with other people. These suggestions aren't meant to be a "conversation by the numbers" formula; they are simply techniques that can help us hold interesting discussions instead of being hopelessly tongue-tied.

From Shy to "HI!"
—————— ⊙ ——————

"That is the happiest conversation where there is no competition, no vanity, but a calm, quiet interchange of sentiments."
— SAMUEL JOHNSON

Tony, a self-described introverted engineer, said, "I used to go to work, go home, go to work, go home. Put me in front of a computer and I was in my element. Put me in front of a couple of attractive ladies and I was out of my element. The problem was, I never used to know what to say. I'd die a thousand deaths searching for something clever to say. Your class was a godsend for me because I realized I didn't have to be witty, clever, or brilliant. All I had to do was ask good 'Tell me' questions.

"I couldn't wait to try out that technique. On the way home from your class, I stopped by a popular restaurant. I took a stool at the bar and ordered dinner. Then I gathered my courage and turned to the woman next to me and asked, 'What do you do?' She was a real estate agent. Before, I would have panicked because I don't know anything about real estate. This time I remembered your tip and said, 'I don't know anything about real estate. Could you tell me what's happening in the market here? Do you think it's a good time to buy?' We had a fascinating conversation, and I learned a lot about the real estate market.

"She had to leave after a while, so I turned to the guy on the other side and asked, 'What do you do?' He was an insurance salesman. Instead of thinking '*Boring*,' I said, 'I don't know anything about insurance. Tell me, do you think a single guy in his thirties needs life insurance?' He turned out to have some good tips about how to get a policy without spending an arm and a leg.

"Those two words 'Tell me' have changed my life. I don't worry anymore about what to say. I know I'll never run out of things to talk about as long as I remember those two words. That restaurant has turned into my own private *Cheers*. Everyone knows my name. I go there a couple of nights a week and sit at the bar and have dinner. It's become a home away from home . . . all because I've learned that a great conversation is one 'Tell me' question away."

Interesting vs. Interested
————————◉————————

"We can make more friends in two months by becoming interested in other people than we can in two years by trying to get people interested in us."
–DALE CARNEGIE

Dale Carnegie's timeless advice is true, yet some of us aren't sure how to apply it. Every time someone finishes talking, we have a choice. We can take back the conversation or we can turn back the conversation. If we consistently take back the conversation, we take the wind out of the other person's sails and come across as being self-centered. If instead we learn to turn back the conversation and draw the other person out, we will be that rare individual who does more than dwell on him- or herself.

How exactly do you turn back conversations instead of take them back? By asking "you" questions instead of making "I" statements. Imagine you've just asked someone if she's seen a good movie recently. She responds, "Yeah, I saw *Twister*." You have a choice. You can state, "Oh, *I* saw that yesterday," or you can ask, "What did you think of it?" Do you see what happens when you make the "I" statement? "I" statements grab the conversational ball back from other people and deflate their enthusiasm. "You" questions draw people out and keep the spotlight directed at them instead of you. The other person will feel you're interested in hearing her thoughts instead of just wanting to spout yours.

Deflate vs. Draw Out
———————— ◎ ————————

"For most people the opposite of talking isn't listening . . .
it's waiting."

-FRAN LEBOWITZ

I witnessed a classic demonstration of this lesson at a cocktail party. I was in a group of people gathered around a former naval aviator who was telling stories about taking off and landing on an aircraft carrier. He animatedly described what it was like getting catapulted off the ship, going from 0 to 150 miles per hour in less than three seconds, and what it was like having a bolter landing, one in which you miss the catch wires and have to throttle up to full power to try another approach.

When he finished with his stories, two people spoke up simultaneously, one performing a perfect representation of a turn-back, the other a classic take-back. The take-back person had obviously just been waiting to put in his two bits and said eagerly, "*I'm* a pilot, too." The turn-back person said sympathetically, "You really miss it, don't you?" Guess which person the aviator turned to?

I constantly relearn this lesson. I used to fly in and out of Honolulu Airport several times a week to present training programs on Oahu. I got to know Sandy, the taxi dispatcher, rather well. On one trip, while waiting for the cab to show up, I asked Sandy, as we say in Hawaii, "Whazzup?" She proudly announced, "My niece just graduated from the Naval Academy." Without thinking I responded, "Oh, I was married at the Naval Academy." You should have seen her face fall. One second, she had been full of pride for her niece; the next, she'd had her satisfaction punctured by my selfish response. I had just yanked the conversational carpet right out from underneath her.

Good news. Or as our son once said, nood gews. It's never too late to "catch and correct." If you become aware that you have just trampled someone's conversational toes, just turn the spotlight back on them with a "you" question. "Oh, did you get to go back for the ceremony?" "Do you have any pictures of her?" In that situation, it was far more important for Sandy to have an opportunity to share her excitement than it was for me to expound on my ties to the academy.

Dump the Dumpers
————————◉————————

"Every time I look at you I get a fierce desire to be lonesome."

— OSCAR LEVANT

Are you thinking, "I'm pretty good at starting conversations and keeping them going. What I'd like to know is how to *stop* them!" As a woman named Cathy said, "I'm afraid to ask people how they are because they'll tell me! At a party last week, I was backed into a corner by this narcissistic bore who talked non-stop. Short of shoving him aside, I didn't know how to escape."

Perhaps you've also met up with a few of these "Well, enough about me. What do *you* think about me?" characters. Or, as Ron Dettinger describes it, "I wouldn't mind her having the last word—but she never gets to it." You're right not to feel you have to spend your evening with an insensitive bore. If you've ever had the misfortune of being cornered by someone who is, as speaker Lee Glickstein says, "hard of listening," it's in your best interests to learn how to disengage diplomatically.

Four Steps to Courteously Closing Conversations
━━━━ ◎ ━━━━

"I've had a wonderful evening. But this wasn't it."
— GROUCHO MARX

From now on, if someone is being so thoughtless as to monopolize the conversation and you want to call it quits, you can do so courteously and confidently with these four steps.

1. *Interrupt and say his name.* Yes, I said interrupt. If someone has been carrying on about himself, you're not being rude by wresting the conversational ball away; *he's* being rude by hogging it. It's said that if you "give a pessimist an inch, he'll take a smile." Bores will take a lot more than that. They'll take your whole evening! Don't suffer in silence while someone maintains a monologue ad infinitum. People pause when they hear their name, and that is your chance to get your verbal foot in the door.

2. *Summarize what he's been saying.* Instead of saying abruptly, "I've got to go now," refer back to a key point he has just made. "I'm definitely going to check out that club. It sounds like it's got some interesting programs." This way the conversation, one-sided as it may have been, comes full circle, and the other person knows you've been listening.

3. *Start wrapping up with "As soon as" or "I wish."* Say, "As soon as I get home, I'll call to get membership information." Perhaps there's no action to be taken. Maybe you've run into a former co-worker at a movie and she's bending your ear about the goings-on at your previous job. This woman had a reputation as quite a talker, and you're not interested in spending the remainder of the evening listening to her prattle. Have the confidence to speak up. "Lenore, I wish the situation had improved at work. It sounds like things are as frustrating as they used to be."

4. *Start verbally and physically departing.* Use a friendly phrase such as "Thanks for bringing that to my attention" or "I'm glad you brought me up to date," and then say, "And now I need to head on home," or "And now I want to go over and welcome a couple of my friends who just arrived." Distance yourself from the other person and break the connection by backing up a few steps while maintaining eye contact. It's impolite to turn and walk away with your back to someone, but it's okay to step back while looking at the person and delivering your departure line.

Gloria Steinem said, "Far too many people are *looking* for the right person, instead of trying to *be* the right person." These talk tools can help you be the right person so you can find more friends. Vow to put these ideas into practice so you can converse with comfort anytime, anywhere, and with anyone.

Sample Starting Today Assignment

"He has lost the art to live who cannot win new friends."
—SILAS W. MITCHELL

TODAY'S ASSIGNMENT IS TO USE these conversational techniques when you talk with people throughout the day. Vow to turn back more discussions than you take back. Ask for advice instead of giving it. Have the courage to courteously close a conversation instead of suffering in silence as someone talks ad infinitum. If you reach out to people and engage them with these talk tools, if you start with "Tell me" questions and follow up with Cues and Ws, you are sure to please the men and women you meet and win some new friends in the bargain. If you ground all these techniques in a genuine interest in other people, you will make friends wherever you go. ◎

Action Plan for Conversing with Comfort

Patricia is attending her husband's annual office party. She usually dreads these things because her husband is busy handling logistics and she has to fend for herself. She has a choice concerning how to approach the evening and how to interact with the people there.

BLOCKERS	BUILDERS
Make statements *"I'm an accountant."*	Ask questions *"How did you become involved with the travel industry?"*
Interrogate *"Do you like being a travel agent?"*	Absorb, express *"What are some of your favorite places to visit?"*
Closed questions *"Don't you get tired of all the paperwork?"*	Open questions *"I've heard about these new computers that research the best fares. How do they work?"*
Deflate *"Oh, I've been to England, too. I saw Princess Di when I was in London."*	Draw out *"You saw Princess Di? What was that like?"*
Take back the conversation *"I thought London was too expensive. We could only afford to go to the theater once."*	Turn back the conversation *"Did you get to go to the theater while you were there? Wasn't* Cats *playing?"*
Suffer in silence *"This guy has talked nonstop for the last half hour. Help! Somebody rescue me."*	Courteously close conversations *"Thanks for the heads-up about that credit card scam. I'll check it out. And now I'm going to find my husband . . ."*

MY PERSONAL STARTING TODAY ASSIGNMENT

Starting today I'm going to _____

_____

_____

Signed _____ Date _____

Cure Self-Consciousness

*"The essence of charm is the ability to lose yourself in
the other person."*
—ELEANOR ROOSEVELT

Are you thinking, "What if I
use these talk tools and I'm *still* self-conscious?" You can turn
self-consciousness into charm by heeding Eleanor Roosevelt's
advice. Instead of saying to yourself "How do I look?" "What
can I say?" or "What do they think of me?" switch your con-
sciousness to other people by giving 'em L. You can lose yourself in other people if you learn to:

L = Look at people's faces intently. Don't let your eyes wan-
der or your mind will, too. Fix your gaze on their face.

L = Lean forward and direct your complete attention on them
and nothing else.

L = Lift your eyebrows to counteract passivity. Raising your
eyebrows activates your interest and energizes you.

L = Listen with your head cocked to one side. This classic
posture of attention causes you to feel more inquisitive.

To demonstrate the power of "Giving 'em L" in my workshops, I often ask participants to pretend they're bored stiff with
what I'm saying. I tell them to imagine I'm droning on and on
and ask them to show me with their body language that they

can't stand it anymore. They all lean back and slouch in their chairs, let their heads loll, their shoulders slump, and their bodies sag; each one assumes a long-suffering facial expression, eyes dull. I ask the group to take a look around the room. It's usually pretty funny to see everyone so thoroughly and obviously indifferent.

Then I ask everyone to pretend pearls of wisdom are rolling off my lips, to act as if they can't wait to hear the next morsel of knowledge to come out of my mouth. Once again, to a person and without exchanging a word, every individual assumes a similar posture. This time they are literally and figuratively on the edge of their seats. They are all leaning forward, looking straight at me, eyebrows lifted and light in their eyes. I ask the group to look around and announce, "*This* is giving 'em L."

When we are truly interested in someone, we automatically assume an energized posture. The good news is, we can adopt an energized posture when we are *not* interested in someone, and it causes us to care more about what they are saying. Assuming such a posture counteracts lethargy and/or anxiety because we're focusing our attention on the other person instead of ourselves. "Giving 'em L" can cure self-consciousness because it is impossible to be self-absorbed when we're fully attuned to someone else.

Listen and Learn
————— ◉ —————

"Listening means taking a vigorous, human interest in what is being told us. You can listen like a blank wall or like a splendid auditorium where every sound comes back fuller and richer."
—ALICE DYER MILLER

I'll always remember a student, a stunning six-foot-two redhead, who found it difficult to relax in public. "I used to feel conspicuous everywhere I went because I'm often the tallest person in the room. I would feel self-conscious because I stood out in the crowd. Your session made me realize that if I'm feeling self-conscious, it's because I'm not listening to the other person. I learned that if I became immersed in what the other person was saying, if I thought, 'How would I feel if I were in their shoes?' I no longer worried about myself. Now, whenever I'm talking with people, I try to involve myself in what they're saying instead of becoming impatient with it. My second-guessing is behind me now that I put other people first."

Take It Easy
——— ◉ ———

"The best way to entertain some folks is to listen to them."
— KIN HUBBARD

Another way to free ourselves from discomfort or embarrassment when meeting people is by ridding ourselves of the erroneous notion that we've got to perform to prove we're worth knowing. As Kin Hubbard has noted, we are more likely to impress people if we employ our ears, not our mouth.

This was great news to a man who had always been the class clown. "Growing up, I was the family entertainer. My parents would demand, 'Say something funny, Ronnie,' and most of the time I would. I enjoy making people laugh, but it put a lot of strain on me to feel I always had to entertain people. I carried that expectation over into my social life. I was always on the lookout for puns and plays on words. It got to be almost an obsession. Whenever something clever occurred to me, I blurted it out whether it was my turn to talk or not. My idea of a conversation was me doing a string of one-liners. As long as I was on and people were laughing, I was confident.

"I took your class because I wanted to learn some other way to interact with people. When you said a key to being liked is to listen more than talk, that was a new concept to me. It helped me see that I was probably annoying people with my comedy routines more than I was impressing them.

"Instead of shooting from the lip, I started zipping it. I'm much more relaxed now that I've stopped trying to be a stand-up comic. My friends have told me I'm a lot more enjoyable to be around now that I'm not trying to be Robin Williams."

Listen Up

"No man ever listened himself out of a job."
—CALVIN COOLIDGE

No one ever listened himself out of a friend either. A former student of mine was on the same flight back to Maui one evening and filled me in on his progress. He said, "My kids are all grown now, and it wasn't until your class that I realized I was still treating them as children. Every time we got together, I was still telling them what to do and how to do it. The weekend after your class, I went over to my son's house for Sunday dinner. Halfway through the meal, I was into one of my 'good old days' stories, and I caught my son looking at his wife and rolling his eyes. It stopped me dead. In that instant, I realized I always talked about myself when I was around them. I never asked about their lives, I only talked about my own.

"I dropped my story and said, 'So, Brian, tell me how work is going for you.' After his initial shock, he started talking about a major project he's been assigned to. When he was finished, I asked Sarah about her job. That evening was a turning point in our relationship. After thirty-five years, I abandoned my *Father Knows Best* role and talked *with* Brian and Sarah instead of *to* them."

Conducting vs. Controlling Conversations

"Listening, not imitation, may be the sincerest form of flattery."
—DR. JOYCE BROTHERS

Honor people with your attention, not your opinions. Talking about ourselves is a way of controlling the conversation. It's a way of saying, "I'm in charge." It arises from a feeling of superiority, the conviction that the other person wants to hear everything about us. In a way, it's a selfish ignoring of the other person's right and need to say something. It's an indication that we're thinking only of ourselves and not of the other person. Recognize that it's fair for both parties to have an equal opportunity to speak. As Lyndon Baines Johnson said, "I already know what *I* think. I want to find out what *others* think." Instead of talking to impress, listen to learn.

Facilitate Fascinating Discussions
━━━━━━━━━━━━━━━ ◉ ━━━━━━━━━━━━━━━

"Good talk is like good scenery—continuous, yet constantly varying, and full of the charm of novelty and surprise."
–RANDOLPH BOURNE

In an ideal world, all conversations would be as Bourne describes them. In the real world, few are. Conversations can be fascinating if someone takes the responsibility for facilitating them. Picture a maestro conducting a symphony orchestra. The maestro doesn't play the music himself, but draws it out of the musicians. He makes sure that all the different sections are featured and the sound is balanced. See yourself doing the same with conversations.

One lady took this suggestion to heart. "I go to a lot of professional meetings and luncheons. We're often seated at those large tables with eight or ten people. I hate it when two people know each other and no one else does. The two buddies engage in a private conversation and ignore everyone else, while the other six people stare at their salads and pretend to be incredibly intrigued with their soup.

"I decided to try your idea and see myself as a conductor. At the next luncheon, I clinked my glass to get everyone's attention and said, 'I don't think we've all had a chance to meet. Could we please go around the table and introduce ourselves?' After introductions, I said, 'We've got about twenty minutes before the program starts, would you like to have a roundtable discussion? Maybe we could each describe a challenge we're facing at work or tell of a recent accomplishment.' Then I made sure to keep the conversational ball rolling. I didn't let one person dominate the discussion, and I made sure that everyone had a chance to contribute.

"At the end of that luncheon, every one of my table mates came up to say thank you. One said, 'I dread these things sometimes because it seems I'm the only one at the table who doesn't know anybody. Not only did your facilitating set up some great networking, but I learned more from our table discussion than I did from the featured speaker. I'm going to use your idea from now on when I go to luncheons.' "

She went on, "I can't tell you how many times people have come up to me since then and thanked me for orchestrating such interesting and useful discussions." Randolph Bourne also said, "A good discussion increases the dimensions of everyone who takes part." It does *if* someone is courageous enough to make sure everyone *gets* to take part, and if someone is confident enough to lead table conversations instead of leaving them to chance.

Cure Shyness
————— ◎ —————

"It is part of the cure to want to be cured."

- S E N E C A

A woman called to share a wonderful story of what happened because of her decision to cure her self-consciousness by focusing on other people. She reported, "I've always loved to sail, but I never knew anyone with a boat, I certainly couldn't afford to buy my own, and I was too shy to offer to crew on other people's boats.

"I had about given up hope of ever getting involved in sailing when I took your class and you gave us that 'go out and meet someone' assignment. That motivated me to drive to our local marina to see if they had an instruction program. After strolling up and down the docks admiring the yachts, I stopped by the harbor bulletin board to read the race announcements. There was a small sign tacked up that said, 'Crew wanted. No experience necessary. See slip 53.'

"Normally I wouldn't have had the confidence to follow up on something like that. I would have immediately thought of all the reasons they wouldn't want me and would have just kept on walking. This time, instead of using my shyness as an excuse for *not* following up, I used your homework assignment as an excuse *for* following up.

"I walked over to the slip, introduced myself to the people working on the boat, and explained I was answering the ad. I said I was a quick learner and a hard worker, and before I knew it, they had asked me to join them for a practice sail the next day. To make a long story short, I am now part of their team and we race almost every Saturday. I can't begin to describe the thrill of being out on the water, racing along under a full spinnaker with the wind at our backs. If I hadn't had the guts to introduce myself, I'd *still* be shy and landlocked."

Be a Friend
———— ◎ ————

"Friendship improves happiness, and abates misery, by doubling our joy, and dividing our grief."
-JOSEPH ADDISON

A nurse was able to use a combination of these techniques to go from "shy to hi." Doris confessed, "I've worked at this hospital for three years and haven't made one friend. It's the unfriendliest place I've ever worked." I asked, "Have you approached anyone?" She said, "I wouldn't know what to say. Plus, how can I be sure they want to get to know me?" I reminded Doris that the question to ask isn't "Will they be interested in me?" The question to ask is "Am I interested in them?" Since the assignment was to introduce yourself to someone you wanted to meet, she decided to try these ideas. She came back with a moving success story:

"The week after class, on three different days I asked co-workers to join me in the employee cafeteria for lunch. When I got there, instead of worrying about what *I* could talk about, I asked myself, 'What would *they* like to talk about?' I asked a couple of good 'Tell me' questions: 'Tell me, what do you do when you're not working?' 'I've got relatives coming in from out of town. Could you tell me some fun places they might like to visit?' Then I just followed up with Cues and Ws. Instead of making *myself* feel ill at ease, I dedicated myself to putting *them* at ease. I really listened to what they were saying instead of just waiting for my turn to talk. Do you know, I made more friends in three days than I have in three years . . . all because I made an effort to be interest*ed* instead of interest*ing*."

Graciously Working a Room
-----------◉-----------

"Listening is a magnetic and strange thing, a creative force. The friends who listen to us are the ones we move toward, and we want to sit in their radius. When we are listened to, it creates us, makes us unfold and expand."
—KARL MENNINGER

Listening is a marvelous gift. Unfortunately, it is done well so rarely that it often makes people unfold and expound and expound. If you are a good listener you have probably already discovered that some people will take advantage of your generous spirit and suck every ounce of energy from you, leaving you with "compassion fatigue."

In "Converse with Comfort" I discuss how you can diplomatically disengage from overlong conversations. Here is another idea you can use to make sure your great listening skills are not abused. A state beauty pageant winner took my workshop because she wanted to know how to better handle the many social occasions she was required to attend. "I've never liked the term 'work a room' because it sounds so mercenary," she said, "but that's what I've been told to do. My advisor says I can't stand in one place and talk with one person the whole evening, I've got to move around. Sometimes that's easier said than done."

She said, "Last week I was at a mall opening and a woman who'd grown up with my grandmother wouldn't let me go. She grabbed my arm and continued to reminisce about the old days. Every time I tried to move on, she'd latch on tighter and say, 'I'm not finished yet. I have to tell you about the time . . .' and off she'd go again. How could I have ended this without hurting her feelings?"

She had brought up a good point. If she's attending an activity in her official capacity, she's not supposed to stay with one person and neglect the rest of the group. It's her role to meet as many people as possible.

I said, "It's not being insensitive of you to want or need to spend time with other guests. It's okay to end a conversation after a few minutes and move on, as long as you give the person to whom you're talking to at any given time your undivided attention. You may not be able to give them the *quantity* of time they want, but you can at least give them quality time. A fully focused five minutes is better than a distracted or impatient fifty minutes."

Dean Rusk said, "One of the best ways to persuade others is with your ears—by listening to them." One of the best ways to get along with others is to listen to them. This ability is so rare that if you have it, you will be welcome and appreciated everywhere.

Sample Starting Today Assignment

"He has the gift of quiet."
—JOHN LE CARRÉ

TODAY'S ASSIGNMENT IS TO PICK three different people and give 'em L. As Le Carré points out, it is often more important to have the gift of quiet than the gift of gab. In these conversations you are going to consciously look, lean, lift, and listen so you become completely immersed in what the other person is saying. Instead of making yourself self-conscious by worrying, "What can I say?" "What can I talk about?" you're going to put yourself in the other person's place and see things from her point of view. You're going to turn your shyness into charm by giving your complete, undivided attention to someone else. If you find yourself talking with several people, perhaps you could do the group a favor by facilitating a fascinating conversation and giving everyone a chance to contribute. ◉

Action Plan for Curing Self-Consciousness

Ron has never felt comfortable around people. He's always said to himself, "I was absent the day God passed out confidence." He's decided to go to a popular singles mixer held at a community center, but is getting more and more nervous as the event grows closer.

BLOCKERS	BUILDERS
Self-conscious	Self-confident
"I always feel so awkward at these kind of things. I'll probably end up being a wallflower."	*"Instead of obsessing about myself, I'm going to focus on putting other people at ease."*
Feel like hell	Give 'em L
"This was a stupid idea. No one has even tried to talk to me."	*"I'm going to look at them instead of over their shoulders."*
Intimidated by people	Involved with people
"Wow, she's beautiful. She'd never be interested in me."	*"This is my first time here. Do you have any suggestions?"*
Feel ill at ease	Put others at ease
"Why can't I think of something witty to say?"	*"So, do you think Unity Church sponsors a singles potluck on Fridays?"*
Controlling conversations	Facilitating conversations
"I think they should have spent more money on refreshments and booked a better band."	*"Have you been here before? Did they have the same band or a different one?*

MY PERSONAL STARTING TODAY ASSIGNMENT

Starting today I'm going to _____

_____

_____

Signed _____ Date _____

Go Solo

*"The man who goes alone can start today; but he who travels
with another must wait till that other is ready, and it may be a
long time before they get off."*
- HENRY DAVID THOREAU

re you uncomfortable trav-
eling alone or attending functions by yourself? Many workshop
participants have told me they would rather not go than have
to go solo. My response is it's an advantage to go by yourself *if*
you see it as an opportunity to be free to do what you want,
when you please.

Would you like to know how to go anywhere, anytime, by
yourself and feel confident? The key is to ask for help or give
help so you feel like an insider rather than an outsider.

Request or Give Help

*"Many of our fears are tissue paper thin, and a single courageous
step would carry us clear through them."*
-BRENDAN FRANCIS

Many of our fears about going places alone are based on the
discomfort we feel at not belonging. We may not feel safe in a
room full of strangers. The object, then, is to find out how to
quickly turn those strangers into friends so we feel a part of the
group, instead of apart from the group. The way to do that is

to let people know we're a first-timer and to ask for assistance or offer assistance.

Remember Tony, the formerly introverted engineer who created his own neighborhood *Cheers*? Here's another of his success stories. Tony decided to try a public dance sponsored by a local Elks lodge. As he drove up to the parking lot in front of the large club, he started feeling intimidated by the sea of strange cars. "I'm not going to know anyone there. Everyone's probably come in pairs. I'll end up being a wallflower."

He said he circled the block three times trying to summon up the courage to go in. "What finally tipped the scales was remembering the song from *Cabaret*: 'What good is sitting alone in your room?' I decided that I didn't have anything to lose. I'd feel better trying it out than wimping out.

"I parked my car, walked in, paid my money, and said your magic words to the first lady I saw. 'This is my first time here. How can I help?' The woman at the registration table said, 'You just stick with me. You can help stamp parking tickets. As soon as we're finished here, I'll take you around and introduce you to everyone.' That's exactly what she did. After the last dance, the lights came on and she said, 'Can you come back next month? We're always looking for single men.' That's just another example of a great time I wouldn't have had if I'd given in to my fears and chickened out."

Going Alone vs. Staying Alone
━━━━━━━━━━━━━━━━━━━◎━━━━━━━━━━━━━━━━━━━

"A smile is a passport that will take you anywhere you want
to go."
-ANONYMOUS

Tony discovered for himself what happens when you give people an opportunity to take you under their wing. I know from experience (having driven cross-country by myself) that just because you *go* alone doesn't mean you have to *stay* alone.

Some people dislike traveling by themselves. They would rather stay in their hotel and order room service than risk going to a restaurant and have people think there's something wrong with them. I found that you don't have to stay by yourself just because you go by yourself. The key is to take your passport—your smile—and the question "What do you suggest?"

Whenever I drove into a new town, I would stop for a cup of coffee at a neighborhood diner (not a major chain). I would tell the waitress, "I'm traveling through town. Any suggestions about interesting things to do while I'm in the area?" More often than not, she'd eagerly share local lore about the best places to eat, stay, and visit. I've had people invite me to go skiing with them, steer me to a local swimming hole, and take me along to a family potluck. Helpful residents clued me in on activities such as rodeos at private ranches, community Fourth of July celebrations, and unadvertised estate auctions that I'd never have known about otherwise. Instead of feeling out of place, I felt a sense of place because they treated me like a friend instead of a tourist.

All by Myself
◉

"The experience of strolling by one's self through the vast mult-itudes of a strange city is one of the most wonderful in life."
– GAMALIEL BRADFORD

Family friend Connie Dubois, now retired, treks to Europe at least once a year to satisfy her love of French culture and art. She prepares for her excursions by listening to language tapes and studying art books.

"I love to travel. Scratch that—I *live* to travel," says Connie Dubois. "I always used to go with someone. It just seemed the proper thing to do, but that was one of those ideas that worked better in theory than in practice. It seemed like my companion and I were frequently at odds. I love to walk, everywhere, all the time; my partner preferred to take cabs. I can spend all day in one gallery; my friend was ready to move on after a couple of hours. I enjoy exploring cathedrals. My friend thinks they all look alike after the first few. I was constantly compromising what I wanted to do just to keep the peace.

"Last year I rebelled and decided to go by myself. It was kind of scary at first, a seventy-year-old woman traveling to Europe on her own, but I ended up having a wonderful time. I was free to do exactly as I pleased. If I wanted to gaze at the Mona Lisa for two hours, I could. If I wanted to get up at six and take a sunrise stroll along the Seine, I could. I'm only sorry I didn't have the courage to try this earlier."

One definition of courage is "determination to achieve one's ends." An important component of confidence is being able to achieve our ends *on our own*. We don't want to have to rely on or wait for someone else to accompany us on our adventures. Connie's decision to travel to Europe on her own made it possible for her to have the experience she'd always wanted.

Solitary Isn't Confinement
◉

"What a commentary on our civilization, when being alone is considered suspect; when one has to apologize for it, make excuses, hiding the fact that one practices it—like a secret vice!"
—ANNE MORROW LINDBERGH

A seminar participant said she loved opera but couldn't find anyone who shared her interest. Joyce said, "My husband bays like a hound dog if I dare play a Pavarotti CD at home." When I asked why she didn't go by herself, she looked at me aghast and said, "I couldn't go by myself!" I asked, "Why not?" She sputtered, "I'd be so uncomfortable. Everyone is in pairs or with other couples. I'd be the only person who wasn't with someone. People would think I was strange."

We discussed Anne Morrow Lindbergh's quote and I told her something my mom used to tell me: "We wouldn't worry what people thought of us if we realized how infrequently they did." Joyce realized that she had passed up ten seasons of superb opera because she was concerned what some strangers might say about her. After the session was over, she marched over to the telephone and ordered subscription tickets. She sent me the playbill for Mozart's *Magic Flute* later that year with a note on it: "Loving every minute!"

Sweet Solitude
———— ◎ ————

"There is no such thing as fun for the whole family."
-JERRY SEINFELD

A wise mother contributed her experience. "I love my family dearly, but I believe you can have too much of a good thing. I used to get burned out hearing 'Mommy, Mommy, Mommy' a hundred times a day. Last year I started giving myself breakfast out, by myself, once a week. Every Thursday I take my toddlers to a play group and then drive to my favorite coffee shop. I sit in a corner, sip my tea, and read a book—without interruption! It's sheer bliss. I don't talk to anyone, and I don't want to. That hour and a half is the only time all week I get to read, so I bury my nose in my novel and the world slips away.

"Every once in a while I'll see someone I know, and I can tell they're waiting for me to ask them to join me. Before I would have worried that friends would think I was being unsociable, but now I'm confident enough to know that I deserve ninety minutes of solitude. That morning is sacrosanct to me. I don't have to apologize for not wanting to share it with anyone."

Judiciously Join In
———— ◎ ————

"Include me out."
-SAMUEL GOLDWYN

What can you do if, contrary to Mr. Goldwyn, you want to be included *in*? A young man said, "I moved to Honolulu a few months ago and I've been miserable ever since. I've always heard about Hawaii's aloha spirit. Hah! I told one of my co-workers how I felt and he told me I was being paranoid. 'People

aren't ignoring you. You've just got to make the first move.'
How do I do that, though? It seems likes everyone knows each
other except me."

What *can* you do when it seems everyone knows each other,
except you? Try this four-step process so you can join in judi-
ciously:

1. Imagine you're at a party and everyone is paired off. Look
around for a group that looks interesting and is not gathered
in a tight circle. People in an intimate discussion do not appreciate being interrupted. People in a loose, irregularly
spaced circle are more open to add-ons.

2. Walk over to the group and stand about an arm's distance
away. You've heard the saying "You're in my space"? Our
space is an arm's length in front of us, to the side of us, and
behind us. In the olden days, we felt threatened if someone
entered that three-foot zone, because we knew we were vul-
nerable to attack. The original reason for our fear of someone
intruding in our space may no longer be valid, but we still feel
uncomfortable when someone, unasked, comes too near.
They are literally and figuratively too close for comfort. Now
slightly lean in, cock your head to one side, and follow the
conversation with your eyes.

3. Either the person speaking or the person next to you will
look at you and raise her eyebrows as if to silently say, "What
do you want?" At that point, say these magic words: "Okay if
I listen in?" Not "okay if I join in?" but "Okay if I listen in?"
This is a subtle way of acknowledging that it's *their* group and
you're not attempting to take it over. In twenty years of using
this technique, I have never had anyone say no. The group
has always parted and made space for me to join them.

4. Once you're in the group, don't grab the conversational
ball right away. Start participating in graduated steps. It's still
their group, and you don't want to wear out your welcome in
the first few minutes. Listen to what everyone else is saying,

and after a while, if you think you have something of value to say, throw in your two bits, and then turn back the conversation to someone else. By getting involved gradually, you will gain acceptance.

On My Own
◉

"I thought: 'It's now or never. Either I cling to everything that's safe and that I know, or else I develop more initiative, do things on my own.' "
—AGATHA CHRISTIE

A traveling salesman with clients in five states took Christie's quote to heart. "I'm on the road three weeks out of every four. I used to get meals from fast-food places rather than face the ordeal of eating in a restaurant by myself. It's not appropriate to socialize with my clients, so when I was finished with my sales calls, I would just head back to where I was staying. I spent many an evening watching TV in a lonely hotel room.

"After taking your course, I resolved to take advantage of my life on the road. Now, when I pull into town, I get the local paper to see if anything special is going on. I've seen Tony Bennett in concert, attended some impressive community theater productions (including the best *West Side Story* I've ever seen), and had good meals at dozens of different restaurants— all because I'm no longer intimidated by the irrational thought that everyone will be wondering what's the matter with me."

Hook Up with Hosts
◉

"To wait for someone else to make my life richer, fuller, or more satisfying, puts me in a constant state of suspension."
—KATHLEEN TIERNEY ANDRUS

"I love the outdoors," reported one female student. "Unfortunately, I live in an area where it's not really safe to go hiking by yourself. I had a scary experience a couple of years ago where I was assaulted in the woods behind my house. I was so shaken up by what happened, I stopped going for runs. It made me sad to think I couldn't even go for a jog in the wilderness without having to worry about being mugged. I mentioned what had happened to a woman at work, and she said, 'Why don't you join the Sierra Club?' She told me they had weekly outings, often with thirty to sixty people participating. I was curious, but I didn't know anyone in the club, so I didn't pursue it until you gave us that assignment where we had to seek out people with a common interest.

"I called their hike hot line and was told where to meet and what to bring. Before your class, I would have felt out of place because I didn't know anyone. You taught me to think of that as an advantage because it gave me the freedom to meet whoever I wanted. You suggested we give people an opportunity to take us under their wing, and that's exactly what I did. When I arrived, I told the trip leader, 'This is my first Sierra Club hike. Any suggestions?' He said, 'Follow me.' I did, and I'm so glad I did. He turned out to be a walking, talking encyclopedia of information about the area. He knew the name of every bird, plant, and tree, and told me the history of every valley. He introduced me to at least a dozen people on the trip from all walks of life. I joined the Sierra Club on the spot, and now I can't wait till Saturday rolls around. If I had waited for someone to show me a good time, it wouldn't have happened. The difference was extending myself to the person in charge and giving him an opportunity to be a host. I'm going to do that from now on whenever I go someplace by myself."

Be a Host
—⊙—

"Mankind is divisible into two great classes: hosts and guests."
—SIR MAX BEERBOHM

I don't think we have to be *either* guests or hosts, I think we can be both. A docent for a museum introduced this idea to me. She said, "I used to be painfully shy. I always stayed in the background and let other people do the talking because I was uncomfortable in the spotlight. Then I started volunteering at our local botanical garden and science/nature museum. After I spent a couple of years behind-the-scenes arranging exhibits, the director asked me to give guided tours. At first I was petrified at the thought, but my love for what I was doing carried me through my initial embarrassment. I was so committed to showing visitors what a wonderful place we had, I lost myself in the process. I realized the tour wasn't about me; I was just a messenger. My role was to make sure our guests enjoyed themselves and learned something of interest.

"I realized I could do the same thing at social events. Instead of staying back and dwelling on my discomfort, I could find people who looked like they didn't want to be there and make sure they had a good time. Of course, most of the times I extend myself, we both end up having a good time."

Frank Tyger said, "Your future depends on many things, but mostly on you." From this day forward, have the confidence to do what you want to do and go where you want to go, regardless of whether someone accompanies you.

Sample Starting Today Assignment

"The happiest of all lives is a busy solitude."
—VOLTAIRE

I THINK THE HAPPIEST OF all lives is a *friendly* solitude. We don't want to have to be around people all the time, and we don't want to be by ourselves all the time. What we want is to feel equally comfortable in both situations. The assignment today is to select an activity in which you'd like to participate or a place you'd like to visit. Jot it down on your calendar and plan on going *by yourself*. Once you're there, you have several options. You can revel in a solitary experience and enjoy having some private time. You can see yourself as a host or

hook up with a host, giving or asking for help. You can join an interesting group, and/or you can give people an opportunity to take you
under their wing. Whatever option you choose, you will be happier for
the experience than if you had stayed home because you "didn't have
anyone to go with." ◎

Action Plan for Going Solo

Don has just joined his professional association and is attending
his first meeting. He's feeling a little out of place because everyone
seems to know everyone else. He has a choice of how to handle this
situation.

BLOCKERS	BUILDERS
Stay home because you don't have someone to go with *"I should have stayed home. This looks like one big clique."*	Go, even though you don't have anyone to go with *"I'm going to attend because I want to meet my peers."*
Feel like an outsider because you don't know anyone *"I feel like a fifth wheel. I'm the only one here who's new."*	Feel like an insider because you ask for help *"I'm going to ask if I can take the the empty chair at their table."*
Feel left out *"No one's even made an effort to welcome me."*	Offer to help out *"Do you need some help stamping parking tickets?"*
Feel helpless *"This is the unfriendliest group. I'm never coming back here again."*	Hook up with a host or be one *"Hi, this is my first time here. Any suggestions about where I might sit?"*
Lonely *"It's just not fun when you don't know anyone."*	Alone and content with your solitude *"This lunch is delicious, and I'm looking forward to the program."*

| Jealous of groups
"Everyone's paired off except me." | Join groups judiciously
"Okay if I listen in?" |

MY PERSONAL STARTING TODAY ASSIGNMENT

Starting today I'm going to _____

_____

_____

Signed _____ Date _____

Make and Keep Friends

*"We are all travelers in what John Bunyan calls the wilderness
of this world, and the best that we find in our travels is an
honest friend. He is a fortunate voyager who finds many.
They are the end and the reward of life."*
— ROBERT LOUIS STEVENSON

Have you discovered true
friends along your journey . . . only to lose them through neglect? Søren Kierkegaard expressed a sentiment shared by many
philosophers: "To love human beings is still the only thing
worth living for; without that love, you really do not live." To
put it more simply, "If we're too busy for friends and family,
we're too busy."

It's time to get back in touch with the pivotal people in your
life. It's time to reconnect with the college roommate you were
once so close to, the neighbor you bonded with, the office mate
that made your job bearable, the fishing buddy you had so much
fun with.

Bring Back Friends
◉

*"What sweetness is left in life, if you take away friendship? Robbing
life of friendship is like robbing the world of the sun."*
— CICERO

The members of the Maui Writers Conference organizational
team "bonded" while preparing for and producing their annual

event. At the end of our successful four-day meeting, we all agreed to stay in touch. In the next few months, we occasionally ran into each other around Maui and promised to get together when we "had more time." Of course we never *got* more time. Do you know *anyone* who ever gets more time? We finally agreed to put our schedules where our mouths were, and vowed to meet once a month for a reading group. In view of our full calendars, we called it All Booked Up.

When that first Monday rolled around, there were a hundred reasons to cancel, but we didn't. As Sydney J. Harris said, "The time to relax is when you don't have time for it." We kept this time for relaxing with each other, even when we had other important obligations. When we were tempted to call and say, "I can't make it this month," we asked ourselves rhetorically, "Don't I have two hours a month for friends?" It put that obligation into perspective for us and helped us keep a commitment to each other that brought hours of sunshine into our lives.

Who's Got Time?

◎

"One of the symptoms of an approaching nervous breakdown is the belief that one's work is terribly important."

—BERTRAND RUSSELL

Some of you may be thinking, "It's easy for you to do something like that. You work for yourself so you can take time off in the middle of the morning. I can't. I can just picture telling my boss, 'I'm off to my book club meeting.'"

Do you make time for your kids' orthodontic appointments? Do you make time for washing the car? Do you make time to go to a movie? Wouldn't you agree two hours a month with friends is as important as those other commitments? Make a date with a friend and keep it—no matter what. Realize that your friends are at *least* as important as any one of a dozen other commitments you keep every month.

I can hear you saying, "Get real. I'm so busy, the last thing I have time for is friends." We need to reframe our thinking, so instead of saying, "I'll get together with my pals *when* it's not quite so crazy," we'll say, "I'm going to get together with my pals *so* it's not quite so crazy."

Colorado keynoter and friend Mary LoVerde addresses this issue in her presentation "June Cleaver Never Fried Bacon in a Bill Blass Dress." Mary maintains that balance is not achieved by working longer, harder, or smarter, but by taking time in the midst of our hectic schedules to nurture ourselves and others through loving relationships and rituals. She believes that when we feel overwhelmed, we often isolate ourselves. Mary suggests we do just the opposite. Instead of retreating and withdrawing, we need to reach out.

That was the lesson I learned from the month-long media tour for my book *Tongue Fu!* The schedule was rather daunting. More than sixty media interviews, TV and radio programs, speaking engagements, and book signings in sixteen cities in thirty days. I couldn't believe how many people in the biz warned me in advance, "You're going to get exhausted." "Have you seen the weather reports? The Northeast is blanketed with blizzards." One person even said, "I just know you're going to get sick. The air on those planes is teeming with germs."

Finally I put my hand up and said, "*Stop!* I'm looking forward to this trip. This is a privilege, not a pain. I can't wait to share the book's success with my friends in all the different cities." A fellow author said, "You can't be serious. This isn't a social trip. You're not going to have time to get together with friends. You'll be lucky just to get from one place to another in one piece."

Fortunately I didn't listen to these skeptics. As a result, the tour turned out to be a month-long birthday party. In every city, someone—a Hawaii neighbor who had migrated to the mainland, a college roommate, or a National Speakers Association buddy—met me at the airport or hotel, helped out with my programs, assisted at book signings, and got me to the plane on time. My enduring memories aren't of the heady celebrity moments, the TV shows, the limo rides, or the fancy hotels, but of the many friends I connected with on the way who so graciously extended themselves. That experience was infinitely sweeter because it was *shared*.

Impose vs. Add Value

◉

"Human beings are born into this little span of life of which the best thing is its friendships . . . and yet they leave their friendships with no cultivation, to grow as they will by the roadside, expecting them to 'keep' by force of mere inertia."

—WILLIAM JAMES

One seminar participant said, "I'd *love* to cultivate friendships with some of the people I've met, but many of them are juggling careers and a family. My kids are grown and out of the house and I'm not putting in sixty-hour workweeks like they are. Every time I ask if they want to get together, they say, 'I'd love to, but I'm jamming right now. Maybe when things aren't quite so crazy?' I don't feel comfortable calling them back because it seems they always have too much to do and too little time to do it in."

Denise had brought up a very real challenge. Many people continue to think that getting together with friends is something you do when all your other obligations are taken care of. That's why it's important to suggest double-duty activities. Impose is defined as "to force into the company or on the attention of another." Instead of imposing, propose an activity that's going to be a win for the other person *and* for you. Few people have time to just get together and talk. That may be perceived as a low priority when the person has dozens of other responsibilities competing for his or her attention. The question is, what activity does the other person want or need to do that the two of you can enjoy together? That way neither of you is taking time out of a busy schedule; you're making the most of a busy schedule. By dovetailing the necessary activity with something both of you want or need to do anyway, you're maximizing value by getting two things done at once.

Double-Duty Activities
⊙

"The eternal quest of the individual human being is to shatter his loneliness."
-NORMAN COUSINS

Denise followed up on this idea with great results. "I asked myself what my friends wanted to do that we could share. The answer to that was an early-morning aerobics class. One neighbor in particular that I'd always admired and enjoyed had mentioned several times that she wished she had the discipline to get up and exercise in the morning.

"I called and proposed we sign up for a six-thirty A.M. aerobics class three mornings a week. I volunteered to pick her up and bring her back and suggested that going together would keep us honest. That was six months (and six inches) ago, and we're both glad we got off our duffs and did this for ourselves.

"The best part is, we've become great friends. We bounce ideas off each other while we're bouncing around. Those mornings together energize us physically and emotionally. Neither one of us could or would have carved six hours a week out of our schedule if it hadn't been tied into a 'useful' activity."

Kindred Souls
⊙

"Loneliness and the feeling of being unwanted are the most terrible poverty."
-MOTHER TERESA

One participant snorted when we were talking about the importance of staying connected. He said ruefully, "I don't have any friends to keep. I moved here six months ago and haven't made one friend."

I suggested Ted seek "kindred souls." Kindred means "of a similar nature or character." A fact of human behavior is we like people who are like us. In fact, if we're surrounded by people who aren't like us, we feel we don't belong.

This was dramatically illustrated by a snippet of information that was given in the bio of a big-wave surfer selected by *People* magazine as one of the Fifty Most Beautiful People in the World. In the copy about him, this man said that while attending high school in Hawaii, he couldn't get a date.

My walking buddy and I were discussing this on our early-morning jaunt. Shannon was astounded that this incredibly good-looking guy felt rejected in high school. She summed it up in two words: "wrong place." There was nothing wrong with the guy, he was just in the wrong place. His only mistake was that he was different. As a nonlocal, he didn't fit in.

Are you in the wrong place? Are you in the midst of a group that is not like you so you're feeling shunned? Are you starting to think, "There's something *wrong* with me?" Maybe, like the big-wave surfer, you're just in the wrong place. Seek out people with a similar nature and character. Find someone who is like you. Search for a group that shares your interests. As soon as you do, you will breathe a sigh of relief because you'll finally, blessedly, feel you do belong.

Community Cause
◉

"To associate with other like-minded people in small purposeful groups is for the great majority of men and women a source of profound psychological satisfaction."

-ALDOUS HUXLEY

Community is defined as a body of persons having a common history or common social, economic, or political interests. When I asked Ted what his interests were, he said he liked cars. I told him about a drag strip outside of town that sponsored amateur races every Saturday night, and suggested he call them up and offer to help. Surely they needed someone to collect tickets, assist with crowd control—something. He dropped me a line several months later and said he had found his community. "*Fi-*

nally I met some people I can be myself with. I get along with these guys because we're into the same thing. I can talk about cars all I want and no one thinks I'm crazy. The drag strip has become my second home, and the crew there has become my second family."

Cater-Made Community
───────────◎───────────

"Friendship is the only cement that will ever hold the world together."
-WOODROW WILSON

Cater is defined as "to supply what is required or desired." The community you live or work in may not be cater-made for you if it's not supplying what you require or desire. In that case, you need to seek similarly inclined individuals.

A military wife discovered the importance of seeking her own community instead of trying to fit into the ones forced upon her. Norma married a divorced senior military officer and moved into base quarters with him. She didn't play bridge, golf, or tennis, and preferred not to help out with the officers' wives' club secondhand shop. Needless to say, after politely declining numerous offers to join in, Norma started feeling the disapproval of several of her neighbors who wondered, not so discreetly, if she thought she was too good for them. It wasn't that Norma was being a snob, she just didn't share their interests.

A former track star in high school and college, she decided to get involved with running again. The next Sunday morning, Norma drove to Kapiolani Park near Waikiki to train with the Honolulu Marathon Clinic. Every year, for the eight months leading up to the annual 26-mile run held in early December, hundreds of athletes show up every weekend to train together. Norma reported, "I met a running buddy that first session. Barbara and I run at the same pace and we're both doing this for recreation, not competition. We started running together four times a week. Barbara was a behind-the-scenes volunteer last year, and she asked me to help organize the water stations.

Thanks to her and the other runners I've met, I've found my place, instead of feeling out of place."

Place is defined as "a proper or designated niche." Have you found your proper place? If not, it's time to find your niche. Ask yourself, "What do I like to do? Where can I find people who share my interests? How can I boost my confidence by finding my own community?"

Seek Out Support Groups

"There can be no peace, and ultimately no life, without community."
—M. SCOTT PECK

Sometimes instead of seeking a community to share your likes, it's more helpful to seek a group that shares your *dis*likes. An executive had battled agoraphobia most of his adult life. This panic disorder causes people to dread going outside because it is physically and psychologically nerve-racking for them to be around people. Every morning this man had to use every ounce of discipline he had to force himself to leave his house, drive to work, attend meetings, and function "normally."

"What saved my sanity was finding an agoraphobia support group. You can't imagine my relief that first evening when I found I wasn't the only person who felt this way. It meant so much to realize that *other* people were going through the same thing. When you're fighting it by yourself, you think you're nuts. Every day, you're tempted to give in to your paranoia, bury yourself under your covers, and never come out. To know that others have conquered it, or at least gotten to the point where they can cope with it, convinced me that I can, too. Those meetings are my life raft."

Do you sometimes find yourself in a sea of confusion with nothing to hold on to? Your daily newspaper lists a variety of support groups in its community section. There are support groups for people with cancer, for adult children of alcoholic parents, for stutterers, for women who have been battered, and for people whose loved pet has died. If you're hurting, other people have experienced what you're feeling, and they're willing to help you through it. Check your paper or call a local family service center to request the phone number of a group that shares your concerns. Aligning yourself with these kindred souls will give you something to hold on to in your time of need.

You Are Not Alone
━━━━━━━━━━⊙━━━━━━━━━━
"Communication is to relationships what breath is to life."
-VIRGINIA SATIR

While buying a pair of tennis shoes, I started talking with the twenty-something manager of the athletic store. Her company's management philosophy was to develop their new supervisors by transferring them from store to store for the first five years. Angela said this was the third state and store she'd been in the last two years, and she was homesick. She checked her mailbox every day, hoping to find a letter, but was often disappointed.

I told Angela that relationships are as necessary to us as oxygen, and the way to have a steady supply is to initiate and maintain communication with the people we love. If the people we love are not nearby, we can keep in touch with letters, faxes, phone calls, or e-mails. I suggested if she wanted to *receive* more letters, she needed to *write* more letters.

She replied, "I'm here from eight in the morning to eight at night. I don't have time to write letters." I asked if she wanted to hear a lesson I learned from my grandmother. She nodded, so I told my tale.

"One Christmas our granny (which was what she liked to be called) was particularly generous with her gifts. On the way out her front door, I gave her a big hug and said, 'Thanks for the great presents.' She said, 'If you really like them, write me a thank-you note.' I promised I would.

"Well, January came and went, no thank-you note. February came and went, no thank-you note. March, no thank-you note. Our family went back to Granny's house for Easter Sunday dinner. Following our holiday meal, my grandmother led me out onto the back porch and asked, 'Sam, didn't you like your Christmas presents?' I said, 'Oh yes, they were great.' 'Why haven't I gotten a thank-you note yet?' 'Oh, Granny, I've just been so busy, I haven't had time,' I said apologetically.

"If you have a grandmother like mine, you know she wasn't about to let me get away with that. She pursed her lips and said, 'Hhhmm, have you watched any TV these last few months?' I nodded. She continued, 'Have you read any books these last few months?' Again I nodded. She made her point: 'Sam, how long does it *take* to write a thank-you note?' "

Write On
— ◉ —

"Excuse me for not answering your letter sooner, but I've been so busy not answering letters that I couldn't get around to not answering yours in time."
— GROUCHO MARX

I asked the young manager, "Angela, do you have ten minutes a night for the people you love? Promise yourself you're going to write one letter every night for the rest of the month . . . and see what happens."

Guess what? Six weeks later, I got a letter from Angela! She said she couldn't believe what had happened. After sending a letter to every member of her family, she had run out of relatives, so she started writing old high school friends, former work mates, even an old boyfriend. She said she now receives at least a letter a day. More important, she doesn't feel alone anymore because she's no longer "out of sight, out of mind." Her full mailbox is a constant reminder of all the people she loves and the people who love her.

Are you wondering what this has to do with confidence? Randolph Bourne believed, "A man must get friends as he would get food and drink for nourishment and sustenance." By taking the time to nourish yourself with friendships, you will like your-self and your life even more—the essence of confidence.

Sample Starting Today Assignment

"There is no physician like a true friend."
—ANONYMOUS

WHO HAVE YOU LOST TOUCH with? Who have you been promising to get together with, someday soon? Is there a support group with like-minded souls somewhere nearby? Where could you find a community that contains people who share your likes or dislikes? Judy Garland asked plaintively, "If I'm such a legend, why am I so lonely?" What she didn't understand is that *loneliness is a voluntary status.* The assignment today is to pick up the phone right now and give that long-lost friend a call. Or pick up your pen and write that long-overdue letter. You won't be sorry you did, you'll only be sorry if you don't. ◎

Action Plan for Making and Keeping Friends

Andrea used to belong to an organization for women in her profession, but she dropped out last year when she gave birth to twin baby girls. She really misses her friends, but she's busy juggling her job and her daughters and figures friendships will just have to wait until her schedule lightens up.

BLOCKERS	BUILDERS
Lose friends	Keep friends
"I don't have time to be in-volved in anything outside the home."	*"I'm going to take three hours a month to go to the club meeting."*

Relationships are luxuries to be done when you "have time" *"I'll get together with friends when it's not so crazy."*	Relationships are essential to life and are maintained all the time *"I'll get together with friends so it's not so crazy."*
Don't want to impose *"I can't ask her to get together. She's already got too much to do."*	Want to add value *"I'll ask if she wants to ride to the meeting together."*
Can't find anyone who shares the same interests *"All my neighbors want to talk about is soap operas."*	Find people with similar interests *"I'm going to call Carole to see if she'll go to that seminar with me."*
Feel you're the only one who's going through this *"I don't know if I can stand this. I feel like I'm stagnating."*	Find other people who are going through the same thing *"What a relief to know I'm not the only one who feels like she's going nuts cooped up at home."*

MY PERSONAL STARTING TODAY ASSIGNMENT

Starting today I'm going to _____

_____

_____

Signed _____ Date _____

Catapult Your Career with SOCIALSAVVY®

"Anyone who waits for recognition is criminally naive."
- ANONYMOUS

Is your career as successful as you'd like? Are you receiving the recognition, pay, and promotions you deserve? Are you confident on the job?

I'll always remember one participant who spoke up and said, "Sam, these techniques work great in the social world, but I need something to help me out in the work world." Ryan complained, "I'm the one bringing in most of our clients, but the promotion I was up for went to a co-worker who's pals with the boss. In my company, if you're not part of the old boy network, you're never going to rise to the top."

Ryan had brought up a good point. You may be an enormously talented, competent individual, but if your supervisor doesn't like you, you're hitting your head on your professional ceiling. Seminar attendees frequently approach and tell me tales of woe about how their good work has gone unnoticed, "I'm the one who stays late to finish projects, but the guy who goes golfing with my supervisor is the one who got the raise," or "It's not fair. I'm holding down the office, but my manager gave the position I wanted to her college buddy."

When I ask these disgruntled employees if they've spoken up about these inequities, the answer is usually no.

The Unwritten Rules of Business
———————— ◎ ————————

"If we're going to play the game, we better know the rules."
– BARBARA JORDAN

Face it. Hard work and talent aren't enough. Like it or not, one of the unwritten rules of business is that people do business with people they know, like, and trust. The question then is, are the people who have the power to give you a raise, promotion, or contract even aware of your existence? Are you known and respected? If not, you must take responsibility for diplomatically bringing your contributions to their attention. Confident people don't sit back and complain when a situation is not to their liking. They do something about it. We must have the courage and the confidence to diplomatically market ourselves instead of passively leaving our career success in the hands of others.

An employee in one of my sessions objected, "Why should I have to market myself? Maybe I'm naive, but I think my results should speak for themselves." A woman in the same session agreed. "Isn't it the manager's responsibility to know who is the best person for the job and to assign the position accordingly?"

"Hah!" retorted a man in the class. "You *are* naive. In my agency, it's a joke every time they announce a position opening. Everyone knows it's going to go to one of the boss's cronies. Other people might as well not even apply."

True, the word *cronyism* has a negative connotation, but let's explore what it really means. *Crony* is simply defined as "a close friend, especially of long standing." We may not like the fact that people give jobs to their friends, but it's a fact of life.

Get Known, Liked, and Respected
————————⊙————————

"How do you spell professional success?
F-A-V-O-R-A-B-L-E V-I-S-I-B-I-L-I-T-Y."
—SAM HORN

I took my SOCIALSAVVY handouts to my local printer to have them duplicated for an upcoming convention. Bob looked through them and commented, "This looks interesting. Tell me more about it." I was explaining the content of the course when he cut me off. "Oh, what you're talking about is, 'It's not *what* we know, it's *who* we know.' I don't play that game," he said with some distaste.

I asked, "You don't play this game, huh? Who takes care of your bookkeeping? Do you do all your own record-keeping?"

"Oh no," Bob replied, "I have an accountant who handles that."

"Uh-huh, and how did you find that accountant?"

Bob explained, "I played in a charity golf tournament and he was part of my foursome. I was impressed with him and, after a couple of exploratory appointments, asked him to take over the financial side of my business."

"Uh-huh. Bob, you just moved into our neighborhood. Did you find your house by yourself?"

"Oh no," he answered, "our real estate agent located it for us. And in answer to your next question, she spoke at our Rotary Club, and I thought she really knew the real estate market in our area."

"Uh-huh," I replied. "Bob, your place was transformed from a bare lot to a green oasis in just a few months. Did you do all that planting yourself?"

"No," he answered, "A landscaper did it for us. He was walking through our neighborhood passing out business cards and offered to give me a free one-hour consultation. He took me around our yard and explained how he could turn it into our own private Eden. I liked his ideas *and* his initiative, and gave him the job."

"Uh-huh," I said. "Bob, you *do* play that game. We all play the game. It's not a *game*; it's how the work world works. It simply makes sense to give business to people we know, like, and trust. After years of writing and speaking on this topic, I've come to the conclusion that it's who we know *and* what we know that determines how well we do professionally."

It's been said, "The world belongs to the energetic." I think the world belongs to those who energetically and confidently promote themselves. So how do we *ethically* establish positive name recognition with potential employers and/or clients? How can we get credit for our contributions? Most important, how can we do this with integrity?

Don't Sell, Serve
——————◉——————

"The more you give people what they want, the more they'll give you what you need."
—ZIG ZIGLAR

We do it by serving, not selling. Most people hate the hard sell, and rightfully so. Pushing ourselves on others is inappropriate and counterproductive. I'm not talking about aggressively selling ourselves and I'm not talking about kissing up. One rather un-refined class participant said bluntly, "I'm no brownnose. I'm not going to suck up to my boss." I'm not suggesting we do. I'm suggesting we tactfully take the responsibility for letting current or potential employers know what we have to offer. How can we accomplish this without alienating decision makers and without compromising our morals? We do it by using *high-principled* techniques instead of *high-pressure* tactics. Instead of missing out on the professional success you deserve, market yourself without marketing yourself with these three SOCIAL-SAVVY steps.

SOCIALSAVVY Step 1. Cultivate a Mentor or Womentor

In this age of downsizing, our job security is only as good as our sponsor. Find someone several levels up in your chain of command who is universally respected. Is there someone at least five years ahead of you on their career path that you admire? Ingratiate yourself to that person. I know, the word *ingratiate* probably has negative connotations for you; however, it simply means "to gain favor or favorable acceptance for deliberate effort." I am indeed proposing that you diplomatically and deliberately curry the favor of the people who control your career, rather than leaving it to chance.

A participant in one of my sessions protested, "I wouldn't feel comfortable approaching someone senior to myself. Why would they want to spend time with me? I don't have anything to offer them." Why, indeed? I complimented him on his sensitivity and agreed, "You're right, it's *not* fair to ask people for their valuable time unless we intend to offer them something in kind. What we *can* do for mentors is to give them an opportunity to share their intellectual wealth. What we can do is give them an opportunity to make a lasting difference for someone else." Seneca observed, "There is as much greatness of mind in acknowledging a good turn, as in doing it." The key to acknowledging your mentor's (or womentor's) good turn is to honor the Four As of Being a Protégé.

A = Acknowledge. When you call, e-mail, write, or walk up to your potential mentor, the first five words out of your mouth need to be "I know you're busy, and . . ." In a delightful discussion at the Maui Writers Conference, author Jack Canfield (*Chicken Soup for the Soul*) told me he had discovered the secret to convincing someone to grant us a favor while researching his book *Aladdin Factor: How to Ask for and Get*

What You Want. The key is acknowledging you know people are busy and that you appreciate them giving you a little of their valuable time. Another way to get a yes to your request is to put parameters on the amount of time—for example, "Could I have fifteen minutes to ask you some quick questions?" or "Can I take you out for a brief lunch to seek your advice? My treat."

A = Ask. Once this person has graciously agreed to share his time and expertise, SHUT UP and listen. A fellow author told me about a writer wannabe who pleaded for an opportunity to pick his brain. My friend finally consented, they met for lunch, and the aspiring author didn't stop talking the entire time. My friend wanted to tell the young man, "You can't learn anything when your mouth is open." Prepare thought-provoking questions in advance and take notes so you're taking full advantage of your benefactor's wisdom.

A = Act. Acting is the way you keep your end of the bargain, the key to making this a mutually beneficial proposition. Since this wise individual cared enough to donate his or her time, attention, and experience, the least you can do is to follow up and take action on at least one of the ideas.

A = Appreciate. Expressing your appreciation is the final part of the agreement, bringing the relationship full circle and making it win-win. Take the time to get back in touch with your mentor to let him know the results his advice produced. Be sure to put this in writing. Phone calls and verbal feedback are nice, but they're no substitute for a handwritten note on quality stationery detailing exactly how this person's suggestion made a tangible difference for you.

> *"The best way to pay for a lovely moment is to enjoy it."*
> **—RICHARD BACH**

Wouldn't you agree the best way to pay mentors for their lovely advice is to express your appreciation and act on it? After almost every seminar, someone will come up and say, "I want to do what you do. Can you tell me how to become a professional speaker?" In my early speaking years, I gave hundreds of hours (and the equivalent of thousands of dollars in consulting fees) to these individuals. I was glad to have serendipitously discovered my calling and welcomed these opportunities to give back.

And boy, did I give back. Of the dozens of people I gave trade secrets to, only a handful were thoughtful enough to write a thank-you note. I realized over time that many of these aspiring speakers didn't fully understand the magnitude of what they were asking. As my schedule filled to overflowing, I realized it was necessary for me to be more judicious about who I gave my time to.

I'm still committed to sharing my enthusiasm for this profession, and now when people approach me, I agree that it's a tremendously rewarding career, suggest they call the National Speakers Association for membership information, invite them to attend one of our local chapter meetings, and refer them to a comprehensive resource book (*Speak and Grow Rich* by Dottie and Lilly Walters). I also offer to mail a couple of articles I've written about this topic, free of charge.

If I sense they're serious about pursuing a speaking career, I'll meet with them for a walk/talk. The last thing I need is to go out to lunch, but I can always use a good walk. I'm glad to meet with them for a jaunt along the three-mile, user-friendly beach path at the end of our street. It's a double-duty activity that's a win for them and for me. And if those people take five minutes to put pen to paper to tell me how they've been able to put some of the ideas we shared into practice, then I consider myself paid in full. Our time together was well and gladly spent.

SOCIALSAVVY Step 2. Become a Visibility Virtuoso

— ⊙ —

"The most effective way to ensure the value of the future is to confront the present courageously and constructively."

— ROLLO MAY

One of the best ways to ensure your professional future is to have the courage and confidence to present decision makers with opportunities to see you in action so they are favorably impressed. In my SOCIALSAVVY workshops we discuss literally dozens of ways to give potential clients or employers a chance to get to know us. One of the most beneficial is to get involved in industry, business, and community organizations in high-profile leadership positions. If you're a banker, join the American Bankers Association. If you're a contractor, get involved with the Associated General Contractors of America. If you're in personnel, volunteer for the Society for Human Resource Managers.

Perhaps you're thinking, "I joined one of those organizations and didn't get anything out of it." We can't expect to get anything out of organizations unless we put something into them. Here's a story that illustrates this point rather nicely.

Our family was standing in line at one of Disneyland's most popular attractions. We were scrunched together with hundreds of other people patiently (and not so patiently) waiting their turn. The family in front of us was having a marvelous time. They were poring over the map, discussing what ride to go on next, where they wanted to have lunch, and where they planned to sit to get the best view of the Midnight Parade.

Meanwhile, the family behind us was miserable. They were complaining about how hot it was, how long the lines were, and how expensive everything was. The father grumbled, "We're never coming back here again. Disneyland just isn't any fun anymore."

Hmmm. Two families six feet apart. One family having a terrific time, the other having a terrible time. It occurred to me that Disneyland itself isn't fun, it's a *forum* for fun. We can have a dreadful time there or a delightful time. It's up to us.

The same is true of professional associations and industry organizations. They can make a worthwhile investment of time and money, or they can be a waste of time and money. It's up to us. Associations don't do anything *for* us, they simply offer opportunities for us to network with peers, develop our expertise, and make it so peers and industry leaders recognize us. We can't just pay our dues, show up at meetings, and expect miracles to happen. We must get actively involved so as many people as possible have a chance to see us in action and come to know and respect us.

> *"Power positioning is 'intentionally placing ourselves wherever luck is most likely to happen.' It is also volunteering for leadership roles where we control the results so we can add value while producing the kind of quality with which we want to be associated."*
>
> **—SAM HORN**

Since most of us don't have much discretionary time, any addition to our calendar has to be a high-payoff activity—the biggest bang for our organizational buck or the biggest gain of our luck. That's why you must be in charge of something rather than simply serve on a committee. If you are a member of a committee, your impact is limited and you don't control the outcome.

A friend offered to help out with programs for her association one year. Unfortunately, the chairperson of the committee had already scheduled several boring speakers in a row. Members complained to my friend that they weren't going to attend meetings unless the caliber of speakers improved. My friend couldn't do anything about the bookings, so her reputation ended up getting tarnished by her association with these programs.

If you chair an event, you can make sure that you're proud of what you produce and that it reflects well on you. A bonus of a high-profile position is that you have a legitimate reason to approach respected experts in your field. You can call the mayor of your city, the editor of your local newspaper, or the CEO of your industry's largest corporation, and ask them to speak. The emphasis, of course, is not on you. Don't use your position to market yourself to these guests. However, if you act with integrity in the course of your hosting duties, they will come to respect you and may be in a position to recommend or hire you at some time in the future.

One woman said, "But I don't have the experience or confidence to head up a committee." Fair enough. There are other ways to get positive name recognition from your peers and potential employers. Offer to contribute a "People on the Move" column for your association newsletter. You don't have to be Hemingway to report promotions, awards, transfers, and other member news, and this is a commitment you can fulfill from home on your telephone. Set aside three hours a month, call different members, ask, "What's up?" and collect the material for your monthly submission.

You could also offer to help out at the registration table or to be a greeter at your professional society's monthly meeting. Whether you're checking names off the reservation list or simply welcoming guests with a friendly smile, you are getting noticed.

A consultant used these techniques to successfully establish a consulting practice after moving to a new state. When Kathy moved to her new home, she didn't know a soul. This savvy lady took several pivotal steps the first week she arrived. She called the local chapter of the American Society for Training and Development and (1) asked if she could sign up for membership at the next meeting, (2) offered her assistance, (3) and asked for the names and phone numbers of three of the most successful consultants in town.

Within one month, Kathy was a contributing editor to the ASTD newsletter, had already met with the three leading consultants in town, and had picked their brains as to how to set up shop. Within six months, Kathy was well known and liked by the corporate community and had more business than she could handle. All because she was a skilled and delightful lady who operated with integrity, and she had focused on serving, not selling. She hadn't made one cold call to solicit clients. Clients had called *her* after reading one of her articles, meeting her at one of the many functions she attended, or hearing good things about her from other impressed professionals.

SOCIALSAVVY Step 3: Be Uncommonly Courteous
━━━⊙━━━

"Life is not so short but that there is always time for courtesy."
-RALPH WALDO EMERSON

Our final technique takes about five minutes and a postage stamp. From this day forward, vow that you are going to write thank-you cards. I'll always remember the time I mentioned this at a public workshop and a woman laughed out loud and said, "You've got to be kidding. I haven't even written thank-you notes for my wedding, and that was two years ago."

I realize the last thing most of us need is another time-consuming task. However, W. H. Auden said, "Noble actions are the most radiant pages in the biography of souls." The noble task of putting appreciative thoughts on pages produces emotional and tangible rewards that make it well worthwhile. From now on, when people contribute to you professionally, you are going to follow up and thank them for their ideas, time, attention, advice—whatever. It is a cordial way to stay connected and to reinforce the positive impression you made.

This is especially important because I don't believe in giving out business cards. *"What?"* you might be saying. My personal philosophy is, *don't* give your card unless the other person asks for it. Why? If you've had a delightful discussion with someone and you wrap it up by hauling out your card and saying, "If you ever need a stockbroker, let me know," you've just cast doubt on the entire interaction. People may immediately assume you were buttering them up for the sales kill. They may conclude you were really after only one thing—their wallet. They'll suspect that the gleam in your eye was not because you enjoyed their company, but because you were excited at the prospect of making some money.

There's a caveat. It is acceptable to *ask* for someone's card *if* you intend to follow up with something of value to them. By all means, say, "If I can have your card, I'll be glad to send that article to you we were talking about," or "If you'd like to give me your card, I'll be happy to call you with that store's 800 number." Then when you send them something of value, include your card, but *don't* make a sales pitch. It's still not appropriate to say, "And if you're interested in starting a stock portfolio, please keep me in mind." Any overt commercial overture will taint the entire transaction. Thank them for the delightful conversation, refer to something specific they said that you appreciated learning, and let them know how much you enjoyed meeting them. Then drop it. They will know who you are and what you do. In their own time, they're likely to get back in touch with you because you've handled yourself in a classy way. By not pressuring them, you have made them confident they can deal with you without your hassling them to become a client.

"Small kindnesses, courtesies, and considerations, habitually practiced in our social intercourse, give a greater charm to the character than the display of great talents and accomplishments," noted Mary Ann Kelly. This was certainly the experience of an interior designer who followed up on the idea to be uncommonly courteous. She reported, "I got a $25,000 contract because of a 25¢ stamp." (This story is obviously from one of my workshops in the eighties!) "I was competing with three other firms to win the bid to renovate the lobby of an office building here in town. All of the other firms had been around longer than mine and had well-established reputations. I'd only been in business for two years, and this was my largest project to date. I was flabbergasted when they awarded me the contract. After working with the building manager for a while, I summoned the courage to ask why I had been selected for the job. She said simply, 'You were the only one who sent us a thank-you note.'

"The manager went on to explain that all four firms had submitted similar designs and budgets. She admitted, 'I didn't know who to choose because it seemed like all of you would do a good job. Then your thank-you note arrived. I really liked the fact that you took the time to follow up. Your card broke the tie and made my decision for me.' "

If you're thinking, "This will work for entrepreneurs, but I'm part of a large bureaucracy. I can't go around sending thank-you notes to people I work with every day." Why not? The thank yous don't have to be formal, they can be handwritten faxes or memos. The point and the outcome are the same. These people will appreciate you for caring enough to send your very best . . . wishes.

Give for the Giving
————— ◎ —————

"We are here on earth to do good to others. What the others are here for, I don't know."

- W. H. AUDEN

One skeptic shook his head in disagreement. "This sounds a little too calculating for me, Sam. Won't people know I'm just trying to get in their good graces?"

I was glad this man had voiced his objection because it's important to clarify that our goal is to give without expectation of reciprocity. I am *not* suggesting we send thank-you notes out of a desire to get in with someone. I'm suggesting we cultivate the characteristic of courtesy, which means taking the time to thank people who have assisted us in some way. Yes, it's true that doing this might reflect well on us, but that's not why we do it. We express our gratitude because that's the kind of person we want to be.

How can we tell if we're extending ourselves with integrity? Ask yourself, "Would I do good for others even if nothing positive happened to me as a result?" If the answer is a resounding yes, then we know we're doing it for the right reasons. Write thank-you notes because the other person deserves to know his or her actions are appreciated, not because your actions might pay off. If you in some way benefit, that's a bonus to be accepted graciously. If you don't, it's equally okay because giving is not meant to be quid pro quo.

You've probably heard the Swedish proverb "The best place to find a helping hand is at the end of your arm." If your professional life is not what you want it to be, it's up to *you* to do something about it. These SOCIALSAVVY ideas can help you achieve the career success you want and deserve.

After I had covered the communication techniques from these last few chapters in a public workshop, a woman named Ginny asked, "What if you do all this and you still don't have a healthy regard for yourself and your powers? I've got a decent career and plenty of friends, but I still don't feel very confident."

"Then," I told Ginny, "your lack of confidence is probably all in your head." If you're thinking this information has been helpful, but you still don't feel completely confident, then turn to the next section, which deals with self-concept. The next few chapters will explain how to become your own best friend, instead of your own worst enemy.

Sample Starting Today Assignment

"Everyone, in the final analysis, is in business for himself."
—ANONYMOUS

TODAY'S ASSIGNMENT IS TO FOLLOW up and use at least one of these ideas to catapult your career. How are you going to cultivate a mentor and create a win-win relationship? How are you going to befriend the decision makers who have the power to give you the raise, promotion, contract, or position you've got your eye on? How are you going to serve, not sell, potential clients/employers with uncommon courtesy? How are you going to position yourself in a high-profile leadership role so you become known, liked, and respected? How are you going to get actively involved in organizations so you can give back to your professional community and give others an opportunity to see you in action and become favorably impressed? In the final analysis, your career success is your business. ◉

Action Plan for Catapulting Your Career with SOCIALSAVVY

Stan has his own car detailing business. Many people don't enjoy or have time to clean their cars, so he makes weekly or bimonthly house calls. He has a number of loyal clients, but he needs more customers to earn a decent living.

BLOCKERS	BUILDERS
Take offense that we're not getting the recognition we deserve *"I should be making a lot more money than this."*	Take responsibility for getting the recognition we deserve *"I'm going to get involved in the local business club so I can make contacts."*
Hard pressure *"I'm going to attend that meeting and give my business card to anyone who will take one."*	High-principled *"I'm going to attend and see if they would like some help with their registration desk."*
Unethical and hard sell *"I'm going to sneak some of my brochures on this back table."*	Integrity and high serve *"Would you like me to organize a table to display members' brochures?*
Attend meetings only *"That meeting was a waste of time. I didn't get one new client."*	Involved in high-profile activities *"Sure, I'd be glad to help out with the Meet the Pros table topics."*

Member of committee and
don't control results
*"They have a lousy lineup. I
don't think anyone's going to
be interested in this program."*

Chair of committee so can
control results
*"Would you like me to line up
the table facilitators? I'll be
sure to ask a variety of experts."*

Give cards and be crass
*"Take my card, and give me
a call if you want your car
detailed."*

Ask for cards and be courteous
*"I'll be glad to send you that
article about that car leasing
service."*

MY PERSONAL STARTING TODAY ASSIGNMENT

Starting today I'm going to _____

_____

Signed _____ Date _____

PART III

Concept: It's All in Your Head

"Every man stamps his value on himself. Man is made great or small by his own will."

- J. C. F. VON SCHILLER

Put the Past in the Past

*"There are some who want to get rid of their past, who if they
could, would begin all over again . . . but you must learn that the
only way to get rid of your past is to get a future out of it."*
— PHILLIP BROOKS

Think back to your early
years. How did the significant others in your life treat you? Did
your parents make you feel loved and wanted? Or were you
raised in a family where it seemed nothing you ever did was
good enough? Did you have brothers and sisters? Did sibling
revelry often turn into sibling rivalry? How about school? Did
your teachers, counselors, and peers make you feel you had
something to offer, or did you feel ostracized and misunder-
stood?

Children believe whatever the important people in their lives
tell them. When we're young, we're not emotionally mature
enough to have our own self-image; we adopt the labels and
beliefs applied to us, whether accurate and fair or not. If our
authority figures told us we were good and had value, we believed them. If they told us we were bad and wouldn't amount
to much, we believed them.

Would you like to hear some good news? No matter how you
were brought up, it doesn't have to determine the quality of
your life now. You have a choice. You can use your upbringing
as an excuse or you can use it as an incentive. It's up to you.
Our history does not have to be our destiny. As George Eliot
observed, "It is never too late to be what you might have been."

Studies of successful people have revealed that many were raised in supportive homes where they were frequently told, "You can do anything you want to do." Surprisingly, though, some successful people came from dysfunctional homes. These determined individuals chose to use their painful family history as a reason for achieving ("I'm going to prove them wrong. I'm going to make something of myself") instead of as a rationalization for *not* achieving ("I can't hold a job because I was held back in sixth grade").

So the question is, did the significant others in your early years make you feel valued or devalued, and have you used that experience to your advantage or disadvantage? The purpose of this chapter is to help you once and for all put the past in the past so you can get a future out of it.

Who's to Blame?
——————◉——————

"Blaming our parents is just a negative way of clinging to them still."
-NANCY FRIDAY

A man said he used to blame his alcoholic, abusive parents for his problems. "My mom and dad are both dead, but they continued to live in my head. I used to play all the messages they told me when I was little boy: 'I wish I'd never had you,' 'You're a poor excuse for a son,' and 'If it hadn't been for you, I would have. . . .'

"I was at a bar one night crying on some woman's shoulder when all of a sudden, she turned to me and asked, 'How old are you, anyway?' I told her I was forty-five. She shook her head and said, 'And you're *still* dwelling on what Mommy and Daddy did to you thirty-five years ago?' With that, she said, 'Get a life!' and stood up and walked away.

"I sat there, stunned. After nursing my beer for a while, I recovered from the shock of what she'd said and realized she had a point. It *was* pretty pathetic for me to be carrying on about something that had happened three decades ago. I realized I couldn't take back what they did to me, but I could take back my life. Now, if I start dredging up those childhood memories, I simply say to myself, 'That was then, and this is now. And now I take responsibility for my life.' "

That Was Then, This Is Now
◉

"At Phoenix House, the highly regarded drug-rehab center in New York, a typical therapy group will start out by listening quietly to all the victim chatter of a recently arrived addict. Then someone will say something like, 'It isn't your mother or society or even the pushers who put the needle in your arm. You did.' Therapy starts there."

—JOHN LEO

What history have you been hauling around? What is something unfair or hurtful that happened years ago that you're still using as a reason for not being the person you want to be? Agatha Christie believed that "many people go right through life in the grip of an idea which has been impressed on them in very tender years." Many people go through life in the grip of a label or experience that was imprinted on them in their early years.

It's been said that "when we miss the target, never in history has it been the target's fault." This may sound a little harsh, but it has a lot of truth in it. Blaming others is a subtle way of saying, "See, it's not *my* fault. It's not that *I* don't have the discipline, the will, the smarts, or the talent. It's this other person or circumstance that is responsible for what's happening to me."

Blaming is an unhealthy abdication of our power (the ability to get things done) because it makes us dependent on others. Confident individuals don't finger other people as the reason they are the way they are. As the saying goes, whenever we point a finger at someone else, we need to remember that three of our fingers are pointing back at us.

It's time to break up the pity party. If it is your habit to point the verbal finger at someone or something else and start blaming them or it for what's wrong in your life, say to yourself,

"That was ____ [months? years?] ago, and now I'm responsible for what happens to me."

Stop the Pity Party
◎

"Self-pity is easily the most destructive of the non-pharmaceutical narcotics: it is addictive, gives momentary pleasure, and separates the victim from reality."
—JOHN GARDNER

"Not everyone's life is what *they* make it," noted Alice Walker. "Some people's life is what other people make it." This quote really hit home for one woman. She said, "I was abandoned by my mom when I was five years old. She dropped me off at my grandmother's house one day, drove away, and never came back. For weeks afterward, I sat on the porch waiting for her to come back and pick me up. She never did. My grandmother did the best she could, but she was too old and tired to raise a child, so she farmed me out to an aunt I'd never even met. Tilly had three kids of her own, and the last thing she wanted was another one. She kept me until I was ten, and then handed me off to another aunt. For the next few years, I got passed from relative to relative like a used piece of furniture. I felt unwanted everywhere I went.

"I carried those scars with me for years. I told my 'poor me' story to anyone and everyone who would listen. I see now that I was looking for sympathy. I wanted everyone to know how hard I'd had it. Then I met Don, who somehow saw beyond my sob story. He told me writer Larry McMurtry's line 'Yesterday's gone on down the river, and you can't git it back,' and helped me see that I would never 'git' anywhere unless I moved on and put this behind me.

"He encouraged me to go back to school and get my GED. Once I started, I never looked back. I'm in college now, studying for my master's in social work. I intend to become a therapist and save others the pain I suffered. I want them to know you *can* make something of your life—regardless of what's happened to you."

If we're lucky, someone like Don comes into our lives and helps us see that nursing animosity makes us sick. We don't have to wait for a wise benefactor to introduce us to this truth, though. The Buddha noted, "The grudge you hold on to is like a hot coal that you intend to throw at somebody else, but you're the one who gets burned." Confident people refuse to waste their lives carrying grudges. It's been said that enlightenment is nothing more than realizing we've been pinching ourselves. From now on, instead of pinching yourself by choosing to concentrate on a painful past, commit to using your energy more constructively. Focus on how you can improve yourself and enjoy your world, instead of dwelling on who hurt you and how, umpteen years ago.

Free to Move On
—————— ◉ ——————

"Freedom is what you do with what's been done to you."
—JEAN-PAUL SARTRE

Are you thinking, "But you don't know what my parents did to me. You don't know how awful they were. There's just no way I can forgive them and put them out of my mind."

You're right, I *don't* know how awful they were. What I *do* know is that if you continue to hold on to the anger you feel toward them, it will haunt your every waking moment. Ralph Waldo Emerson said, "Skepticism is slow suicide." So is resentment. The question isn't whether what they did to you was terrible. The question is, does it serve *you* to keep it alive? Does it help to carry all that emotional venom in your mind and heart? If you do, you are killing the person you want to be. If you hate what happened so much, why would you want to keep reliving it? You are free to put it behind you. I'm not saying it's easy. I'm saying it's *necessary* if you want to lead the life you want to lead.

Forgive Yourself
—————◉—————

*"Forgiveness saves the expense of anger, the cost of hatred, the
waste of spirits."*
—HANNAH MORE

While one of my groups was discussing this idea of putting the
past in the past, a participant spoke up and said, "So far, all
you've talked about is what other people did to us. What I regret
about my past is what *I* did to someone else. I was a real jerk
in my first marriage. I was so immature, all I ever thought about
was what I wanted. I cheated on my wife. She put up with it for
six years and then asked for a divorce. The thought of losing
her brought me to my senses, but it was too late. She said she
couldn't trust me anymore, and I can't say I blame her. I can't
believe I blew that relationship. I've tried to reapproach her, but
she doesn't want to have anything to do with me."

Mike had brought up a good point. Sometimes the painful
past we're carrying around is regret for what *we've* done. In that
case, we need to evaluate our actions; extract the value so we
can keep it from happening again; if possible, make amends to
the injured party; forgive ourselves; and move on.

Mike said, "How am I supposed to forgive myself for what I
did? It was stupid."

I told Mike his remorse was understandable, but he might want
to remember Henry Ward Beecher's wise words " 'I can forgive,
but I can't forget,' is only another way of saying, 'I will not forgive.' Forgiveness ought to be like a canceled note, torn in two
and burned up, so that it never can be shown against one."

"Mike, we are fallible. We do dumb things. We can't take back
what has happened; we *can* extend a genuine apology to the
person we hurt. If the other person isn't in a place to accept it,
then we simply let them know we're sorry and wish we could
undo what happened. Since we can't, all we can do is tell that
person how much we regret what we did, and then move on,
determined to act more conscientiously in the future."

Aldous Huxley advised, "If you have behaved badly, repent, make what amends you can, and address yourself to the task of behaving better next time. On no account brood over your wrongdoings. Rolling in the muck is not the best way of getting clean."

To keep from "rolling in the muck" and probing a mental wound (as your tongue would a sore tooth), start using the phrase "I used to . . . [whatever the destructive behavior was]," followed by "And now I . . . [whatever the desired behavior is]." Instead of dwelling on regretful acts, mentally close the books on them and behave more constructively in the future. For example, "I used to think only of myself and I hurt a lot of people I loved. And now I'm more sensitive to other people's feelings and treat them with the respect they deserve."

Sample Starting Today Assignment

"The reason people blame things on previous generations is that there's only one other choice."
—DOUG LARSEN

THE ASSIGNMENT IS TO IDENTIFY one thing from your past you're still clinging to. Who or what are you blaming for not being all you can be? Resolve to put the bitter lessons of the past behind you. American journalist Sydney Harris noted, "We have not passed that subtle line between childhood and adulthood until we move from the passive voice to the active voice—that is, until we have stopped saying 'It got lost,' and say, 'I lost it.'" Today, if you start to point the finger at something or someone as the reason why something's wrong with your life, choose instead to say, "That was then, and this is now," or "I used to . . . and now I . . ." Take active responsibility for your behavior. Choose to become better instead of bitter. ◉

Action Plan for Putting the Past in the Past

Rob invested almost all of his savings in an import-export business a friend had started. Unfortunately, his friend's company went bankrupt and Rob lost everything. Rob is fifty years old and has to start all over again.

BLOCKERS	BUILDERS
Using the past as an excuse *"I never want to see Tom again. He's ruined me."*	Using the past as an incentive *"I learned an expensive lesson."*
Resentment and regret *"I can't believe I let Tom talk me into investing. What a jerk."*	Responsibility *"From now on, I'm going to be more careful where I invest my money."*
Hauling around history *"Why didn't I spend more time investigating? I would have found out he was undercapitalized."*	Healing from history *"I'm going to put that experience behind me. I'll know better next time."*
Anger *"I ought to sue him. He really suckered me."*	Enlightenment *"If it looks too good to be true, maybe it is!"*
Can't forget *"I'll never get over this. I'm ruined."*	Can forgive *"I wish this hadn't happened, but it did. I'm going to get on with my life."*

MY PERSONAL STARTING TODAY ASSIGNMENT

Starting today I'm going to _____

_____

_____

Signed _____ Date _____

Spring Free from the Comparison Trap

"All the wrong people have inferiority complexes."
- SLOGAN ON COFFEE MUG

Do you ever find yourself paling in comparison to others? Do you ever feel jealous of someone who appears smarter, wealthier, or better looking than you?

Understand that comparison is the root of all unhappiness and the ruin of self-esteem. When we compare ourselves with someone else, we feel superior or inferior to that person. Neither feeling is desirable. We don't want to feel better than other people—that's arrogance. And we don't want to feel other people are better than us—that's unworthiness.

The goal is to have a solid sense of self-worth that is not dependent on where we are or who we're with. How do we obtain that? By promising ourselves that from now on, rather than comparing ourselves to other people, we're going to admire or aspire.

Admire or Aspire

—————— ◉ ——————

*"We need to be taught to admire, to surrender ourselves
to admiration."*

—WILLIAM HALE WHITE

I agree with Mr. White. It's natural for us to feel envious of
others, to want what other people have. The problem is, it's not
healthy. We need to learn how to admire instead of envy. From
now on, instead of comparing ourselves with other people
("She's so smart. I feel like a dunce next to her" or "Look at
his salary. He makes twice as much money as I do") choose to
admire ("Good for her/him") or aspire ("How can I . . . ?").

A woman called with a satisfying success story. "The Monday
after your class, I decided to rejoin my health club. I used to go
to the gym three times a week, but had gotten out of the habit.
Believe me, my body had paid for this inactivity. I stuffed myself
into my exercise clothes and drove over to the gym. I walked
in for my first workout, took one look at all those hard bodies
leaping around in their leotards, and wanted to turn and walk
right back out the door. I felt so embarrassed about how I
looked, compared to everyone else in the room. Then I remembered what you said: 'If you don't quit comparing, comparing
will cause you to quit.'

"You were right. Comparing was about to cause me to give
up something I wanted to do. I decided to use your advice.
First, I admired: 'Good for them. They're really in shape.' Then
I aspired: 'How can I improve my physical condition?' The answer to that was obviously *not* to go home and inhale a pint of
ice cream. I'm happy to report that admiring and aspiring
moved me from envy to action. Instead of running home and
feeling sorry for myself, I stayed and tackled the Stairmaster.

"I continue to use your advice, and it's made a big difference.
Every once in a while when I'm working out, I'll glance at the
person on the treadmill next to me and start to feel intimidated
because they're going faster, steeper, or longer. If I stayed fo-

cused on the other person's superior performance, I'd become demoralized. Instead, I simply refocus my attention on my intentions to become more fit and congratulate myself for acting on my intentions. Every time I do that, I'm motivated to continue instead of quit.''

Turn Insecurity into Action
⊙

"A show of envy is an insult to myself."
-YEVGENY YEVTUSHENKO

Be aware that other people's strengths don't diminish our value. Just because someone else is attractive doesn't mean we're not. Just become someone else is well paid doesn't mean we're not fairly compensated. Instead of measuring ourselves against other people to see how we stack up, it's better to recognize their good qualities without reflecting them back on ourselves. Realize that comparisons kill contentment.

Choose instead to silently compliment the person ("Wow, she's bright" or "He is well paid") without mentioning yourself. Instead of envying them for what they have, appreciate them for what they've accomplished.

If you still feel a twinge of jealousy and want what they have, then ask yourself, "How can I develop more expertise?' or "How can I increase my income?" These pro-active responses turn insecurity into action. Instead of tormenting yourself by focusing on what you *don't* have, ask "How can I . . . ?" and focus on how to acquire what you'd like to have.

Transform Rivalry into Respect
⊙

"Ambition is the grand enemy of all peace."
-ANONYMOUS

Personally, I think rivalry is the grand enemy of all peace. It's impossible to have peace of mind if our sense of self-esteem requires us to be better than the people around us. Rivalry, defined as "one of two or more striving to obtain something that *only one* can possess," is unhealthy because it is based on the classic one up/one down premise. The belief that only one person at a time can possess competence is the antithesis of confidence (defined as a healthy regard for ourselves and our powers). We don't want our feeling of competence to be at the expense of others', and we don't want their competence to be at the expense of ours. True confidence is based on the premise that competence doesn't have to be either/or—it can be *both*.

This concept was never better demonstrated to me than by a young friend of our son. We celebrated Andrew's tenth birthday with ten of his friends at a nearby beach park. The surf was booming that day and the boys were having a great time skim-boarding into the waves and flipping into the water. After Andrew performed a particularly spectacular somersault, his competitive spirit got the best of him. He strutted up to his pal Hari and said challengingly, "I can get better air time than you can."

Hari looked at Andrew and said simply, "I don't care." With that, he dashed into the ocean without a backward glance. Hari's noncompetitive response stopped Andrew in his tracks. He stood there for a moment, stunned, and then shook it off and ran into the surf after Hari. At the age of ten, Hari already instinctively knows that the object isn't to show up his pal, it's to share good times with his pal.

The next time someone tries to one-up you, could you simply say, "Good for you," or "I don't care," and then go about your business? It will probably stop that person in his tracks and put a stop to his attempt to establish a rivalry. And if you find yourself tempted by rivalrous tendencies, remind yourself that we're not here to beat or defeat other people. We're here to be companions, not competitors.

I Don't Care to Compare
―――――――― ◎ ――――――――

"When nobody around you seems to measure up, it's time to check your yardstick."

—BILL LEMLEY

With all due respect to Mr. Lemley, I think it's time to *chuck* our yardsticks. Taking someone else's measure traps us in a no-win "Who's better or worse?" battle. Odetta said it eloquently many years ago: "The better we feel about ourselves, the fewer times we have to knock someone down to feel tall." Genuinely confident people don't need to belittle other people to feel good about themselves, and they don't belittle themselves if they're around someone who happens to be better at something than they are.

This concept helped a recently divorced woman get over her inferiority complex. Lisa said, "My confidence was really suffering. Last year my husband asked for a separation, and I was forced to reenter the workforce. After being a homemaker for thirty years, I found the work world quite a shock. I got a job as a receptionist for a company where I was surrounded by bright young college graduates who all seemed to know more than me.

"I was overwhelmed by all those newfangled office gadgets. I was a low-tech person in a high-tech world. There was this story on the e-mail circuit about someone who called Repair and complained that the cup-holder on the front of her computer had broken off. The tech was stumped until he realized she was referring to her CD-ROM drawer. Everyone in our office had a good laugh at that except me—that's what I thought it was, too!"

I told Lisa that the first step to overcoming her inferiority complex was to stop comparing herself with her peers. Instead of belittling herself with "I'll never be able to use the DOS system as well as they can," she could better herself with "How can I learn to use the DOS system?" Instead of "She's got an MBA at twenty-six and I don't have a BA at fifty-six," she could say, "Good for her for finishing her MBA at such an early age," or "How can I go back to school and get my BA?" Instead of being intimidated by her teammates' level of expertise, she could see this as an excellent opportunity to expedite her own professional development.

The second step was for Lisa to start recognizing what *she* was bringing to the table. I explained that focusing on others' strengths sometimes causes us to lose sight of our own. Just because her co-workers were computer whizzes didn't mean Lisa didn't have something to offer. The hallmark of a good team is that its members have a balance of skills. Lisa was a gracious woman with a warm, friendly personality. I told her she was the ideal person to handle the agency's front desk because of her outstanding interpersonal and organizational skills. Her lack of a degree in no way hampered her ability to establish positive first impressions with customers, and give them the quality of service that made them want to come back.

Lisa reported back. "Thanks to that workshop, I've realized it's a privilege to work with talented people, not a pain. I've stopped comparing myself to my younger colleagues, and give myself credit for what I have to contribute."

Envy Immobilizes
—————◉—————

"I can't write a book commensurate with Shakespeare, but I can write a book by me."
-SIR WALTER RALEIGH

Do you sometimes talk yourself into a state of despair by focusing on what someone else has already achieved, instead of what you want to achieve? Have you ever given up before you even started because you thought you couldn't measure up to what someone else has already accomplished? If so, you are suffering from the avoidable consequences of comparison.

A professional speaker used Sir Walter Raleigh's idea to overcome her writer's block. She used to get depressed every time she walked into a bookstore and saw the dozens of titles on the business/self-help shelves. She concluded that the last thing the world needed was another book on her subject. She wondered, "What could I possibly say that hasn't been said hundreds of times before?" It finally occurred to her that this wasn't the question to ask. Do composers immobilize themselves by lamenting, "Why write a song about love? It's already been done?" She finally understood that her envy was immobilizing her. As long as she continued to compare herself with those best-selling authors, she would never start her project. She realized the question to ask was "Do I have something of value to say? Will people benefit from hearing my message?" The answer to that was yes. You are reading the result of my decision to concentrate on what *I* had to contribute instead of what others had already achieved.

A friend used a variation of this idea when she attended a national convention. During introductions around the lunch table, everyone told of their recent triumphs. One lady had appeared on *Oprah*, another had just returned from Singapore, and one had been featured in a front-page *USA Today* article. Maggie said she felt herself shrinking smaller and smaller as everyone reported in with their impressive feats. "I had been pleased with my career progress until I heard all these glowing accounts of standing ovations, first-class travel, and big-name clients. I slunk back to my room, wondering if I even belonged there. Then my eyes fell on the photograph I always place in my room when I travel. My family's happy faces reminded me that I had a good life, too. I saw that focusing exclusively on my table mates' successes had caused me to overlook my own."

Maggie created a clever way to counteract this all-too-common tendency. The next morning, before going downstairs, she slid a small snapshot of her family inside the back of her name tag. Throughout the day, anytime anyone boasted of the lucrative contract they had just landed or bragged about the number of frequent flier miles they had racked up, she would sneak a peek at her picture. One glimpse was enough to remind her of all she had to be grateful for, freeing her to be glad for them, instead of jealous.

Compare Yourself with Yourself

—————————⊙—————————

"Forget your opponents, always play against par."

-SAM SNEAD

A father who had attended one of my presentations came up to me in an airport and said, "You don't know how much your suggestions on comparison helped me. I live next to a retiree who spends hours every day puttering around his house. His yard is so perfect, it could be featured in *Better Homes & Gardens*. It had gotten to the point where I couldn't relax on weekends anymore because I felt so darn guilty. I kept thinking to myself, 'I should be outside cutting back the bushes or cleaning the storm drains.'

"After your class, I started mentally complimenting him. Whenever I drive past his house, I think, 'Your place looks great, Dan,' or 'You did a super job on your yard.' Then I stop there instead of driving myself crazy with comparisons. I've realized I don't *want* to aspire. I don't want to invest the time and effort it takes to have an immaculate house. I can say 'Good for you' without feeling bad about me."

Good point. We can choose *not* to aspire. Aspire is defined as "to seek to attain or accomplish a particular goal." We can admire what someone else has without wanting it for ourselves. As Dan discovered, we may not choose to go through what we have to go through to acquire it. We can mentally congratulate people for their accomplishments . . . and then move on. You can give people their due without it reflecting poorly on you.

Comparison Creates Competition
◉

*"There is nothing noble in feeling superior to another person. True
nobility is in being superior to your former self."*
-HINDU PROVERB

A woman named Lydia spoke up in a seminar and said, "When
I was growing up, everyone used to compare me to my older
sister, who was prettier, smarter, and more popular than I was."

Lydia asked, "Did you see the movie *League of Their Own*
about the women's baseball league during the war? There was
a line in there that made me laugh out loud because it pretty
well summed up my situation. In one scene, someone asks the
parents if they have any children. The mother proudly puts her
arm around her star pitcher and says, 'Yes, this is our daughter,
Dottie,' and then she turns to her other girl and says, 'And this
is our other daughter, Dottie's sister.' "

Lydia continued: "I couldn't wait to graduate from high
school and go to college in another state so I could establish
my own identity. It took me years to feel comfortable around
my sister, but I finally achieved it because I stopped competing
with her. She has her life, and I have mine. I just let it be,
without it reflecting on me."

This woman had brought up an interesting insight. Children
of celebrities often have a tough time growing up in the shadow
of their famous parents. Kids who have a multitalented sibling
can feel overshadowed by their high-achieving brother or sister.
The only way for these kids to develop a solid sense of self-
esteem is to stop using their successful parents or siblings as a
yardstick for their own worth. Ideally, they would be able to
develop a strong sense of self regardless of the star status of
their loved ones. If that isn't possible, these kids may need to
do what Lydia did: get out from underneath that big tree and
go plant themselves somewhere else. In doing so, they can give
themselves an opportunity to grow.

One fellow disagreed. "Are you saying all competition is bad?"

Good point. Is healthy competition an oxymoron? The answer is in the question. Competition in which we compulsively strive to be better than other people so we feel better about ourselves is destructive. Competition in which we're inspired to do better without having to beat other people is constructive. George S. Patton advised, "Don't fight a battle if you don't gain anything by winning." To modify General Patton's advice, we don't gain or win anything by battling other people. We don't want to have to belittle someone else to feel big. True confidence is having the security to feel we don't have to feel superior to others.

Just Say No to Jealousy
◎

"Jealousy is . . . a tiger that tears not only its prey but also its own raging heart."
−MICHAEL BEER

A woman named Sheila told me of her experience with jealousy. "I'm a stay-at-home mom. I used to be jealous of my cousin because she's a big-time businesswoman. My days are filled with diapers, carpooling, and pot roast. Her days are filled with designer suits, limousines, and power lunches. Whenever our families would get together for holiday gatherings, she'd be full of stories about her travels to exotic destinations. I'd be full of stories of trips to the doctor for ear infections.

"Last Christmas we were standing at the kitchen sink doing dishes and she confessed that she'd always envied me. I was flabbergasted. Why in the world would she envy me? She told me her fast-track life was glamorous, but that her biological clock was on overtime. She felt empty every time she saw me surrounded by my adoring brood. I admitted my secret yearning for her jet-set lifestyle and we shared a good laugh.

"We've become close since then and have worked out a once-a-month swap. She takes the kids for an outing every month so Auntie gets to experience the joys of motherhood (and my husband and I get to be lovers again). On another day, I dress up and meet her at a business luncheon so I can experience the vicarious thrill of her fast-track career. I still marvel at the years I wasted being jealous of her 'ideal' lifestyle when all the while she was envying mine."

Eliminate Envy
————— ⊙ —————

"Every man in the world is better than someone else. And not as good as someone else."
—WILLIAM SAROYAN

Sheila had discovered yet another consequence of comparison. It leads to envy, which is almost always based on a complete misunderstanding of the other person's situation. Envy, the "painful or resentful awareness of an advantage enjoyed by another with a desire to possess the same advantage," is hardly an attractive quality. In fact, La Rochefoucauld said, "The truest mark of being born with great qualities is being born *without* envy." While it may be too late to have been born without envy, we can at least make sure we're not borne away by it. The best way to avoid traveling down a covetous path is to (remember the refrain!) turn our envy into admiration or action.

A male participant said, "My wife and I are both actors. A couple of years ago, her career took off and mine didn't. I tried to be happy for her, but it destroyed my ego when she got picked to be in a play and I didn't. Then she landed the lead in a major production, and I didn't even get called back for a second audition. I'm ashamed to say I didn't handle it very well.

"We were on the verge of a divorce when she talked me into going to counseling. The therapist helped me see that our future hinged on my ability to maintain my sense of self in the face of my wife's success. It would never work as long as I competed with my wife and felt that I, the man, had to be on top in our relationship to feel good about myself. We are now secure in our love for each other, because I don't base my worth on how my career is going in relationship to my wife's. My feelings for her, and my feelings about myself, no longer depend on whose name is on top of the marquee."

Turn Envy into Appreciation

———————— ◉ ————————

*"I have never admired another's fortune so much that I became
dissatisfied with my own."*

-CICERO

A mother spoke up in a session and said, "What you said about
comparing causing us to lose sight of our own value is so true.
I have four sisters who live in four different states. Every time I
talked to them, it seemed like all I ever heard about was their
perfect children. This one just got straight As, this one just made
Eagle Scouts, this one gets up early every morning and cleans
his room without being asked. My sons struggle to get Bs and
Cs, and they're not even *in* Boy Scouts. My kids have never
once in their entire lives cleaned up their rooms without my
reminding them about it ten times.

"After talking with my sisters, I felt like going to bed and
pulling the covers over my head. They made me feel like my
family was a complete failure. All of a sudden, my kids weren't
good enough. They were the same kids they'd been when I'd
answered the phone twenty minutes before, but somehow
they'd been diminished in my eyes. They hadn't changed, but
my perception of them sure had. After taking your class, I decided I wasn't going to keep score anymore. I wasn't going to
do my sons the disservice of playing 'Who's the best and bright-
est?' I'm going to be happy that my nieces and nephews are
doing well *and* I'm going to be happy that I have two healthy,
active boys. As you said, quit the either/or, up/down comparing
contest and appreciate what you've got."

From now on, could you mentally congratulate others on
their successes instead of keeping score? Could you remember
that true confidence is not arrogance (feeling better than other
people) and it's not inferiority (feeling other people are better
than us)? Confident people choose to see fellow human beings
as companions rather than as competitors, and choose to feel
compassion toward them rather than competing with them.

Sample Starting Today Assignment

"We should strive against envy, for if indulged in, it will be to us a foretaste of hell on earth."
—SIR RICHARD BURTON

THE ASSIGNMENT TODAY IS TO ask yourself, "Who am I comparing myself with? Does any good come out of it? Who or what am I envying, coveting, or competing with? Could I admire or aspire instead? Could I 'leggo' of my ego-busting envy and turn it into ego-boosting action? Could I replace rivalry with respect? Instead of intimidating myself by looking at other people's achievements, could I appreciate my own? Rather than immobilizing myself because someone else has accomplished more, could I acknowledge my own contributions?" Remember, the goal here on earth is not to be better than other people; it is to be the best person you can be. Instead of striving to be *the* best, strive to be *your* best. ◉

Action Plan for Springing Free from the Comparison Trap

John has decided to take up golf because he's heard it's a great way to meet clients. Unfortunately, he's not too good at it. He's tired of getting beat every time out. He has a choice of how to react.

BLOCKERS	BUILDERS
Compare	Admire
"Look at Dave's drive. I'll never be able to hit mine that far."	*"Wow, what a great drive. He's so long and straight off the tee."*

Arrogance
"Well, at least I beat them on that hole."

Appreciation
"They have really spent a lot of time on their games. Good for them."

Inferior
"They're so much better than I am. This is humiliating."

Acceptance and/or action
"Maybe I can talk with the pro about a lesson. He'll help with these putts."

Unworthiness
"What a mistake. I don't even belong out here."

Aspire
"I think I'll pick up one of those golf videos and watch it this weekend."

Rivalry
"Joe's double-bogied the last four holes. If I can just par this one, I'll score better than him."

Respect
"What a beautiful iron to the green. He has great touch on the ball."

Compete
"I know I can beat Andy. He's the weakest next to me."

Contribute and/or compassion
"I can at least laugh at myself so we can enjoy ourselves."

MY PERSONAL STARTING TODAY ASSIGNMENT

Starting today I'm going to _____
_____
_____

Signed _____ Date _____

Who Do You Think You Are?

"The most powerful thing you can do to change the world is to change your own beliefs about the nature of life, people, and reality to something more positive ... and begin to act accordingly."

— SHAKTI GAWAIN

How do you talk to yourself? Do you second-guess your every move, ridicule your every misstep? Can you do anything right in your own eyes?

Oprah Winfrey observed, "It all boils down to self-hatred. That's the source of all problems on the planet, actually." Hate is such a strong word. Unfortunately it's how many people feel about themselves. The word *hate* is synonymous with *detest, abhor, loathe*. Wow. Can you imagine living with someone twenty-four hours a day who detests and abhors you? That's exactly what we do when we make hateful comments to and about ourselves.

It's time to change our self-talk so it supports rather than sabotages us. Our goal is to eliminate internal verbal abuse and initiate more positive beliefs so we can begin to act accordingly. How can we do that? By making daily deposits into our Confidence Account.

Give Yourself Credit

◎

"Shy people undervalue what they are and overvalue what they are not."
—DOROTHY SARNOFF

Imagine my delight when I looked up the word *credit* in the dictionary and found that it means "the balance in a person's favor in an account." That's exactly what we're talking about. It's time to create a more favorable balance in your Confidence Account, to value who you *are* instead of who you are *not.*

Every time we say something to or about ourselves, we make either a deposit into or a withdrawal from our Confidence Account. If we say something demeaning, scornful, critical, or sarcastic, we debit our account. If we say something supportive, encouraging, or complimentary, we add to our account. As we would do with any bank account, our goal is to build a healthy balance.

The problem is, many of us deplete our Confidence Accounts by making more withdrawals than deposits. We bankrupt our self-concept by paying more attention to what we do wrong than to what we do well. Credible is defined as "worthy of belief . . . worthy of esteem or praise." We all, on a daily basis, do things worthy of praise, yet we rarely give ourselves credit for them. Our goal is to increase the number of deposits we make into our Confidence Account on a daily basis. We want to boost our credibility in our own eyes so we come to believe in our hearts and minds that we have value.

If You Can't Say Something Nice . . .

━━━━━━━━━━━━━━◉━━━━━━━━━━━━━━

"The most powerful agent of growth and transformation is something much more basic than any technique: a change of heart."

- J O H N   W E L W O O D

How can we make this idea more tangible? By, literally and figuratively, counting our blessings. When I first started offering my confidence course in Hawaii in 1982, we would meet for three consecutive Saturday mornings. I would assign homework at the end of the sessions and ask participants to report back the following week. The first assignment was simple. One day that week, students were to count the number of times they said something negative to themselves. From the second they woke up to the second they went to bed, they were to jot down every time they made a disparaging comment to or about themselves, whether it was silent or out loud. If they wanted to get extra value from the assignment, they could take the time to record what was said. I wanted them to realize how many times a day they were putting themselves down—often without even knowing it. The feedback was astonishing. The number of negative statements ranged from 23 to an all-time high of 344!

One middle-aged woman said, "This assignment accomplished its purpose in the first hour. By seven-thirty in the morning, I had already called myself lazy and had scolded myself for always being late. I had yelled at my kids for not getting ready fast enough, and then got upset with myself for being a witch. I took one look in the mirror and told myself I looked like a fat slob. I never realized I had this destructive internal dialogue going on all the time."

That's the point. Most of us don't even realize the dozens of detrimental remarks we direct at ourselves daily; however, that doesn't lessen their destructive impact.

The second part of the assignment was to, on a different day, count the number of *positive* things the students said to themselves. Guess what? The count was always dramatically lower than the negative list. Many people said only three or four positive things about or to themselves—all day long.

Silent Pats on the Back
-------------◉-------------

"Correction does much, but encouragement does more."
-JOHANN WOLFGANG VON GOETHE

I'll always remember the woman who asked plaintively, "Why are we so *hard* on ourselves?" Good question. There are many reasons. Some of us are perfectionists, some of us inherited this tendency from hypercritical parents, and most of us take normalcy for granted. For example, an employee can be on time every day for five years straight. If one morning he arrives fifteen minutes late, *bam*, he gets in trouble. We often do the same thing to ourselves and the people around us. We're playing a great game of tennis, leading 5–2, and then we double-fault. What do we do? We dwell on the "stupid mistake." Our child proudly shows us his report card. He's got As, Bs, and one C. What do we concentrate on? The C! It seems to be human nature to notice the exceptions, not the rule.

I also think that many of us were taught not to brag when we were kids. Boy, did we take that to heart. Not only do we not boast about our accomplishments to other people, we don't even acknowledge them to ourselves. Since we can't say anything nice about ourselves in public, we don't say it in private either. The fallout of this harmful habit is that we cease seeing our good qualities because we never draw attention to them. If all we focus on are our mistakes and shortcomings, that's all we feel we have.

We need to reverse this destructive tendency before it does irreversible damage. Jack Paar once said, "Looking back, my life seems like one long obstacle race, with me as its chief obstacle." Have you been the chief obstacle in your life? If so, it's time to learn how to get out of your own way.

Count Your Blessings

◎

"If you count all your assets, you always show a profit."
-ROBERT QUILLEN

Starting today, we're going to literally and figuratively count our blessings on a daily basis. We're going to celebrate what we do well and congratulate ourselves for what we do right. They can be little things: "That was nice to let that car merge onto the freeway." "Good for me. I got out of bed this morning when the alarm went off instead of rolling over and going back to sleep." It's not necessary (or recommended) that you go around telling others about your mini-victories; just tell yourself. Consciously increase the number of deposits you make in your Confidence Account so you see yourself more favorably.

A seminar participant approached me during one of our breaks and said, "You know that quote you read to us?" He was referring to Alexandre Dumas's observation that "a man who doubts himself is like a man who enlists in the ranks of the enemy and bears arms against himself. He makes his failure certain by being the first to be convinced of it." The student exclaimed, "That's me! I say things to myself I wouldn't say to my worst enemy. I realize now, I have been my worst enemy! I always tell myself I'm going to screw up, and when I do, I think, 'I knew it!'"

Pop Psychology?

◎

"I was going to buy a copy of The Power of Positive Thinking *and then I thought: What the hell good would that do?"*
-COMEDIAN RONNIE SHAKES

Have you been your own worst enemy? Dale, a college basketball player, said, "I inherited perfectionism from my parents. If I made twenty points in a game, they wanted to know why I didn't make twenty-five. I ran for student body president in high school and lost by five votes. Dad told me I would have won if I'd campaigned harder. I got 1423 on my SATs, and Mom thought I could have scored higher if I'd 'applied myself.' Nothing I ever did was good enough. Now, I'm not happy unless I'm first. Coming in second is not good enough."

As Henry Miller observed, "There are no perfect beings, and there never will be." I suggested that instead of criticizing himself for being imperfect, Dale start giving himself self-congratulatory pats on the back. "Instead of beating yourself up because you didn't beat everyone else, congratulate your close approximations to desired behavior. "What's that?" asked Dale.

"Have you ever watched babies learn to walk? At first they shakily pull themselves up and lean against a table, chair, or desk. Then they take a wobbly step or two, promptly lose their balance, and go down. What do you do? Scold them and say sternly, 'No, no, no, not like that. *This* is how you're supposed to do it!' I don't think so. You probably clapped your hands in glee and cheered enthusiastically, 'Yeah! You took your first steps!'

"See the difference? We don't expect babies to walk perfectly the first time. We compliment their effort, point out their close approximation to desired behavior, and encourage them to try again. We need to do the same thing to ourselves. Dale, the next time something doesn't go perfectly, give yourself credit for what you *did* accomplish instead of criticizing yourself for what you *didn't* accomplish. Praise yourself for your effort and encourage yourself to try it again."

The Price of Perfectionism
━━━━━━━━━━━━ ◉ ━━━━━━━━━━━━

"The sin of perfectionism is that it mutilates life by demanding the impossible."
—JEROME FRANK

Dale agreed to do this and wanted to know if there was anything else he could do to reverse his perfectionism. I suggested that he establish more reasonable expectations. "From now on, whenever you set a goal or establish an expectation for yourself, just ask, 'Is this significantly challenging and achievable in the not-too-distant future?' Are you willing to try something to find out firsthand why too-high expectations hurt us more than help us?" "Sure," Dale said gamely.

I said, "Pretend your goal is to play basketball as well as Michael Jordan. That is certainly challenging, but is it achievable in the not-too-distant future? Probably not. A more reasonable and specific expectation might be to play well enough to make your all-conference team. There's a good chance you can accomplish this, so you'll be motivated to do your best. The feasibility of your expectation will inspire you to go for it."

Dale disagreed. "Why shouldn't we have big expectations? My dad always taught me if we don't aim high enough, we settle too low."

Establish Feasible Expectations
◉

"I always wanted to be somebody, but I should have been more specific."

—LILY TOMLIN AND JANE WAGNER

"I realize that's a popular philosophy," I replied, "but I think the 'shoot for the stars; if you miss, you still hit the moon' approach backfires more than it helps. Some people feel a lofty goal motivates them to be their best. I believe it more often causes them to abandon the goal because they're never going to be able to reach it."

I asked Dale to stand up. "How high are these ceilings?" I asked. "About fourteen feet," he ventured. "Dale, could you please jump up and try to touch the ceiling?"

Dale crouched, gathered his energy, and sprung up into the air. It was an impressive leap, but he wasn't able to reach the ceiling. "Try again," I suggested. He added a couple of inches to his next jump but still wasn't even close. "Try a couple more times." He did, with an equal lack of success.

I said, "Dale, you could train with master rebounder Dennis Rodman himself. You could practice your vertical leap, exercise for hours a day to get in top physical condition, and you *still* wouldn't be able to touch that ceiling.

"What would happen to your spirit after all this? How would you feel if you were doing your best to accomplish this goal, but you realized that no matter what you did, you'd *never* be able to touch that ceiling?"

"Pretty depressed," Dale admitted. "I'd want to quit."

I nodded. "That's what happens when we set impossibly high goals for ourselves. In the beginning, we enthusiastically apply ourselves, and if we don't succeed, we just try harder. Over time, though, disappointment sets in. We become depressed and finally conclude it's not worth trying anymore because we're never going to be able to win." As novelist Graham Greene observed, "Despair is the price one pays for setting himself an impossible aim."

Give Grief vs. Give Credit
————————————————⊙————————————————

"Words of comfort, skillfully administered, are the oldest therapy known to man."
-LOUIS NIZER

"Instead of setting yourself up for failure," I continued, "select a *specific* expectation, a goal just beyond your reach. You can't touch it now. If you could, that's not significantly challenging. Then start working to achieve it.

"As you progress toward your goal, remember you have a choice. With every attempt you make, you can give yourself *grief* or you can give yourself *credit*. Giving yourself grief will discourage you. Giving yourself credit will encourage you. Which is better? Resolve to give yourself silent POBs (pats on the back) every time you expend effort and every time you make progress. Turn that enemy within into an advocate."

Are you thinking, "Am I just supposed to ignore mistakes?" Good question. We're not supposed to pretend we don't make mistakes, we just don't want to persist in giving ourselves grief about them. From now on, we're going to pay attention to what we do well *and* we're going to put those mistakes to work for us by turning them into lessons instead of failures. The next chapter will explain how we can do that.

Sample Starting Today Assignment

"Have patience with all things, but chiefly have patience with yourself. Do not lose courage in considering your own imperfections, but instantly set about remedying them—every day begin the task anew."

—SAINT FRANCIS DE SALES

YOUR ASSIGNMENT IS TO MAKE at least fifty mental deposits into your Confidence Account today (that's only three or four an hour). Give yourself silent pats on the back every time you do something nicely, thoughtfully, or skillfully. If you establish a goal or expectation for yourself today, ask yourself if it's significantly challenging and achievable. Instead of giving yourself grief if you don't do something perfectly, give yourself credit for effort and progress. Instead of criticizing what you do wrong, compliment your close approximations to desired behavior. Rather than ridiculing your imperfections, set about remedying them. ◎

Action Plan for Who Do You Think You Are?

Darlene has always been her own worst critic. Her parents taught her that "if it's worth doing, it's worth doing well." She's taken that advice to the extreme. If she bakes a cake and it doesn't rise the way it's supposed to, she throws it away. She spends hours writing one letter, trying to get every word right. She second-guesses everything she says and constantly criticizes herself for what she should have said.

BLOCKERS	BUILDERS
Destructive self-talk *"Look at those cookies. They're overdone. I'm ashamed to serve them."*	Constructive self-talk *"Good for you for making cookies from scratch. Next time I'll take them out a couple of minutes earlier."*
Castigate *"Why do I always mess things up?"*	Catch yourself doing right and congratulate *"That was thoughtful of you to take the time to make cookies for the PTA fund-raiser."*
Ridicule *"I'll never be as good a cook as Esther."*	Respect *"At least you're always trying new recipes."*
Give grief for mistakes *"Why didn't I check the oven earlier?"*	Give credit for effort and progress *"At least I made an effort. I could have just taken the easy route and gotten store-bought."*
Impossible expectations *"From now on, I'm going to watch them every minute to make sure they come out perfectly."*	Achievable increments *"Next time I'll set the timer five minutes early so I can see if they're getting done too fast."*

MY PERSONAL STARTING TODAY ASSIGNMENT

Starting today I'm going to _____

_____

_____

Signed _____ Date _____

Set Up a Success Spiral

"We are going to have to find a way to immunize people against the kind of thinking that leads to self-devastation."
— DR. JONAS SALK

What do you do when something goes wrong? Do you personalize or persecute? Do you get angry with yourself for what went wrong, or get angry at the other person? These are natural reactions, yet both lead to self-devastation.

From now on, if something doesn't go your way, put it in perspective and plan how it could be handled better next time. Ken Keyes, Jr., said, "No matter how horribly we have judged our past actions, each day our life begins anew." It does *if* we live and learn. From now on, when you make a mistake, give yourself credit for effort (as stated in the last chapter), and then immediately figure out how you can handle that situation more effectively in the future (or how you can keep it from happening again). Instead of finding fault, find solutions.

Internalize vs. Externalize
———————————◉———————————

"Notice the difference between what happens when a man says
to himself, 'I have failed three times,' and what happens
when he says, 'I am a failure.' "

—S. I. HAYAKAWA

A friend was able to put this idea into practice at a recent conference luncheon. She approached two well-known people who were deep in a discussion at their table. She stood behind them, patiently waiting for them to notice her. They continued to talk, ignoring her. After several moments, it became obvious that they had no intention of turning away from their conversation. Sue walked away, rather red-faced.

Sue commented, "If that had happened a couple years ago, I would have been humiliated. I would have internalized—'How stupid of me'—or I would have externalized—'What snobs. They think they're too good to talk to the little people, huh?' Either I would have beat myself up mentally, blown it out of proportion, and vowed never to talk to anyone famous again, or I would have focused on how *rude* they'd been and written them off as arrogant prima donnas.

"Instead, I used your advice and assessed it objectively. I realized it hadn't been appropriate to intrude on their obviously intimate conversation. If I had been more sensitive to their closed body language, I would have seen that they didn't want to be interrupted. I vowed from then on not to horn in on people who were talking privately."

Turn Disappointments into Discoveries

————————◉————————

*"It is a mortifying truth, and ought to teach the wisest of us
humility, that many of the most valuable discoveries have been
the result of chance rather than of contemplation, and of
accident rather than of design."*

–CHARLES CALEB COLTON

One school of thought maintains that there are no accidents.
According to this way of thinking, accidents and mistakes occur
to teach us a lesson. If we don't figure out what we're supposed
to learn, that accident occurs over and over again until we do.
A minister once remarked, "Want to make God laugh? Tell him
your plans." If something doesn't go as we planned, that doesn't
mean it was a failure. Ask yourself, "What am I to discover
here?" Instead of writing that experience off as a disappointment, see it as part of a puzzle you're supposed to figure out.
What was the purpose of that puzzle piece? Where does it fit
into your life? How and where can you use it to your advantage?
That experience will be a waste of time only if you don't extract
something of value from it—because then you'll have to go back
and do it over again. Now *that's* a waste of time!

Kids are masters at turning disappointments into discoveries.
A fellow author who was visiting Maui invited me to join him at
his oceanside hotel for an afternoon of "talk story." I explained
I didn't have a babysitter for my sons and he said to bring them
along; they could swim while we caught up. When we arrived,
there wasn't a single person at the pool or on the beach. The
skies were gray and overcast, and it was obvious the inclement
weather had kept the vacationers indoors.

Allen was disappointed on the boys' behalf, but the cool,
breezy weather didn't faze them one minute. *"Pool!"* they
shouted and promptly dove in. For the next three hours they
frolicked on the lawn using a small coconut as a ball, built sand
castles on the deserted beach, turned the plastic chaise longues
into slippery water slides ("Whee!"), and thoroughly enter-

tained themselves with nothing but their imagination and energy.

Allen watched their antics in amazement. "Kids are incredible," he said. "They have a rollicking good time whether or not the sun is shining." His observation about kids' determination to make the most of any situation was so true. I told him about another time the boys had turned a disappointing event into a delightful good time.

Tom and Andrew were to have an end-of-the-season swim party after their last soccer match. When we drove up to the pool, we were unpleasantly surprised to find it closed, with the entrance gate padlocked and no way to get in. Several of the parents became upset and concluded that the party was going to have to be canceled or rescheduled. Meanwhile, the kids had grabbed a ball from the coach's van and had started playing soccer in the parking lot. They were oblivious to their parents' dismay and were just involved in their game. Finally, one resourceful mother suggested we spread our blankets out in the dirt and have our pizza picnic anyway. We did, and everyone ended up having a thoroughly enjoyable afternoon.

The boys taught us adults a valuable lesson that day. Events don't have to go as planned to be a success! Whether or not an activity turns out as hoped, you can still have fun. What are some "whether or nots" in your life? From now on, remind yourself that if something doesn't work out the way you originally wanted it to, you have a choice. You can become disappointed and write off the event as a failure, or you can be resilient, discover the value and/or message, and enjoy yourself anyway.

Don't Self-Destruct, Self-Diagnose

──────────◉──────────

*"Have the unflinching determination to move on your path
unhampered by limiting thoughts of past errors."*
-PARAMAHANSA YOGANANDA

Are you thinking, "What if what went wrong isn't as frivolous as
an afternoon swim or an end-of-the-season soccer party? What
if I made a serious mistake that has real consequences?" Confident people don't limit themselves by dwelling on thoughts of
past errors; they focus their thoughts on how they can improve.

A man in a session said he was devastated because he hadn't
been selected for his ideal job. Toby admitted, "I blew the interview. I stayed out late the night before with my buddies, and
I sleepwalked through the entire thing. The interviewer said,
'Over fifty people have applied for this position. Why should we
hire you?' I hadn't prepared, so I just sat there and mumbled
out a nonanswer. He wrapped up our meeting by asking if I had
any questions for him. That's one of those open-ended questions you can hit out of the ballpark, but I couldn't think of
anything to say! I knew when I walked out the door that they
weren't going to hire me. I'm really mad at myself for blowing
that opportunity."

I said, "Toby, you can get upset because that interview didn't
turn out the way you wanted, or you can get busy figuring out
how to make sure the next one *does*. A Zen saying is 'All experience is education for the soul.' It is *if* you turn perceived
failures into lessons by self-diagnosing instead of self-
destructing. Instead of dissing yourself for doing it wrong this
time, determine how you can do it right *next* time."

Don't Get Upset, Get Busy

────────○────────

*"You don't always get what you want—but you always get
what you need."*

—ANONYMOUS

Toby called several weeks later to share his good news. "I followed your advice. Instead of getting more depressed, I asked myself what I could discover. I realized that maybe I wasn't meant to have that job, which meant there must be something out there more appropriate for me. I told myself I wasn't going to find it sitting at home and sulking.

"I thought a good place to network was at the monthly meeting of my professional association. I started talking to a new member who had just joined our organization. He has his own small business called the Computer Doctor. His motto is 'We make mouse calls.' This guy had been laid off from his company and used his severance pay to set himself up as an entrepreneur. He found that many people don't know how to operate, program, or fix their PCs, and they hate the inconvenience of having to take their equipment into a dealership. He comes into people's homes, sets up their system, trains them, and makes repairs if necessary. Six months after coming up with the idea, he already had more business than he could handle. A lightbulb went off in my mind. Did he want a partner?

"Rich and I hit it off from the moment we started talking. To make a long story short, I'm now working with him. I love this job because I get out of the office and into the field. I'm back to the hands-on stuff where I get to meet customers one-on-one and troubleshoot their computer problems. Three weeks ago, I didn't even know this kind of work existed, and now I couldn't imagine doing anything else."

A participant approached me after I told Toby's story in a seminar. The attendee said with a smile, "My dad had a different way of saying, 'Don't get upset, get busy.' If I was frustrated and about to throw in the towel on something, he'd say, 'Sometimes you might think you're at a dead end when actually you're just sitting on it.' " What is something you recently attempted that ended in frustration? That disappointment doesn't have to be a dead end unless you give up.

You Can Stay Down or You Can Get Up

───────── ◉ ─────────

"My sun sets to rise again."

-ROBERT BROWNING

What a poetic way to view disappointments. What Browning is saying is *he* rises after a stumble instead of staying down. Can you commit to doing the same? What situation has recently left you downcast? Are you staying in the dumps about it? Are you allowing it to immobilize you? Could you rise out of your doldrums with renewed optimism, ready to try again? As Mary Pickford said, "If you have made mistakes, even serious ones, there is always another chance for you. And supposing you have tried and failed again and again, you may have a fresh start any moment you choose, for this thing that we call 'failure' is not the falling down, but the staying down."

That's an eloquent view of mistakes. Former football coach Mike Ditka put it a little more simply: "Success isn't permanent, and failure isn't fatal."

Reverse the Neurotic Spiral

───────── ◉ ─────────

"Man, did he make a wrong mistake."

-YOGI BERRA

What does all this have to do with confidence? When we make a mistake, we have a choice. If we punish ourselves for less-than-perfect results, we will make ourselves feel worse, which will cause us to regret what happened. As a result, we may avoid similar situations in the future so we don't risk further humiliation. If we do find ourselves in those circumstances again, chances are we'll be afraid the mistake will reoccur ("*Please* don't let me forget what I'm supposed to say"). What we fear will probably happen because it is what we're thinking about ("I hope I don't hit it in the trap").

This cumulative process is called the Neurotic Spiral. Negative self-talk after a bad performance imprints fears and anxieties, which increases the likelihood of another unsatisfactory experience, which creates a self-fulfilling prophecy, which makes us even more reluctant to put ourselves in that situation again. That's a "wrong" mistake! If we censure ourselves with hypercritical inner dialogue, our confidence spirals downward and quickly disappears. We need to understand once and for all that we can't berate ourselves into becoming a better person.

Instead, I propose we set up a Success Spiral. If something goes wrong, immediately give yourself credit for the effort you expended and figure out how you can handle the situation better in the future. Cheer your victories. Make "good" mistakes by coaching them with the words *next time* so you "fail forward." Keep your mind focused on what you accomplished that was of value. Make progress your goal rather than perfectionism. Compliment yourself every time you show improvement. Give yourself silent pats on the back every time you step out of your comfort zone and try something new. Recognizing and rewarding yourself for your small triumphs leads to increased self-esteem, which motivates you to take more risks, which increases self-respect, which gives you the confidence to put yourself on the line again—a sort of reverse domino effect. All the while, you're accumulating what I call mental momentum—a growing feeling of positive self-regard and a willingness to try new things. Want more specifics? Read on.

The Do's and Don'ts of the Do's and Don'ts
─◎─

"Always change a losing game, never change a winning one."
-VINCE LOMBARDI

While we're speaking of momentum . . . I just finished watching golfer Greg Norman lose the 1996 Masters by blowing a six-stroke lead in the final round. By the end of the telecast, on-air analysts were already calling it the biggest collapse in the history of professional golf.

For the first three days of the tournament, Norman experienced Maui's law, the obverse of Murphy's law: everything that *could* go right—*did*. That mental critic who second-guesses our every move was silent and Norman was playing pure, sweet golf.

Then things started going wrong. At that point he had a choice. If he let those doubts and fears creep in, his positive momentum would be lost and his confidence would instantly start spiraling downward. I know it's easy for me to armchair-quarterback, but that's probably what happened. It was just Greg and his head out there, and his head won. He started focusing more on the don'ts than the do's . . . and it was downhill from there. Those final twelve holes turned into Norman's worst nightmare. As Wilson Mizner once said, "Failure had gone to his head."

The Prophets of Doom
◎

"If you keep on saying things are going to be bad, you have a good chance of being a prophet."
-ISAAC BASHEVIS SINGER

If Norman could only have crowded out those doubts by filling his mind with positively phrased commands, he could possibly have been able to regenerate that positive momentum. If he had filled his mind with desired rather than dreaded behavior, he could perhaps have regained his confidence.

Greg Norman, bless his heart, handled his Masters defeat like the classy champion he is. In his gracious interview following the debacle, a press conference many lesser men would have ducked out of, he quietly said, "I'm still a winner. I just didn't win today." Good for him! He refused to buy into the negative labels that were being unfairly forced upon him. I'm convinced Greg Norman *will* win a big one soon because he displayed resiliency, the ability to recover from misfortune. When champions get knocked down, they don't make excuses. They extract the lesson that will enable them to do better next time and move on.

Greg Norman's winner mentality helped him transcend this experience. Do you have a winner mentality? Have you recently suffered a humiliating defeat? Resolve to self-diagnose instead of self-destruct. Don't get mad, get busy figuring out how you can improve next time. Can you stand one more quote from a football coach? Coach Vince Lombardi said, "Confidence is contagious. So is lack of confidence." Instead of criticizing yourself and heading down that Neurotic Spiral, vow to "catch" confidence by cheering yourself up the Success Spiral.

The Don't Downhill
———————◉———————

"Man often becomes what he believes himself to be. If I keep on saying to myself that I cannot do a certain thing, it is possible that I may end by really becoming incapable of doing it. On the contrary, if I have the belief that I can do it, I shall surely acquire the capacity to do it even if I may not have it at the beginning."
–MAHATMA GANDHI

The damage caused by don't words was so evident at our sons' Little League baseball game last night. Parents and coaches alike were all yelling well-intentioned advice. "Don't back away from the ball." "Don't turn your head." "Don't swing so hard."

"Don't worry about getting hit." "Don't let that pitcher intimidate you."

Do I have to tell you how the game went? The boys' heads were so filled with what *not* to do *wrong*, they stood little chance of doing anything *right*. If only the parents and coaches had filled their sons' heads with more positive directives ("Keep your head still." "Swing slow and easy." "You're a hitter!"), the boys might have performed better.

I laughed out loud when I watched the outtakes that ran in the end credits of the movie *Little Rascals*. A voice off camera said again and again to the young star, "Don't look at the camera, honey." The whole time, of course, the young girl was gazing directly into the lens. How could she do anything else?

Do yourself and the people around you a favor. Refuse to let the word *don't* derail your train of positive thoughts. Instead, phrase mental and spoken orders positively so you're giving your brain constructive rather than destructive instructions. Your confidence depends on it.

Sample Starting Today Assignment

"The mind is only as strong as its weakest think."
—ANONYMOUS

TODAY'S ASSIGNMENT IS TO SET up a Success Spiral if something goes wrong. If something doesn't go the way you want it to, don't get mad, get busy. Instead of letting a disappointment depress you, determine how you can handle it better next time. Resolve to self-diagnose instead of self-destruct so you can turn mistakes into lessons. As Anne Stewart expressed it, "Don't think of it as failure. Think of it as time-released success." Focus on what you *want* to do (rather than what you don't want to do) in a situation so you can set up and maintain positive mental momentum. ⊙

Action Plan for Setting Up a Success Spiral

Nolan entered several of his favorite photographs in the state fair competition. Not only did he not receive a ribbon, one judge critiqued them as being "amateurish and common." Nolan has a choice of how to respond to this disappointment.

BLOCKERS	BUILDERS
Neurotic Spiral *"I never should have entered that contest in the first place."*	Success Spiral *"Well, at least I had the courage to try something I wanted to do."*
Self-destruct *"This is humiliating. What was I thinking?"*	Self-diagnose *"I wonder why the judge thought they were common."*
Lament *"Those contests are usually rigged anyway. The judges probably give all the ribbons to the professionals."*	Learn *"I'm going to call the judge and ask for his suggestions on how I can improve."*
Disappointed in the failure *"That was a waste of time. I'll never do that again."*	Discover the lesson *"How can I take shots that are more involving and thought-provoking?"*
Set up negative momentum *"What if my friends see my photographs and realize I didn't get a ribbon?"*	Set up positive momentum *"There's a photography class at the college by that National Geographic photographer. Maybe I'll take that."*
Get upset *"That was so rude of that judge. What a cheap shot."*	Get busy *"I'm going to call and sign up for that course today. It'll be a lot of fun."*

MY PERSONAL STARTING TODAY ASSIGNMENT

Starting today I'm going to _____

_____

_____

Signed _____ Date _____

Who Cares What People Think (I Do, I Do)

*"To be nobody but yourself—in a world which is doing its best,
night and day, to make you everybody else—means to fight
the hardest battle which any human being can fight, and
never stop fighting."*

— E. E. CUMMINGS

A friend was buying a coat at an out-of-town department store and paying for it with a personal check. The clerk called over to the shift supervisor, "I need approval!" Smiling, her manager called back, "I like your dress!"

Everyone wants approval; it's *needing* it that causes problems. Anthony Trollope knew that "no one holds a good opinion of a man who has a low opinion of himself." Yet some of us do it backward. We base our opinion of ourselves on what other people think of us. Our every waking minute is governed by WWPT ("What Will People Think?"). What we wear, what we say, and how we act are all designed to win acceptance. This is asking for trouble and can be avoided if we follow Marcus Aurelius's advice: "How much trouble he avoids who does not look to see what his neighbor says or does or thinks, but only to what he does himself."

Looking to other people for acceptance puts us on a confidence roller coaster. One minute we're up because we feel people like us; the next minute we're down because we feel they don't. The goal is to turn an anxiety for approval into emotional independence. Instead of a self-esteem that dips and soars depending on where we are and who we're with, we want a self-assurance that stays with us wherever we go.

Choose to Be Sociable *and* Unsociable
◉

"When given a choice, take both."
-LAURENCE J. PETER

You may be thinking, "But wait a minute, didn't you just say that we *should* care what people think, that we should extend ourselves in an effort to make them like us? And now you're saying we shouldn't? Isn't that contradictory?"

Yes, that's exactly what I'm saying. As with most things in life, the healthy course of action is not either/or . . . it's both. The editors of *The Practice of Kindness* said, "It is one of the most fundamental paradoxes of human existence that we live our lives as unique individuals, and yet the deepest spiritual meaning of our lives resides in our connection to all things."

It's important to be our own person *and* to be part of a community. It's important to be the final judge of our own actions *and* to consider other people's opinions. In this book, I suggest ways to enrich your life with friendships *and* I suggest ways to be comfortable being by yourself. Later in the book, I discuss the importance of slowing down our busy lives *and* I discuss how to become more of an adventurous risk taker. Further on, I propose that we serve other people by meeting their needs *and* that we serve ourselves by speaking up for our own.

These options aren't mutually exclusive. George Eliot once observed, "The strongest principle of growth lies in human choice." One of the strongest characteristics of confidence is being able to *choose* how we want to be in a variety of situations. If you read something in this book and think, "Didn't she say something different in an earlier chapter?" the answer is probably yes. That doesn't mean one idea is right and the other is wrong. It means *both* are appropriate for different situations, and you get to choose which to use and when.

A Quiet Center
◉

"Whenever you find a human being with peace of mind, you will find a person who has a quiet center."
-NORMAN VINCENT PEALE

In the last fifteen years, I've interviewed just about anybody and everybody who expressed an interest in this topic (the wonderful thing is, *everybody* is interested in this topic!). I have also distributed a confidence questionnaire to workshop participants, newsletter subscribers, and friends. One of the questions on the questionnaire was "Who is a confident person you know?" This question resulted in a fascinating discussion with a fellow team mom while we were scoring our sons' Little League baseball game. She mulled it over for a while and then smiled gently and said, "My grandmother was the most confident person I ever knew. She was a tiny woman, but she had a serene strength because she seemed completely comfortable with herself. She wasn't the type of person to go around saying she was confident, she just was. She had a kind of clarity and simplicity, without an ounce of boastfulness. She was probably the most important person in my life, because she showed me what it was possible to be like."

Do you know someone like this? A quietly confident person who seems perpetually poised? Instead of desperately trying to prove themselves, this person exudes a quiet center. "I care not what others think of what I do," claimed Theodore Roosevelt, "but I care very much about what I think of what I do. That is character." An interesting thought, isn't it? If we look to others for approval, if we base our behavior on what other people think, our character is always shifting. Only when we answer to ourselves is our character (and confidence) stable.

Listen to the Voice from Within

————————— ⊙ —————————

"Let me listen to me, and not to them."
—GERTRUDE STEIN

I had an opportunity years ago to see if I could keep a quiet center knowing that my actions might be met with disapproval. While attending a luncheon at a local Maui resort, I watched seventy-year-young Hildred Kaholokula weave a lei po'o (Hawaiian for head lei). I was leaving later that evening for a mainland speaking tour, and Hildred asked if I was looking forward to it. I confessed to having mixed feelings. I love traveling and enjoy the people I get to meet at my presentations; however, I get homesick. I laughed and said wistfully, "I wish I could take Maui with me." With a genuine gesture of aloha, Hildred took the lei po'o off her head, put it on mine, and said, "Now you *can* take Maui with you!"

I wore her head lei on that trip and have been wearing hakus (another word for head leis) for my business activities ever since. On that first trip, a woman approached me before my seminar and said, "I was married in one of those!" A transplanted Hawaiian who worked as a security guard at the Los Angeles airport said, "It's been years since I've seen one of those." A curious individual asked, "Where did you get that? It's beautiful." Hildred's gift was a catalyst for many delightful conversations on that tour, and has become a lovely way to take home with me on many subsequent trips.

A few months later, the owner of a speakers' bureau pulled me aside at a conference to offer some feedback. She said, "Sam, you should know that no one is *ever* going to take you seriously as long as you wear that thing. People will think you're some hippie chick that just got back from a Renaissance Fair." Her comments prompted me to wonder whether I should continue wearing a head lei.

Trusting our own judgment doesn't mean discounting other people's opinions. It means listening to input, evaluating it for merit, balancing it with our own experience and feelings, and making a decision based on all the evidence. I've found it often helps to write out a chart of pros and cons so we can see objectively whether our actions are wise or otherwise. That's what I did with this issue. The question is, do I wear a haku or not?

After weighing the pros and cons, I decided to continue to wear my lei po'o (except if a meeting planner or TV host requests that I not wear it, and then of course I honor their wishes). Every once in a while I'll get a scornful up-and-down look or a snide comment like "Oh, don't *you* look cute!" Many more times, I meet delightful people who ask what the beautiful flowers are for, and I'm able to share Hildred's story. If I find myself losing the courage to wear it, I know I'm worrying ex-

CONS	PROS
⊙ Some people will think I'm weird and avoid me.	⊙ Some people will be curious and approach me.
⊙ Some people will conclude that it's a gimmick I wear to get noticed.	⊙ I know in my heart that it is a gift I wear because it's a meaningful trademark.
⊙ Some people may write me off because they conclude that I'm "one taco short of a combination plate."	⊙ Some people will want to know more about it because they have a connection to the islands.
⊙ Because it's different and doesn't conform to the norm, I'm occasionally subject to derision and suspicion.	⊙ I believe if we're doing things with integrity and not hurting anyone, we should have the confidence not to conform to the norm.

cessively about what people will think. As soon as I remind myself to have a quiet center, I once again feel blessed to be able to wear this symbol of aloha.

Me? Codependent?
Do You Really Think So?
◉

"A man who finds no satisfaction in himself, seeks for it in vain elsewhere."

-LA ROCHEFOUCAULD

A self-confessed people pleaser spoke up in one of my classes. "It's not easy overcoming a compulsive need for approval, but it can be done. I spent the first half of my life trying to get everyone to like me. You've heard the line 'I'm so codependent, I have to ask my friends if I'm having a good time'? That was me. My brother told me I should get that new insurance for codependents—it's called 'my fault.' Then I saw this poster that said, 'If you don't run your life, someone else will.' My immediate reaction was 'Everyone runs my life *except* me.' I started asking myself what *I* wanted instead of always doing what other people wanted.

"I've been single for a long time and I've grown tired of waiting around for someone to ask me out. I wanted to place an ad in the Personals section of our local paper, but I could just imagine people saying, 'Amy is so desperate, she had to advertise to get a date.' I finally thought, 'I don't care *what* they might think, I want to meet some interesting men.' Do you know, the first week the ad ran, I got thirty-five responses! I met five of the men for coffee (each separately), and I'm continuing to see three of them. None are the love of my life, but we have fun. One likes old movies, so we go to film festivals, one is a racquetball nut, and the other is an antiques buff, so we roam the countryside on weekends searching for the perfect find. I'd *still* be lonely if I'd caved in to my concerns about what people might think."

Turn Approval Anxiety
into Self-Acceptance
————————— ◉ —————————

"Within you there is a stillness and sanctuary to which you can retreat at anytime and be yourself."
—HERMANN HESSE

A workshop participant used these ideas to give himself the courage he needed to attend his high school's twenty-fifth anniversary homecoming dance. Norm said, "I thought seriously about not going because I was worried what people were going to say about me. You've heard that line about reunions being where everyone gets together to see who's falling apart? That's what I was afraid of. Back then I was the star running back, prom king, and student body president. Now I'm losing my hair, I'm carrying around fifty extra pounds, and I couldn't sprint a hundred yards if I had to."

Norm realized he was about to talk himself out of attending this once-in-a-lifetime event because he was concerned about the raised eyebrows of his former classmates. "Instead of worrying what *they* might think, I asked myself, 'What do *I* think? I think I want to go back and see my high school buddies and the football coach who helped me get a college scholarship.' I decided to go and have a good time, and let people say what they will."

Norm called the week after the reunion to say he was so glad he'd trusted his instincts instead of his apprehensions. His old football coach had pulled him aside and confided privately to him that Norm was the most talented athlete he'd ever had the privilege of coaching. He ran into pals he hadn't seen in years and they reestablished the rapport they'd had in high school. "I can't believe I came *this* close to missing out on all that fun."

Trust Account
————— ◉ —————

"You may be deceived if you trust too much, but you will live in torment if you do not trust enough."

—FRANK CRANE

Think of something you want to do but are worried about what people might think. Can you trust your instincts and listen to yourself instead of acquiescing to your inner version of the voices of others? Trust, the "assured reliance on the character, ability, strength of someone," is almost synonymous with confidence. Think about it. If you trust someone, you have confidence in them. If you trust yourself, you have confidence in yourself. From now on, balance all pro and con input, and then trust your judgment to make the final decision as to what's right and wrong, good and bad. The goal is to be psychologically self-sufficient.

I will always remember a "hail and farewell" I attended shortly after marrying my husband, a naval captain at the time. The party was packed with senior military officers and their wives. At that time, officers were actually graded on their wives. Whether or not they were promoted up through the ranks depended somewhat on whether their wives were "assets" and "commandant material." Throughout that long evening, I did my best to be charming. I asked questions, listened attentively, drew people out, and concentrated completely on the person speaking to me.

This is a very rewarding way to be *and* it can be very draining. At one point in the evening, I glanced around the room and saw the wives of two admirals sitting together on a couch over in the corner. They were deep in an animated conversation, oblivious to the rest of the group. Their duty that night was to mingle and meet, to be sociable hostesses. Yet at some point they had decided to hell with duty and had chosen to honor their friendship and take advantage of this opportunity to spend some time together. I admired their pluck in the face of probable disapproval.

I'm sure most evenings (senior military personnel often go to these sorts of functions several times a week) these women were the picture of decorum. But on this night, they had decided to be "salty old women," as defined by Caroline Bird in her book *Lives of Our Own*: a woman who "doesn't suffer fools gladly anymore, speaks her mind, and isn't afraid of what people think." I bet these ladies didn't regret it for a minute. Goethe observed, "As soon as you trust yourself, you will know how to live." These women trusted themselves and really lived that evening.

Sense of Humor = Self-Assurance
◎

"When Sears comes out with a riding vacuum cleaner, then I'll clean the house."
—ROSEANNE

A housewife said, "Roseanne is my hero. I've never been your typical apple-pie mom. I'd rather be out playing in the sandbox with my kids than cleaning the dust out of the closets. My next-door neighbor Joyce is just the opposite. It's like the Waltons are alive and well and living on our block. Home-cooked meals (from scratch!) every night. Ironed (?) clothes. A spotless home.

"Most of the time, my kids look like Pigpen from the *Peanuts* comic strip. Our house looks . . . well, used. And as my husband would be quick to tell you, my family knows dinner is ready when they hear the can opener and/or the smoke alarm. Debbie Domestic I'm not.

"I started getting sensitive about this after Joyce came over to our house a couple of times. She was too nice to say anything about it, but I could tell she was in a state of shock. I remembered something Roseanne had said on TV the night before: 'The way I see it is, if the kids are still alive when my husband gets home from work, then hey, I've done my job.' I told Joyce that and she cracked up. The joke eased the tension between us and everything was okay again. Instead of getting uptight because I'm not a perfect homemaker, I relaxed and felt comfortable with who I am. I've collected a couple of other good lines that come in handy whenever someone stops by and the place is a pigsty. One of my favorites is from Joan Rivers: 'Housework. I hate it. You make the beds, you do the dishes . . . and six months later, you have to start all over again.' "

Who Asked Your Opinion?
——————————— ◉ ———————————

"When I want your opinion, I'll give it to you."
-LAURENCE J. PETER

One woman said, "I agree that one of the keys to not worrying what other people think is having a comeback for dreaded questions. I learned this in your Tongue Fu! class. My husband and I have decided not to have children. You wouldn't believe the grief we get about this. Perfect strangers ask when we're going to have kids, and when we tell them we're not, they assume we *can't* have children and start asking all kinds of intimate questions like 'Have you tried in vitro?' or 'Have you considered foreign adoptions?' We don't like people prying into our personal lives, and this was really beginning to bother us.

"Then you told us about Fun Fu! We agreed that it's better to be amused than offended by off-the-wall comments. We realized that one reason we'd become so sensitive to other people's opinions was because we didn't have a confident way of expressing ours. Being tongue-tied about this issue had caused us to internalize these people's beliefs and doubt our own. We had stopped trusting our own judgment and had bought into what others thought. Our task, then, was to come up with something to say so that never again could people's intrusiveness about this sensitive issue unnerve us.

"About a week after your class, we were at a community potluck and a group of us were watching some kids whoosh down a water slide. One person said, 'It's fun watching the munchkins, isn't it?' My husband said spontaneously, 'Yeah, children make a great spectator sport.' We looked at each other and laughed out loud. We knew we had found our answer. Now, when people ask us that question, we look them in the eye, deliver our 'spectator sport' line, and move the conversation on to something else. We're secure with our decision again now that we no longer let tactless remarks undermine our confidence in the choice we've made."

What's a question people ask that causes you to doubt yourself? Is there a situation that makes you uncomfortable because you're concerned people will disapprove? Can you come up with a noncombative Fun Fu! response so you can be the picture of poise in the face of insensitive inquiries?

Remember the story about Lisa, the divorced homemaker who started focusing on her contributions instead of comparing herself with her younger ad agency colleagues? She got so many laughs every time she told the cup-holder/CD-ROM drawer story that she started collecting others. When people ask her what kind of computer she has, she tells them, *"Beige!"* She explains playfully that she thought microchips were very small snack food, and that semiconductors were part-time orchestra leaders. Instead of being embarrassed by her lack of computer skills, she can now be amused.

Michel de Montaigne said, "The greatest thing in the world is to know how to be self-sufficient." How can you become more self-sufficient? How can you come to rely on your own instincts instead of acquiescing to other people's opinions? Vow to take into account input from a variety of sources, and then when the final decision is to be made, go with your gut.

Sample Starting Today Assignment

"If you feel like your life is a seesaw, perhaps you're depending on other people for your ups and downs."
—ANONYMOUS

Starting today, as soon as you begin to worry "What will people think?" replace it with, "What do *I* think?" By all means, take into account other people's opinions and input, then balance them with your own. Weigh the pros and cons and consider all evidence before deciding what to do. Value your own beliefs as much, if not a little more, than you do others. Create your own quiet center instead of constantly seeking approval or acceptance. Climb off the Self-Esteem Seesaw and learn to depend on yourself for your feeling of worth. The French have a lovely phrase, *"bien na sa peau,"* which means "comfortable in your own skin." As soon as you learn to listen to your inner voice and trust your instincts, you will be comfortable in your own skin. ◎

Action Plan for Who Cares What People Think (I Do, I Do)

Beth has a bone spur and her doctor has ordered her to wear athletic shoes with cushions at all times to allow her foot to heal. Beth works for a large company where corporate attire is the norm. As soon as she gets to work in her business suit and tennis shoes, she starts getting a lot of strange looks. She has a choice of how she handles people's reactions.

BLOCKERS	BUILDERS
What will people think?	What do I think?
"People are going to think I'm a nerd wearing these shoes."	*"For the first time in months, I can walk without pain."*

Others' opinions are all that count
"Maybe I should just wear my heels at the office, and put my shoes on at home."

Objective evaluation
"Do I want my foot to heal or not? If I put my heels back on, this bone spur is just going to get worse."

Codependent
"I'll ask Tonia what she thinks."

Independent
"I'm going to do what I know is best."

Distrust
"People aren't going to understand why I'm doing this. They'll just think I'm a weirdo."

Trust
"In the bigger scheme of things, this isn't that important. I'm going to take care of my foot."

Constant quest for approval
"I'll just explain to people why I'm wearing these shoes so they don't write me off as a geek."

Quiet center and *bien na sa peau*
"I'm glad to know my foot can be treated. I'm looking forward to getting back into aerobics."

MY PERSONAL STARTING TODAY ASSIGNMENT

Starting today I'm going to _____
_____
_____

Signed _____ Date _____

PART IV

Competence: What Are You Capable Of?

"Life is not easy for any of us.
But what of that?
We must have perseverance and, above all,
confidence in ourselves.
We must believe we are gifted for something,
and that this thing, at whatever cost,
must be attained."

- MARIE CURIE

Tap into Your Talents

"If a man has a talent and cannot use it, he has failed. If he has a talent and uses only half of it, he has partly failed. If he has a talent and learns somehow to use the whole of it, he has gloriously succeeded, and won a satisfaction and a triumph few men ever know."

— THOMAS WOLFE

What is your gift? What are you good at? Are you using the whole of it?

When I ask participants in my confidence workshop what they're good at, some people can't think of anything. To be competent, "having requisite or adequate ability or qualities," is almost synonymous with confidence. If we don't feel we do anything well, how can we feel good about ourselves?

Confidence is feeling "I can." A woman in a seminar spoke up and said, "No wonder I feel inadequate. I *can't* do anything well. It seems like everyone has a talent except me."

I asked Sheila what she liked to do. "Well, I like to sew." "Do you sew very often?" "Yeah." She shrugged. "I sewed this dress. I sew most of my clothes." The other women in the room oohed and aahed. Several said they wished they could sew. One asked if Sheila could tailor clothes. Sheila demurred, "It's nothing to make a big deal about. I've been sewing all my life." One of the other women hastened to correct her. "Sewing may be second nature to you, but it's the eighth wonder of the world to me. I have a whole closet full of clothes I can't wear because there's something wrong with them. Either the hem is torn, the waist has lost its elastic, or the pocket's ripped. Could you fix them?" Sheila didn't hesitate. "Sure."

A couple months later, I got a letter from Sheila with her new business card enclosed. "Sewing has been such a part of my life for so long that I didn't know that these days it's considered a lost art. Do you know, from that one class, three ladies brought me clothes that needed tailoring? They were so pleased with the job I did, they referred me to their friends, and now I have a nice little side business. Guess what I call it? Sew and Sew."

Have you become so close to one of your talents you don't see it anymore? Could you, like Sheila, look at your abilities with a fresh perspective? Could you take stock of your skills and realize that while some may be old hat to you, they're valued by others? Sheila increased her confidence because she gave herself credit for being competent. Can you do the same?

Have a Hobby
——— ◉ ———

"No one with a good hobby is ever lonely for long."
—BERAN WOLFE, M.D.

What skill would you like to acquire? What hobby would you like to pursue? Thomas Szasz said, "People often say that this or that person has not yet found himself. But the self is not something that one finds. It is something that one creates." You can create more confidence by finding what you're good at and finding time to master it.

A former student did this by rediscovering the joy of painting. She said, "When I was in high school, we had a wonderful art teacher. This was before the days of liability, so every week we had a field trip into the neighborhood around our school. Our teacher would lead us to a local park near our campus and we would draw dogs, kids, houses, trees in bloom, caterpillars— whatever caught our eye. Once a month she would meet us at a gallery or museum on a Saturday morning and give us our own private guided tour of the great masters. She instilled in every single one of us her passion for painting. I came home particularly proud one day because she had stopped by my desk, looked over my shoulder, and said, 'You have a real talent for drawing.' I couldn't wait to tell my mom, but when I did she brushed it off with 'You can't earn a living as an artist. Painting won't pay the bills unless you want to paint houses.'

"I was crushed. All the fun went out of my artwork. She turned something I loved into something trivial and meaningless. When that class was over, I never picked up a pen or brush again . . . until the week after your seminar. When you asked what activity used to bring us joy, I realized I had been happiest in those high school art classes. Those hours at the parks, galleries, and museums were the purest fun I've ever had. I decided to bring art back into my life and signed up for a local drawing class at the YMCA.

"That first class convinced me it was the right decision. The teacher even reminds me of my old high school teacher; they share the same philosophy that 'painting is silent poetry.' Someone once told me they never feel lonely as long as they have a good book with them. I feel the same way about drawing. I carry my pen set with me almost everywhere I go now. Sometimes at lunchtime I'll go outside, watch the stream of people go by, and draw whoever or whatever catches my fancy. I can't believe I gave up something I loved so much because of one insensitive remark. Drawing is going to be part of my life as long as I can hold a pen in my fingers."

Uncover Your Abilities
———— ◉ ————

"A ship is safe in port—but that's not where a ship was meant to be."

-ANONYMOUS

What ability have you abandoned? Did you have a talent that someone talked you out of? What interest did you give up because someone diminished it with a cruel or inconsiderate comment? It's time to reclaim the pleasure that accompanies doing something you love, well. Talents that are kept hidden away don't do us any good.

Erma Bombeck (God bless her soul) noted, "Not a day goes by that I don't hear from closet writers who have a book inside them fighting to get out. The wannabe writer has to commit by putting all those hopes and dreams on the line. It's time to stop talking about someday and get the book written."

I'll always remember an incident that happened at the 1995 Maui Writers Conference. One of the joys of this event is that it attracts people from all over the world who have put their hopes and dreams on the line. Attendees included a sixteen-year-old high school prodigy who believed he'd written the "next *Star Wars*," a seventy-two-year-old former journalist, a self-described hermit who came out of hiding to shop her memoirs, and an extremely successful New York ad executive.

The ad executive said, "I'm here because of a chance meeting with my high school creative writing teacher. I went back for my son's PTA open house. I was walking down the hall when my former teacher came running out of her room and flagged me down. She told me I was the most gifted writer she'd ever had and wanted to know what I was doing. When I told her I composed jingles, she said, 'But you must write. You can't turn your back on your talent.' So"—here he grinned—"I'm here with what I hope will be the next Great American Novel."

Make Yourself a Master
————————— ◉ —————————

"Genius is nothing but continued attention."
-CLAUDE HELVÉTIUS

I think mastering a skill is nothing but continued attention. During an interview, I was asked by a reporter where I had gotten my confidence. That intriguing question caused me to reach back in my memory to try to pinpoint what had first contributed to my feeling confident. The answer, I realized, was riding horses.

My parents bought a huge, gentle draft horse for us kids

when I was five years old. Elko was part teacher, part babysitter. My sister, brother, and I could climb all over and under him, and we did. Thanks to his patient good nature, I grew up unafraid of horses. I thought I could ride anything. When I look back, I marvel that any five-year-old could control a 1,200-pound animal. Being in charge of a beast of that size—telling him when to go, when to stop, where to go, and how fast—gave me a feeling of mastery that's still serving me today. I realize now how fortunate I was ("Thanks, Mom and Dad") to be given an opportunity to get good at something at such an early age.

Were you given opportunities to develop talents while you were growing up? The good news is, it's not too late if you weren't. As an adult, you have the freedom to pursue your own interests and develop your choice of skills. And if you do, you'll benefit by giving yourself a sense of mastery that will result directly in increased confidence.

Cultivate Your Competence
────────────◎────────────

"I'd gone through life believing in the strengths and competence of others; never in my own. Now, dazzled, I discovered that my capacities were real. It was like finding a fortune in the lining of an old coat."

—JOAN MILLS

Developing a wide variety of skills does not guarantee success. It guarantees *choice*. This was wonderfully demonstrated by a woman named Bonnie, who said, "One of the reasons I fell in love with my husband was because he's a Renaissance man. I'd never met anyone who was so good at so many things. Jack can cook haute cuisine and fix a carburetor, he can play Bach or Bo Diddley on the piano, he can hit a home run out of the ballpark and he's kind to his mother. When I asked how he got so talented, he said modestly that his parents had given him a liberal arts degree in life. While he was growing up, his folks had introduced all five of their kids to culture, literature, gardening, art, sports, animals, house repair—you name it, they did it. At the dinner table every evening, they discussed current events, worked on crossword puzzles, tested each other on vocabulary words, and shared what they'd learned that day. He's had his choice of occupations because he's got such a deep reservoir of talent from which to draw." She concluded with a smile, "I call him, 'Jack of all trades, master of some.'"

As Bonnie had pointed out, sometimes it's to our advantage to get good at a *variety* of talents instead of specializing in one. I present public workshops for the Learning Annex organization in several cities on the East and West Coasts. I'll always remember the man who took my class and reported in our introductions that he was "systematically working his way through the course catalog."

This adventurous individual said, "I take an average of three or four classes a month. My only criteria is that I can't have done it before. I've taken classes on back massage, wine tasting, meditation, kayaking, making your own greeting cards, and baking your own bagels. I see life as a huge buffet. Why limit yourself to the pasta salad? Taking all these different classes has definitely given me more confidence because I know a lot about a lot of things."

Bowled Over
— ◉ —

"Things are going to get a lot worse before they get worse."
—LILY TOMLIN AND JANE WAGNER

A woman reported back after attending a presentation, "My company has a bowling league every Thursday. I thought this was the perfect double-duty activity. I could gain a hobby while meeting new friends. That first night was humiliating. Our team came in dead last, mainly because of me. I scratched three times and had the lowest score of anyone there. I'm not going to make many friends this way!"

I told Lorna I was glad she had contacted me. Normally I cover the three Ss of skill acquisition in my seminars, but I hadn't done so in the one she'd attended because I'd decided to focus on other points in our abbreviated 45-minute session.

I asked, "Lorna, do you remember the first time you rode a bike? Do you remember how awkward it felt and how often you fell? Then, after familiarizing yourself with the fundamentals, you were able to wobble down the street without running into anything? Finally, after still more practice, you got to the point where you could hop on and head off without even thinking about balance, pedals, and handlebars? We go through those same three stages whenever we try to acquire a skill."

The Three Ss of Skill Acquisition

"The thing is to be able to outlast the trends."

- PAUL ANKA

S = Second-guess. At this stage, nothing is certain. We question our ability to do it right. We wonder what we're doing wrong. We feel shaky and may even feel silly or stupid because of our amateurish performance. We're tempted to quit, but know if we do, we'll never acquire this ability.

S = Second base. At this stage, we're halfway home. We've accomplished something, yet we still have a way to go before we've achieved our goal. We're encouraged by our progress, yet still need to practice and perform the fundamentals if we want to succeed.

S = Second nature. At this stage, the skill can be done on automatic pilot. The fundamentals have become so ingrained, we don't even have to think about them, we just do them.

"Lorna, when learning something new, the thing is to outlast the trials and tribulations. The key is not to give up when you don't get immediate, perfect results. It's unrealistic to expect to be a great bowler right away. That doesn't mean you should quit. It means you should hang in there, knowing you'll get better if you just keep applying yourself. Seneca said, 'Dare to be naive.' We have to be willing to be amateurs if we want to learn anything new."

I suggested, "The next few times you bowl, tell your teammates you're a beginner. Thank them in advance for their patience, and let them know you appreciate any tips they might have. People won't resent your novice status as long as you give them an opportunity to be experts.

"You can take your new hobby seriously without taking yourself too seriously. You can sincerely try to improve your game while laughing at your mistakes. It might be helpful to remember the *Cabaret* philosophy. Remind yourself it's far better to be out there cultivating a talent and enjoying the camaraderie of newfound friends than sitting alone in your room."

Have you recently tried a new activity with less-than-stellar results? Or have you tried to reactivate an old hobby and become frustrated because you couldn't perform at your previous high level? Maybe you went skiing over the weekend and found yourself falling on intermediate slopes when you used to be able to schuss down hard runs with ease. Learn from Lorna's lesson. Does that mean you should hang up your skis and write off your favorite winter sport? No, it means you should remember not to compare yourself to what you *used* to be able to do. Instead, immerse yourself in the joy that you're healthy and outside doing something physically rewarding. Be glad you've brought something you love back into your life. As Theodore Roosevelt once said, "Do what you can, with what you have, where you are." Instead of becoming upset about what you can't do, choose to appreciate what you *can* do.

Sample Starting Today Assignment

"Unless you try to do something beyond what you have already mastered, you will never grow."
—ANONYMOUS

THE ASSIGNMENT TODAY IS TO try to do something beyond what you have already mastered so you can increase your feeling of competence. What is a skill you can acquire so you have ongoing proof of your talent? What is a hobby you can plan to bring back into your life so you have a perpetual source of joy? How could you learn a variety of skills so you can become a modern-day Renaissance man or woman? Vow to persevere through the three Ss of skill acquisition so you can reap the rewards of being good at something.

Charles M. Schulz, creator of the *Peanuts* comic strip, said, "Life is like a ten-speed bike. Most of us have gears we never use." Most of us have talents we never tap. Resolve to take one of your talents out of mothballs, dust it off, and put it into practice so you can make the most of your life. ◉

Action Plan for Tapping into Your Talents

Laura, a nurse, grew up dancing ballet. For years she spent almost every afternoon at the studio and every weekend in performances. In high school she discovered boys and stopped dancing. Laura needs some physical activity to counter the stress of her job, but she's afraid she's lost all her agility.

BLOCKERS	BUILDERS
Unable to do anything well	Able to do things well
"I probably will dance like I have two left feet."	*"I know it'll come back to me with a little practice."*

Trying to *find* self
"*I'm not good at anything any-more. All I do is work, work, work.*"

Working to *create* self
"*I'm going to get back into dancing. I used to feel so good about myself when I was fit and performing.*"

Turn back on talents and aban-don hobbies
"*Who am I kidding? I'm forty years old. I'm not as limber as I used to be.*"

Try old talents and actively en-gage in hobbies
"*I'm going to call the studio and see when their next series of lessons start.*"

Make excuses for not having any skills
"*I was thinking about taking a guitar class, but I'm proba-bly too old to pick that up now.*"

Make time to learn a variety of skills to have choices
"*I'm going to call the YMCA about that guitar class. I've al-ways thought it would be fun to be able to play.*"

Feel incompetent and quit be-cause of imperfect results
"*This is just too frustrating. I just can't put myself through this.*"

Feel competent and persevere through three Ss of skill acqui-sition
"*I can do anything I want if I put my mind to it and don't give up.*"

MY PERSONAL STARTING TODAY ASSIGNMENT

Starting today I'm going to _____

_____

_____

Signed _____ Date _____

Play of the Day

"The tragedy of life is what dies inside a man while he lives."
- ALBERT EINSTEIN

Are you saying, "I'd love to pursue a hobby, but who's got time?" Do you have a bad case of "I used tos"? "Well, I used to be a good photographer." "I used to be a good guitarist." Do you believe fun is frivolous?

Many of us have given up the things we used to enjoy out of a sense of duty to others. Pat Nixon reflected, "I have sacrificed everything in my life that I consider precious in order to advance the political career of my husband."

Free Yourself to Have Fun
◉

"A woman can best refind herself by losing herself in some kind of creative activity of her own."
-ANNE MORROW LINDBERGH

What have you sacrificed and why? Several years ago, I was diagnosed with a pituitary tumor. My physician asked, "What's going on in your life?" I filled him in on my jam-packed schedule. I was jumping on planes several times a week to travel to speaking engagements while trying to write, be a wife, and raise my kids.

My doctor counseled, "Many of the patients I see are so busy taking care of everyone else, they haven't been taking care of themselves. After a while, their body gets sick and tired of being ignored and does what it has to in order to get their attention. You *have* to start taking time for yourself." I launched into my litany of reasons why that wasn't possible. After handling all my other priorities, I just wanted to collapse at the end of the day. There wasn't time (or energy) left over for myself.

My doctor persisted and asked what I did for recreation. I laughed out loud. "Recreation? Who has time to play?" He insisted, "What do you do for fun and exercise?" I admitted I used to play tennis. My wise doctor advised, "It isn't selfish of you to take time to do something that gives you joy, it's *smart*. If you don't make time for play, you're going to have to make time for illness. It's time to reverse your thinking. Stop saying, 'I'm too busy taking care of other people to take care of myself,' and start saying, 'I'm going to start taking better care of myself so I can take better care of other people.' "

That doctor not only gave me permission to have fun, he gave me a prescription to have fun. He made me realize that if we don't take time to play, we'll pay . . . in sickness rather than health. I was lucky that my medical wakeup call wasn't terminal or irreversible. This tumor can be controlled with prescription medication. What is it going to take to get your attention? What will it take to convince you that one of the best things you can do *for* yourself is to start taking better care *of* yourself? And that means balancing our increasing workload with recreational activities that bring us joy.

Busy, Busy, Busy
—————◎—————

"I told the doctor I couldn't relax. He said, 'Force yourself.' "
—RON DETTINGER

Do you sometimes feel like a hamster caught on an ever-faster wheel? What have you sacrificed in your mad rush to get it all done? At what cost? As Mahatma Gandhi said, "There's more to life than increasing its speed."

What really brought home to me how busy we all are is what

happened at Tom and Andrew's end-of-season baseball potluck. Everything was store-bought! There were cakes and cookies from bakeries, heated-up lasagna in foil pans, bags of potato chips, canned soft drinks, Pizza Hut pizza, and Kentucky Fried Chicken. Most of the parents felt lucky just to get off work in time to attend the last game of the season. No one had time to go home and cook the traditional casserole. No one had time the night before to make fruit salad or cupcakes from scratch.

That was such a symbol to me of the little things that get sacrificed in our sped-up society. It made me realize that I had never baked chocolate-chip cookies with my sons. Never. Not once. They had never gotten to lick the batter (which everyone knows is the best part) off the spoon. It made me wonder what other rites of passage we were passing up in the name of being too busy.

My husband and I asked each other what our parents had done with us that we had never done with our kids. We produced a whole list of stuff. We had never planted a garden with our kids and tasted sun-warmed tomatoes fresh off the vine. We had never taken our kids to a parade. We had never made strings of popcorn and hung them on our Christmas tree. We decided we were going to make room for these timeless traditions instead of getting caught up in the never-ending list of chores and responsibilities.

Just Say, "Yes"
—————— ◉ ——————

"For fast-acting relief, try slowing down."
–LILY TOMLIN AND JANE WAGNER

What a concept! Slow down? Impossible! So much to do, so little time. It's unreasonable to think we can slow down the entire pace of our lives. We can slow down parts of our lives here and there, so we're not *constantly* on the go.

One of the ways we do this is to just say yes at least a couple of times a week when the boys ask us to do something. I was working on the manuscript one evening when Andrew came upstairs with a hopeful look on his face and a simple request. "Mom, will you play Bingo with me?"

A hundred reasons to say no. Bedtime was in fifteen minutes. The dinner dishes hadn't been done. I had a *lot* of work to do. Bills needed to be paid.

Then I really looked at my son, registered his wistful eyes, his hopeful expression . . . and found myself spontaneously saying yes.

Andrew's face filled first with astonishment, then delight. He quickly ran to get the game before I could change my mind. He scooted downstairs and recruited his brother. We stretched out on the bed, selected our lucky boards, laid out the pieces, and started calling out numbers. We didn't play very long. There weren't any fireworks, epiphanies, or profound insights. Just a few moments of companionable togetherness.

A week later, Tom suggested, "Let's go for a walk and roll." That's a family phrase for our evening ventures into the neighborhood when Andrew Rollerblades, Tom rides his bike, and I hoof it. Once again I was about to beg off when I thought, "Why not?" Minutes later we were marveling at the stars and Tom astutely observed, "The sky has a better view than your screen saver."

A fellow parent once wisely observed, "Children spell love differently than we do. They spell it T-I-M-E."

Next time someone you love impulsively asks you to read a story, watch them dance, shoot hoops, go for a picnic, or join them for a bike ride, surprise them and yourself by saying yes. Your many responsibilities will wait. Friendships may not, and your son or daughter's childhood will not.

Recreational Refreshers
━━━━━━━━━━━ ◉ ━━━━━━━━━━━

"If you let yourself be absorbed completely, if you surrender to the moments as they pass, you live more richly those moments."
—ANNE MORROW LINDBERGH

Making time for these spontaneous pauses that refresh is a way to surrender to the moment and bring loving fun back into our lives without having to make wholescale changes. What could you start saying yes to? You don't have to do anything radical, just take a mini-sabbatical. These positive "time-outs" are a way to create the quality of life you've always wanted. As friend and speaker/author Paul Pearsall would point out, it's a way of living *in* the moment rather than *for* the moment. If you're wondering how this ties into confidence, remember that anything that causes us to live more richly adds to our self-regard. The more we make our life what we want it to be, the more powerful we feel.

So what's your play of the day? Promise yourself that no matter how busy you are, you will take fifteen minutes sometime during the day to recreate yourself.

Less Is More
━━━━━━━━━━━ ◉ ━━━━━━━━━━━

"Ambition is a lust that is never quenched."
—THOMAS OTWAY

Do you find yourself tempted to do more and more? They don't call it blind ambition for nothing! Some of us are compulsively driven to do more, buy more, get more, and have more. A savvy entrepreneur in Washington, D.C., introduced me to the idea that bigger is not better. Cal owned an outdoor-adventure company. He planned raft trips, ski weekends, hot-air-balloon rides; you name it, he booked it. He had hundreds of loyal clients who counted on him to provide some type of fun outing every weekend. I was impressed with how popular and successful his operation was, and approached him one day bubbling over with ideas about other possible ventures.

Cal patiently listened to my enthusiastic proposals, and then calmly stated that I was right, he *could* expand his business, but he wasn't going to. Stumped, I asked why. Cal replied, "Sam, I'm happy the way I am. If I added all these activities, I'd just have more problems. Sure, I'd make more money, but I'd also have more personnel headaches, legal concerns, financial obligations, and administrative responsibilities. Plus, I wouldn't have the freedom to take a month off whenever I choose to." He smiled serenely and added, "The key to contentment is knowing when enough is enough."

Recreate Yourself
—————— ◎ ——————

"It is in games that many men discover their paradise."
-ROBERT LYND

Are you ready to say, "Enough is enough?" Recreation is defined as "refreshment of strength and spirits after work." Unfortunately, many of us feel our work is never done, which means we never have time for leisure. That means we never get refreshed. Our spirit becomes depleted, our energy disappears, and our lives become less and less to our liking.

As Ralph Waldo Emerson put it, "It is easy to live for others. Everybody does. I call on you to live for yourselves."

A man in Hawaii took action on Emerson's quote and rediscovered his "paradise lost." "I used to live to surf. Now that I'm (it pains me to say this) middle-aged, I never have time for it. I've got a family to feed, a mortgage to pay off, lawns to mow, and a two-hour commute every day. Your session helped me realize that surfing once a week isn't a waste of time, it's an investment of time. It's not indulgent for me to do something I love, it's essential. I got together with a couple of my old surfing buddies, and every Sunday morning we head for the ocean. That one morning out on the waves helps me hang on to the person I used to be and gives me something uniquely mine to look forward to."

In Pat Conroy's fascinating book *Beach Music*, the character Jordan Elliott is asked why he surfs. He answers simply, "It's like praying without any words." What activity gives you an opportunity to pray without words? What can you do that re-energizes rather than de-energizes your spirit?

De-energize vs. Re-energize
◉

"Most of the time I don't have much fun. The rest of the time I don't have any fun at all."
–WOODY ALLEN

Several years ago, I presented a concentration workshop for an insurance firm. I quoted the popular observation that "No one on their deathbed ever said, 'I wish I'd spent more time at work,' " and asked the employees what they did that was fun. One manager burst out, "*Fun?* You've got to be kidding. My life is one big pressure cooker. From the second I arrive at the office, it's one crisis after another. I often work through lunch and never leave before seven o'clock. Even then, I usually take paperwork home and come in on weekends. I'm a real desk potato."

I explained to the group that "expectations are the root of all unhappiness." Many of us operate under an unrealistic expectation that eliminates the chance to be satisfied with our lives. This astonishing insight deserved to be introduced in a compelling way that would stop all of them in their mental tracks and shock them into considering its truth. I asked everyone to be silent for a minute so they could reflect on how this idea pertained to their life. Then with a dramatic flourish I revealed a transparency that read, "Understand you will *never* be all caught up."

Many of us are working (and working!) under the erroneous assumption that if we just work hard enough, long enough, and smart enough, we'll get everything finished. We have the outdated assumption that if we apply ourselves assiduously enough, we'll be able to walk out our office door at night with the satisfaction that everything that's supposed to be done, is. WRONG. Ain't going to happen.

In this age of increased work responsibilities, we'll never be able to complete everything that's supposed to be finished. The sheer volume of responsibilities will not *de*crease; in fact, it may even *in*crease. That's why it's so important for us to change our belief that we're bad people if we don't get everything done. Just because we have unfinished tasks at the end of the day doesn't mean we're inefficient or lazy.

Stress is feeling overwhelmed and out of control. Many of us are overwhelmed by our out-of-control workload, which means we're in a constant state of stress. Since we can't completely eliminate that stress, the healthiest thing we can do is counterbalance it. How do we do that? By making room for recreation in our lives. Playful activities generate *eustress*, which re-energizes us. Feeling panicked because we're perpetually behind generates *distress*, which de-energizes us.

At Your Leisure
━━━━━ ◉ ━━━━━

"If you are losing your leisure, look out! You may be losing your soul."
—LOGAN PEARSALL SMITH

Several months later, I saw the insurance agent at a follow-up program for his company. He reported, "It had never occurred to me until that seminar that it was my job to have fun. I'd always thought play was a reward for getting all your work done. After that workshop, I noticed in the newspaper that one of my favorite authors was giving a free lunchtime reading at a nearby bookstore. I figured, why not check it out? It was a great way to spend a lunch hour. Since then, I go to a brown-bag book signing almost every week. I've met everyone from Dave Barry to Dennis Rodman. I really look forward to my weekly quota of culture. This has put fun back in my life, for free, for an investment of about an hour a week."

How can you put fun back in your life, for free, for an investment of an hour a week? That one hour of play could get you through the day.

Sample Starting Today Assignment

"It is a happy talent to know how to play."
—RALPH WALDO EMERSON

THE STARTING TODAY ASSIGNMENT IS for you to set aside fifteen minutes for your own personal play of the day. What are you going to do today that is fun? How are you going to bring more joy into your life? What are you going to do to take care of yourself so you're better able to take care of others? Understand that the more joy you have, the more of a blessing you will be to have around. How are you going to refind yourself through recreation? Remember, it's not a waste of time, it's an investment of time. ◉

Action Plan for Play of the Day

Janice is taking care of her elderly parents, who both need around-the-clock attention. She loves them dearly *and* she is becoming physically and mentally exhausted.

BLOCKERS	BUILDERS
Taking care of everyone else *but* yourself	Taking care of everyone *and* yourself
"I'll take some time for myself when my sister can help out more."	*"I'm going to take some time for myself so I can recharge my batteries."*

Can't force yourself to have fun
"That would pretty selfish of me to be off taking a yoga class when my folks need me so much."

Free yourself to have fun
"I'm going to take an hour twice a week to go to yoga class with Bev."

Speed up the pace of life
"If I hurry up, I can vacuum and do the laundry while they nap."

Slow down the pace of life
"I'm going to take a nap while they nap."

Only children can play
"There's hundreds of things to be done, and I have to be responsible."

Play like children
"I'm going to put on my oldies CD and vacuum à la Mrs. Doubtfire."

Rushed
"I'll dash over to the store and then run these letters over to the post office."

Recreate and refind
"I'm going to get out the photo albums tonight and go through them with Mom and Dad."

Say nay to play
"I'd like to go for a swim, but chores aren't finished yet."

Play of the day
"I'm going to jump in the pool and cool off for a few minutes."

MY PERSONAL STARTING TODAY ASSIGNMENT

Starting today I'm going to _____

_____

_____

Signed _____ Date _____

Help Others Create Confidence

"Few things help an individual more than to place responsibility upon him and to let him know that you trust him."
– BOOKER T. WASHINGTON

Are there people in your life who lack self-esteem? Would you like to help them become more confident? *Don't* help them. What? I learned the hard way that well-intended efforts to help someone gain confidence often achieve the opposite result.

Tom's first-grade teacher called to set up a parent-teacher conference. During our meeting, Mrs. Echeverri complimented Tom's schoolwork and said he was a bright boy. She then paused and seemed to gather strength for her next, rather personal observation. She cleared her throat and plunged in. "Sam, I perceive that Tom lacks confidence."

Well, knock me over with a feather! How could that be? I *teach* confidence! I had dedicated myself to making Tom confident from the day he was born. I had praised his accomplishments and given positive strokes galore. If he couldn't figure out a math problem, I helped him with it. If he couldn't tie his shoelaces, I showed him how. If a playground bully picked on him, I stepped in.

Mrs. Echeverri listened patiently to my disbelieving reaction to her unexpected news. After hearing me out, she gently advised, "Sam, you don't help your kids when you help your kids." She went on to say, "Every time we do something for our children that they can do themselves, we rob them of self-esteem." Why? If every time our kids run into trouble they run to us to take care of it for them, how are they ever going to learn to take care of themselves? If something goes wrong and they bring it to us to fix, we are teaching them to depend on others to solve their problems. We are undermining rather than enhancing their self-regard. Instead of feeling "I can," they feel "I can't." As John D. Rockefeller noted, "Charity is injurious unless it helps the recipient to become independent of it."

Don't Rescue Me
————— ◎ —————

"Real joy comes not from ease or riches or from the praise of men, but from doing something worthwhile."
—WILFRED T. GRENFELL

I'm not suggesting we abandon people in need. I'm not saying we should turn our backs on people in trouble. I'm saying we should help people help themselves. Handouts *don't* help. Helping too much breeds *helplessness*.

This appears paradoxical. How do you help someone without helping them? We guide instead of rescue. We ask instead of tell. Teachers know their job is not to do students' work *for* them, it is to enable them to do it for themselves. A good teacher doesn't say 2 + 2 = 4, 3 + 3 = 6. A good teacher *asks*, 2 + 2 = ?, 3 + 3 = ?. The word *educate* has its origins in the word *educere*, which means "to lead forth." Some parents keep up a constant stream of advice, telling their kids what to do and how to do it. Somewhere they got it into their heads that's what parents are supposed to do. Wrong. Instead of lecturing our children, our job is to let them learn. To paraphrase Wilfred T. Grenfell, *real* confidence comes not from praise or from criticism, but from doing something well yourself.

I Have Confidence in You
━━━━━━━━━━ ◉ ━━━━━━━━━━

*"We awaken in others the same attitude of mind we hold
toward them."*

—ELBERT HUBBARD

I never realized that my unspoken message when I helped my
sons was "I don't believe you can handle this. Here, let me
handle it *for* you." If I didn't trust them to do it, how could
they trust themselves? Encouraging my sons to handle things
for themselves is not abandoning them, it's allowing them to
evolve into confident, self-sufficient citizens.

I read an article about a family in Florida that had adopted
fourteen children. Their home looked like Grand Central Station
with all the comings and goings of the active youngsters. The
mother commented, "Sometimes I feel I deserve an honorary
chauffeur's license. I only wish I could accumulate frequent
driver miles. My philosophy is 'I'll drive them anywhere they'll
sweat.' We don't watch, we do. Instead of sitting inside on weekends and watching baseball, we go outside and play baseball."

This woman knows she can't give her kids confidence, she
can only give them opportunities to become confident. She's
an excellent example of how to put kids in a position where
they can discover and develop talents that will contribute to
their well-being. She knew the hours spent on the road each
day shuttling them from one activity to another was an investment in their competence and confidence.

Let Them Do It
◉

"You cannot help men permanently by doing for them what they could and should do for themselves."
- ABRAHAM LINCOLN

A supervisor said, "I used to work for a real dictator. He was the kind of guy who had his coffee mug inscribed, 'If you don't come in on Saturday, don't bother to come in on Sunday' . . . and he was only half kidding. I was promoted up through the ranks to supervisor, and I was determined to be different. I instituted an open-door policy so employees felt they could talk to me anytime they wanted. Boy, did that backfire! I had a steady stream of employees coming in and dumping their troubles in my lap. After about six months of this, I took a management class and the instructor told us about the monkey theory.

"If an employee walks in with a problem—say, he's mad at Charlie because Charlie's always talking—that problem is a monkey on the employee's back. If I respond with the word *I* ('*I* think you ought to do this,' or 'I'll see what *I* can do about it,' or '*I*'ll talk to Charlie about that'), that monkey takes a big leap off the employee's back and lands on mine. The employee strolls out of the office with a load off his shoulders because I've just taken the responsibility for solving his problem. Guess what he's going to do next time he runs into difficulty? Right. Run right back into my office so I can take it off his hands."

John explained, "I've learned to use the word *you* instead of the word *I* and to ask questions instead of answering them. Instead of saying, '*I* think you should . . . ,' I ask, 'What would happen if . . . ?' Instead of saying, '*I'll* talk to him about it,' I say, 'Have you thought of . . . ?' I started giving guidance instead of game plans."

Smart man. John began empowering his employees rather than undermining them. Instead of rescuing his staff members, he held them responsible for resolving their own challenges. Instead of solving, he started suggesting.

Responsibility = Respect = Worth

◉

"Responsibility is the thing people dread most of all. Yet it is the one thing in the world that develops us, gives us fibre."

-FRANK CRANE

Robert Anderson said, "There's nothing so rewarding as to make people realize they are worthwhile in this world." We can make people feel worthwhile by involving them in activities they find worthwhile. A PTC (parent-teacher coordinator) at a brand-new school was appalled to see their initially spotless campus turned into a pigpen only three weeks after classes had started. Lectures about littering fell on deaf ears. Finally, with the support of administration and parents, Rita announced at a school assembly that *every* student was *required* to participate in a campus cleanup day that following Saturday.

Rita said with a smile, "As you can imagine, there was a lot of complaining and 'Do I have tos?' Saturday arrived and I put everyone to work, weeding, raking, painting over graffiti, picking up trash, replanting trees, and washing down sidewalks. I played dance music over the school loudspeakers to create a carnival-like atmosphere. We held a potluck lunch at noon to reward all the workers. You should have seen the kids' faces glow with pride as they looked around the campus and saw the results of their labor. The place sparkled, and they had done it. Do you know several of the students asked if they could do it again next quarter? For many of them, it was the first time they had felt good about themselves in a long time. Instead of sitting home and staring at the boob tube, they had done something useful with their Saturday. They liked what they had accomplished, and as a result, they liked themselves."

Work It Out

------ ◉ ------

*"A lot of what passes for depression these days is nothing more
than a body saying that it needs work."*

- GEOFFREY NORMAN

I believe that a lot of what passes for low self-esteem these days
is nothing more than a person needing responsibilities. A friend
who's the principal of a private academy has pinpointed the
primary determinant of success in her school. After tracking students' records for more than seventeen years, Dr. Dorothy
Douthit has found that the factor that *most* contributes to outstanding achievement is not intelligence, financial background,
or parental involvement—it's chores.

Children who are required to do chores develop positive self-
esteem because chores fulfill all the 6 Cs of confidence. Kids
feel they're contributing something of value that makes a difference. They feel competent because they're developing skills
and have tangible proof of their abilities. They feel in control
because they're taking charge of their environment instead of
being its victim. They develop courage when they conquer challenging tasks such as mowing the lawn, and chores force kids
(particularly teens) to communicate with their family so they
feel connected instead of isolated. As a result of all of the above,
children develop a healthy self-concept.

The positive side-effects of chores work for adults, too. As
George Washington noted, "Human happiness and moral duty
are inseparably connected." Doing our duty may not always be
fun, but it can help to make us happy.

Sample Starting Today Assignment

"One of my main goals on the planet is to encourage people to empower themselves."
—OPRAH WINFREY

THE ASSIGNMENT IS TO IDENTIFY someone you care for who could use some confidence, and to figure out how you can encourage her to empower herself. Help by not helping. Resolve to give suggestions, not solutions. Give this person opportunities to develop competence so she feels "I can." Instead of trying to raise this individual's self-esteem through words, give her opportunities to raise her self-esteem through *work*. By giving her a chance to resolve her own dilemmas, she will experience the satisfaction and enhanced self-image that result from a job well done. ◉

Action Plan for Helping Others Create Confidence

Frank's son Matt seems to lack confidence. This has been a source of consternation for Frank because he's always tried to be a good father. He goes to Matt's games and helps him with school projects. He's realized maybe he's been helping him "too much" and that Matt needs to become more self-sufficient.

BLOCKERS	BUILDERS
Help others by doing it for them	Help others do it for themselves
"Having trouble with the algebra problem? Here, let me show you how to do it."	*"Having trouble with that algebra problem? Have you tried to multiply the fractions?"*

Undermine people by solving their problems *"I think Coach should be playing you at first base instead of Jimmy. I'm going to talk to him about it."*	Empower people to solve their own problems *"If you want to play first base, why don't you ask Coach if you can try out for the position?"*
Rescuing people from duties *"It's okay if you don't mow the lawn this weekend. I know you've got a big game tomorrow morning."*	Holding people responsible for their duties *"I understand you've got a big game, and it'll take about an hour for you to keep your promise to mow the lawn."*
Try to give people confidence through words *"You should think more highly of yourself. You're smart and athletic. You've got a lot going for you."*	Give people opportunities to gain confidence through actions *"I'm glad you're getting involved in Boy Scouts. It's a wonderful chance to develop a variety of skills."*

MY PERSONAL STARTING TODAY ASSIGNMENT

Starting today I'm going to _____

_____

_____

Signed _____ Date _____

PART V

Contribution: Make Your Life Matter

"The purpose of life—is a life of purpose."

- ROBERT BYRNE

Leave a Legacy with the Four Es

"The service we render others is the rent we pay for our room on earth."
- SIR WILFRED GRENFELL

hy are you here? Do you wake up looking forward to the day because you have a deeply felt reason to live? It's said, "Activity without purpose is meaningless." What is the purpose that gives your activities meaning? Do you feel your life matters?

One of the surest ways to have an unwavering sense of self-worth is to serve others. Dancer Ginger Rogers expressed it another way: "The only way to enjoy anything in this life is to earn it." To enjoy true self-confidence, we've got to believe we're earning our keep. What are you doing to earn your keep?

Could You Contribute Something, Please?

"When you cease to make a contribution, you begin to die."
-ELEANOR ROOSEVELT

The obverse of Roosevelt's quote is also true. When we start to make more of a contribution, we begin to really live. I know some people feel we all have intrinsic worth simply because we're alive. They believe we don't have to do anything to be worthy, we just *are*. I understand that point of view, and I disagree with it. I think we have been given an opportunity to be here and that we have an obligation to give back.

A gentleman contributed his lesson about what it was like to feel that he was no longer giving back. "All my life I had looked forward to retirement. I could hardly wait to sleep in every morning, to have no phones to answer and no bosses to answer to.

"It was great for that first year. I played a little golf, my wife and I went on a couple of cruises, we took our kids and grandkids to Disneyland, I built a screened-in patio on the back of the house. After a while it got stale. I was living the life of leisure and wasn't enjoying it. The lazier I got, the less I liked myself. One day my wife handed me an article from our local newspaper. The 4-H Club was being disbanded because the leader was leaving town and a replacement hadn't been found. The reporter said it was particularly sad because the kids were going to have to cancel their trip to the state fair.

"I had been raised in 4-H, as had all five of my kids. We'd raised rabbits, hogs, and sheep, and had shown horses. My wife said, 'Why don't you take over?' I offered some weak protests, but she persisted: 'You've got time, and you know how important the fair is to these kids.'

"Well, to make a long story short, I called and volunteered. I helped the kids prepare their animals and we all went to the state fair. One of our boys even won grand champion with his steer and got first place in showmanship. His smile when they announced his name over the P.A. system was thanks enough for me and was worth more than all those fancy cruises put together. It's nice having a reason to get up in the morning again."

This man had discovered for himself the truth in George Bernard Shaw's observation that "a perpetual holiday is a good working definition of hell."

The Good Life vs. A Good Life
———————————— ◎ ————————————

*"What is the use of living if it not be to strive for noble causes and
to make this muddled world a better place for those who will
live in it after we are gone?"*

—WINSTON CHURCHILL

I had the privilege of speaking at a Young Presidents Organization international convention. I enjoyed presenting my Tongue Fu! techniques to these executives from around the world, and appreciated having the opportunity to hear some of the other presentations. Tom Morris, a professor of philosophy at Notre Dame, closed the conference with a profound keynote. He started by asking the audience, "What are some words that come to mind when you hear the phrase *the good life?*" The audience contributed words like *wealth, travel, prosperity, luxury,* and *fame."*

Tom then asked, "What does it means to live *a* good life?" Aaahhh, the difference one small word can make. Now participants were contributing words like *integrity, family, honesty, service,* and *values.*

Morris went on to postulate that many people are facing a personal crisis because they're seeking *the* good life instead of *a* good life. In the process, they're discovering the good life often results in a superficial success. They have everything they want on the outside, but they're empty on the inside. It is only when they seek to lead *a* good life that they start feeling the deep-seated satisfaction that comes from knowing they're doing something to make this a better place for those who will live in it after they're gone.

Surface Success vs. Service Success

◉

"There must be more to life than having everything."
—MAURICE SENDAK

Have you been trying to live the good life or a good life? A millionaire developer took my course years ago and confessed that his schedule was full, but his soul wasn't. He had everything he wanted and nothing he valued. He raced boats, ate at the world's finest restaurants, dated the city's most beautiful women, and still didn't like himself or his life.

I asked what his definition of success was. He said, "I used to agree with that Christopher Morley quote 'There is only one success—to be able to spend your life in your own way.' Now I'm not so sure, because I've been spending my life my own way, and it's not enough."

Someone in the same class protested that he couldn't understand this guy's gripe. He said, "I'd love to have a chance to have everything I want. If you'd like to give me all your money, I promise I won't complain."

I explained to the class that I too have come to disagree with Morley's view of success. When writing on deadline, I used to find myself wishing the world would go away so I could work in peace. Now I quickly correct myself because I know how lucky I am to have distractions in my life and how bereft I'd be without them.

Fellow speaker Maggie Bedrosian helped me arrive at this perspective. We ran into each other at a convention and she asked how I was doing. I started telling her. Maggie interrupted me and said, "Sam, tell me in one word how you're doing."

This challenging question deserved a from-the-gut answer, so I reached down and tried to bring up the single word that described exactly how I was feeling. I said, "Maggie, I'm . . . *conflicted*."

She asked, somewhat surprised, "Why?"

I explained, "Yesterday at this time, I was on the beach with my sons. Tom and Andrew were charging into the surf, slapping their boogie boards down on the waves, riding them all the way in, and then running right back out to do it all over again. I looked at them and thought to myself, 'There's nothing better in life than this. Why am I leaving them for two weeks?' I didn't even want to get on the plane.

"Today I'm here at the conference, exchanging ideas, meeting fascinating people, and my mind is racing with all the different things I could do to grow my business. I'm excited just thinking about all the possibilities. I feel so torn between these two worlds. One part of me wants to stay home and be a mom, the other part of me is yearning to be a career woman."

Maggie said wisely, "Sam, the words you use to describe your experience *define* that experience. As long as you say you're conflicted, that's what you're going to be. You need to come up with a more positive way to describe how you feel."

For the next three days, I mulled over her insight. I knew she was right and that I had to come up with a more enlightened word to describe and define my experience. The perfect response finally occurred to me and I couldn't wait to share my epiphany with Maggie. I saw her walking out of a meeting room and ran over to deliver my good news. "Maggie, I've figured it out. I'm not conflicted, I'm *blessed*. I'm not torn between two worlds, I've got the best of both worlds."

The Best of Both Worlds

—— ◉ ——

"The way to love anything is to realize that it might be lost."
-G. K. CHESTERTON

Maggie's assignment helped me generate a new way of looking at my life. She helped me see how fortunate I am to have both a family and a business I love. We've probably all heard that we have to be careful what we ask for because we just might get it. I now know that I don't want the world to go away so I can write in peace. If the world went away, then the only thing in my life would be work. Wouldn't that be a sorry state of affairs?

I want to maintain the perspective that being able to spend life in my own way means no one needs me or wants my attention. Having to occasionally spend life the way other people want me to is preferable to having no one care *how* I spend my life. Yes, it can be irritating to be yanked away in the middle of a project; it's a frustration I'm lucky to have to deal with.

At Your Service

◉

"By the time we've made it, we've had it."

−MALCOLM FORBES

I asked the developer how he could describe and thereby define his situation differently. Instead of feeling bored, perhaps he could feel blessed that he has the resources to make a difference. He had become accustomed to other people serving him; maybe it was time for him to serve others. I asked what he felt passionately about. At the time he couldn't think of anything, but later on he started supporting the Junior Achievement organization. He realized that life had come easily for him, but that wasn't the case for many young people. He subsequently set up scholarships for first-time entrepreneurs so they could attend trade schools and/or get their degree. He is now one of the city's largest philanthropists setting up small-business "incubators." He started concentrating on giving back instead of getting back and has turned his surface success into a far more satisfying spiritual success.

Albert Schweitzer said, "I don't know what your destiny will be, but one thing I know: the only ones among you who will be really happy are those who have sought and found how to serve." How do you serve others? How can you contribute to your community?

I'll always remember a young woman who approached me after a book signing and said, "I envy you. You're so passionate about what you do. I'm not passionate about anything." She explained, "I was given everything by my parents. I went to a private school. We belonged to a country club. Our family traveled to Europe in the summer and skied in Aspen in the winter. I had all the best things growing up. That seems like it would be an ideal situation, but the problem is, I've never wanted for anything, so now I don't want anything."

I had never thought of it before, but she was right. It is a blessing to feel passionately about something. As we continued our conversation, it became evident that she *did* feel strongly about something—about *not* feeling passion. I suggested she become a spokesperson for her generation. She could interview her peers and write articles, perhaps even a book, about this generation that grew up with everything and now doesn't hunger for anything. In that way, she could be of service by articulating their dilemma and sharing solutions she has been given by other twenty-somethings who have transcended this quandary.

Internal vs. External Wealth
———————————— ◎ ————————————

"A man travels the world over in search of what he needs, and returns home to find it."

—GEORGE MOORE

Thousands of interviews have convinced me that confidence is an "inside job." Instead of looking for something to make us happy, the key is to become someone who makes himself and others happy. You can figure out how to do this by asking yourself, "Who has made a difference for me and how?"

Please think of an individual who has influenced you. Who is someone who has had a positive impact on you? It can be someone you've known all your life or someone you encountered for only five minutes. It could be a parent, a teacher, a minister, a supervisor, a sibling, or a spouse.

I love to ask this question because, over the years, I've heard incredibly moving stories about the long-lasting impact one person can have. To my surprise, an interesting trend has emerged. While there is no consistency in the *type* of person that has an impact on us (i.e., there's no predominant age, gender, or relationship), there is consistency in *how* people make an impact on us. There seem to be four basic ways people make a difference, and each begins with the letter E. Before revealing the Four Es of Influence, let me introduce a couple of other interesting responses to the question "Who is someone who has positively influenced you?"

Bad Examples Count

"I didn't fail. I succeeded in setting a bad example."

—GRAFFITI

Some people say, "I can't think of a *positive* role model. I can think of someone who was so awful that in a way they positively influenced me because I promised I'd never be like them." That counts! As one man said, "My father was a terrible person. I won't even go into what he did to us, but we lived in constant terror. I vowed I would never raise a hand to my kids, and I never have. I wouldn't wish that experience on anyone, but in a way, I'm a better father because of what he put me through." As my computer screen saver says, "Some people's purpose may simply be to serve as a warning."

Another man told how a coach's bad example inspired him to behave differently. "I was always the last kid picked for teams. I was kind of uncoordinated, but I loved sports. I'll always remember our eighth-grade annual physical fitness test. I could never throw the ball as far as the other boys, no matter how hard I tried. No matter how high I tried to jump or how long I tried to leap, I was never as good as the jocks. The last event was the mile run, and I thought, 'Finally, something I can win.' I knew the race wouldn't go to the swiftest but to the one who had the guts to run through pain.

"Most of my classmates started out too fast. I was content to keep a slower pace, knowing they couldn't sprint the whole way. By the end of the first lap, kids were gasping, wheezing, and holding their sides. I started passing people. I still remember the joy I felt at knowing that my strategy had worked. My lungs burned and my legs felt like they weighed a hundred pounds apiece, but I kept up my pace. I figured this was my only chance to come in first at anything. Those last few hundred yards seemed like an eternity. I kept my eye on the finish line and told myself over and over that I could do it. I crossed the finish line and collapsed in a heap on the ground.

"One by one, the others straggled across, moaning and groaning. The bell rang and we started walking back to the locker room. The coach commiserated with the other kids, who were all complaining how tired they were. I kept waiting for him to congratulate my first-place finish, point out my valiant effort, compliment my determination, *something*. He never even looked at me."

Give Attention
───◉───

"When it comes to giving, some people stop at nothing."
-GEORGIE JESSEL

"This may seem like a small thing now, but back then, it crushed me. I made a promise to myself that when I was an adult I would praise the less popular kids instead of focusing solely on the stars. I would give recognition to the ones who were doing their best, even if they came in last. And I have. I'm a P.E. teacher now, and I make it a point to reward each and every one of my students. If they're trying hard, they deserve to hear about it. I wouldn't have believed it at the time, but what happened to me that day served a good purpose. It motivated me to give a lot of kids the attention I wish I'd gotten twenty years ago."

Another surprise response to the question is when someone says, "*I'm* the one who's positively influenced me." These people can't identify anyone who reached out to help them; they had to help themselves. One woman said, "I'm the only one from my family who has ever graduated from college. My parents always told me I was worthless and that I'd be lucky to find a minimum-wage job. I put myself through school while working two jobs. I pulled myself up by my bootstraps, got out of that godforsaken town, and made something of myself." That counts, too.

Our goal is to do for others what was done for us—or to do for others what we *wish* someone had done for us.

The Four Es of Influence
━━━━━━━━ ◉ ━━━━━━━━

"Some people strengthen their society just by being the kind of people they are."
–JOHN GARDNER

So, what are the Four Es of Influence? People strengthen us and society in the following four ways:

E = Example. We admire or respect the way someone behaves and think, "I want to be like that." Or, as mentioned earlier, we *don't* like someone's behavior and we say, "I'm going to be different from that."

E = Encouragement. This person believes in us and tells us, "You can do it." It's said, "Encouragement is oxygen to the soul." This person breathes life into our efforts. Their conviction on our behalf causes us to believe in ourselves.

E = Excellence. Someone holds us accountable for superlative performance or high standards of behavior. This person doesn't let us be lazy. We may not like such people, but we're indebted to them because they make us perform up to our potential.

E = Education. Someone teaches us a skill that enables us to feel competent or gives us information that increases our knowledge.

Who have been your mentors? Which of these Es did they do for you? Perhaps the person who most positively influenced you was a combination of all of these. The question now is, how can you use these Es to positively influence others? How can you set an example, be an encourager, hold yourself and others accountable for excellence, and be an educator so that you can make a difference for the people around you?

Sample Starting Today Assignment

"Try not to become a man of success but rather try to become a man of value."
—ALBERT EINSTEIN

THE ASSIGNMENT TODAY IS FOR you to identify one specific way you are going to start leaving a legacy by positively influencing others. By serving others with the Four Es (described in more detail in the next four chapters) you will be earning your keep. As Winston Churchill expressed, "We make a living by what we get, but we make a life by what we give." The key to constant confidence is to know that you are a contributing member of society, to know that you have value and are adding value. ◉

Action Plan for Leaving a Legacy

Elana is the wife of a successful corporate executive. They have a luxurious lifestyle and she doesn't have to work. She's tired of going out to lunch with the ladies and wants to do something more meaningful with her life.

BLOCKERS	BUILDERS
A life of leisure = *the* good life *"The biggest decision I have to make is what shoes to wear with my outfit."*	A life of purpose = *a* good life *"I'm going to find some way to make a difference for the community."*

Surface success = focus on getting
"I've got everything money can buy. Why am I so unhappy?"

Service success = focus on giving
"What do I care about that I can contribute?"

External wealth
"I just need to take a trip somewhere. That will cheer me up."

Internal wealth
"I used to love being in plays when I was in high school. Maybe the local theater group needs volunteers."

Don't feel passionate about anything
"Nothing excites me. How can I be so bored and have so much?"

Feel passionate about adding value
"I'm going to offer to sponsor scholarships for girls who can't afford to take drama classes."

Feel no obligation to give back
"Nobody's reached out to help me. Why should I care about others?"

Feel an obligation to give back
"So many people have positively influenced me. I'm going to pass on their legacy by helping others."

MY PERSONAL STARTING TODAY ASSIGNMENT

Starting today I'm going to _____
_____
_____

Signed _____ Date _____

Set an Example

*"In influencing others, example is not the main thing, it's the
only thing."*
– ALBERT SCHWEITZER

W hat kind of example are
you setting? If someone interviewed your co-workers and asked
them what kind of person you were, how would they describe
you? If someone asked your family members what you were like,
what would they say?

For a moment, step outside your your own skin and look at
yourself through other people's eyes. We often get so caught
up in our own feelings that we feel justified in our actions. "I'm
irritable because I didn't get much sleep last night." "I snapped
at that person because he caused me to miss a deadline." "We
bad-mouthed our co-worker because she had said unkind things
about us." *We* know why we behave the way we do. Other people don't. They experience us without the emotional lens that
filters our perspective of our behavior.

Seeing ourselves from someone else's point of view can be
an eye-opening experience. I was unexpectedly given this opportunity when I read my son's school journal (with his permission). His teacher had assigned a series of thought-
provoking exercises. One page asked the students to describe
their parents. Questions included "What do your mom and dad
look like?" "Where were they born?" "What kind of work do
they do?'

What caught my attention was Andrew's answer to the question "What is your mom's favorite interest or hobby?" Guess what Andrew put? "The *phone!*" It doesn't matter that I work out of my home on Maui, so 95 percent of my business is conducted with off-island clients via telephone. What matters to my son is that it seems I'm always on the phone. Since I do it so much, he concludes that I must love it. His perception helped me realize the unspoken statement my behavior was making.

What statement is your behavior making? Our goal is to set an example of integrity, even when the people around us aren't. Or as National Speaker Association founder Cavett Robert is fond of saying, "Dear Lord, please help me be the kind of person my dog thinks I am."

What Kind of Role Model Are You?
◉

"Children have never been good at listening to their parents, but they have never failed to imitate them."

—JAMES BALDWIN

A mother of five children said, "It may seem like children aren't paying attention, but they're watching and copying our every move. Last week while I was driving my kids to preschool, a truck cut right in front of me. I swerved to avoid it and almost lost control of our car. I was so mad that I caught up to the truck driver and yelled out my window to let him know exactly how I felt about his driving."

The mother continued with her story, "That wasn't the smartest thing I ever did. Not only did I put us at risk, but the next day the swear words I'd shouted out the window came out of my five-year-old's mouth. When I scolded her, she looked at me with tears in her eyes and said, 'But, Mommy, that's what you said yesterday.' I decided right then to set a better example with my language. If my kids hear me saying something, it'll only be a matter of time before they're saying it." This mom had discovered for herself the truth in Ben Franklin's observation that "a good example is the best sermon."

Common Decency Isn't

———————— ◎ ————————

"One must think like a hero merely to behave like a decent human being."

-MAY SARTON

These days, just being a decent human being will make you a hero to someone. We often think of heroes as individuals who act courageously in the face of danger. However, when asked "Who's your hero?" many people pick individuals who simply acted with integrity when dealing with the sometimes daunting challenges of everyday life.

A friend of ours was proclaimed to be a *she*ro by her fellow workers. Connie never knew the profound impact she was having on her peers until they honored her with a retirement party. After thirty plus years of service for this state agency, Connie walked into the office on her final day of work and was met by dozens of balloons, a bouquet of roses, gifts, and a decorated cake, all donated by her co-workers. One by one, they spoke of how Connie's perpetually positive personality had made a difference for them. Several mentioned how privileged they felt to work with someone whose consistent decency had given them the strength to take the high road when they were tempted to do just the opposite. One secretary said that Connie's warm smile and greeting each morning was sometimes the most pleasant thing that happened to her all day. Connie felt she hadn't done anything to deserve all these accolades. What she didn't give herself credit for was the powerful effect a positive person can have on the people around him or her.

The Power of Positive People

"Cheerfulness keeps up a kind of daylight in the mind, and fills it with a steady and perpetual serenity."

—JOSEPH ADDISON

We had the good fortune to witness an everyday hero in action. Several years ago our family got blizzarded in the mountains on our annual Christmas vacation.

Skiing was out of the question, so we hunkered down in the general store, sipped hot cocoa, played board games on the wooden picnic tables, and watched Dave, the owner/cashier/ honorary mayor and all-around great guy in action.

The phone rang and Dave dispensed a weather report and tire/chain advice. The door whooshed open and a bundled-up local galumped in, saluted hello, and checked the walk-in freezer to see if his special-order turkey had arrived. Newcomers peppered Dave with questions ranging from which wine to buy to whether the 49ers had won. A resident ladled out a bowl of homemade chili and added the total to his bill, which was kept in a shoe box behind the counter.

Through it all, Dave greeted return visitors by name, replenished shelves, tacked up lost mittens, shoveled snow, rang up sales, and made coffee.

I realized the community revolved around this man. The neighborhood stayed connected through this individual whom everyone had "in common."

If a group is fortunate, whether it's a PTA, neighborhood, corporation, or family, it has a "general-store guy."

At work, a general-store guy is anyone whose pleasant (sometimes even charismatic) demeanor and exemplary behavior infuse the group with the feeling they're part of something special. This person usually has a warm, friendly smile for everyone and an attitude of optimism—no matter what. His energy and integrity set a standard and provide the soul for what might otherwise be an impersonal place where employees simply do their jobs and little else.

Unfortunately, the person in charge isn't always like this. In fact the head of a business may be the opposite of this. No matter. Someone else can fill the role. It can be the secretary who's been there forever or the hardworking custodian. It can be the supervisor who inspires everyone to be their best. In a family, it can be the child who is always cheerful. This person is the glue that holds everything and everyone together, the sunshine in what might otherwise be a bleak world.

Who is the general-store guy/gal in your organization or family? Is it you? Could it be you? Could you become the one who sets the example? Instead of following everyone else's lead ("No one else cares, why should I?") could you take the lead ("I care even if no one else does")? Could you become the visible conscience of your group?

It's on My Conscience

"Labor to keep alive that little spark of celestial fire—conscience."
—GEORGE WASHINGTON

Ooohh, what a lovely phrase—celestial fire. What does conscience mean, anyway? "The sense of . . . the moral goodness or blameworthiness of one's own conduct, intentions, or character together with a feeling of obligation to do right or be good."

That sums it up, doesn't it? That's what we're aspiring to—to do our best to be morally good, to conduct ourselves in a right or good way. When I brought this word up in a seminar, there was amused skepticism. One man said, "This seems like such an old-fashioned word." Another woman added, "Conscience doesn't seem to be a driving force these days. It seems our moral code is more like 'What can I get away with?'" Still another person added that the prevailing philosophy about right and wrong seems to be "anything's okay—as long as you don't get caught."

That may indeed be how some people think. Do we want it

to be the way we think? Can we have a healthy regard for our-selves if the example we're setting is to get away with as much as we can? Can we truly have a quiet center if we knowingly do wrong and don't care—as long as no one finds out?

Constant Character
◉

"Character is how we act when we think no one is looking."
-ANONYMOUS

Confidence is doing the right thing when no one will know the difference. Confidence is having the character to do the right thing when others are doing otherwise. Confidence is having the courage to do the right thing when others would have us do otherwise.

A therapist friend asks her patients, "What is something your parents said to you over and over again?" When she posed that question to me, my immediate response was "do the right thing." I remember my parents saying this every time I faced a moral dilemma, especially whenever I was trying to skate out of something I didn't feel like doing. If it was really cold and windy outside and I asked if I really *had* to go to the barn to feed the horses, they'd say, "Do the right thing." If the store clerk un-knowingly gave us extra change and I asked if I really had to give the money back, they'd say, "Do the right thing." I am indebted to my parents for instilling the knowledge that we need to act in ways of which we can be proud. What matters is not whether other people are acting in the same way or whether they notice, approve, or agree with what we do; it's that we have the courage, character, and confidence to do *what* we're supposed to do *when* we're supposed to do it.

Words to Live By
—————————◉—————————

"Somewhere between my ambitions and my ideals, I lost my ethical compass."
—JEB MAGRUDER

In today's society of disintegrating values, we need to have a moral map to guide us. We need to clarify and recommit to the values that direct and add meaning to our lives. An English proverb states that "The example of good men is visible philosophy."

In almost every one of my workshops, I ask participants "What is your philosophy?" The point is to have a mission statement that guides our actions and keeps us on track in tough times. We discuss a variety of inspiring quotes (called Fu! for Thought) that can help us handle adversity with grace and gentle determination. At the beginning of the session, most participants couldn't tell you what their philosophy is. As one amazed student put it, "It's kind of like driving through life with your hands off the steering wheel, isn't it?" Yes, it is.

I ask participants to take ten minutes to craft a philosophy/mission statement that captures the way they want to be. I suggest they keep it brief. Having to articulate your outlook in fifty words or less turns confusion into clarity. I then suggest participants post their mission statements. When faced with ethical dilemmas, all they have to do is glance at their card, and their motto can help them decide how to proceed. What's a slogan that captures the way you want to be? Placing it in a high-traffic area where you'll see it frequently can help you become the living personification of your principles.

Mission Possible
━━━━━ ◉ ━━━━━

"When we look for the best in others, we find it in ourselves."
-ANONYMOUS

A woman in one class labored over this. I had given the group ten minutes to work individually or together to create a philosophy that captured the essence of what they were about. Roberta finally adopted a modified version of my mission statement: "My purpose is to make a positive difference for as many people as possible while maintaining a happy, healthy lifestyle with family and friends."

She went on to share this insight when it was her turn to report what she'd come up with, "Do you know what I realized? Last Friday night my husband and I spent almost half an hour at the video store trying to decide what movie we wanted to see. I spent more time trying to select that video than I have trying to figure out how I want to live my life!"

Roberta got back in touch with me several months later to say she pinned her mission statement on her bulletin board and placed a copy of it in her wallet. She said, "That little ten-minute exercise has made such a difference. It helps me make the right decisions on a daily basis, instead of giving in to temptation and straying from my determination to be a good person."

To Sue or Not to Sue?
━━━━━ ◉ ━━━━━

"Ethics is obedience to the unenforceable. You do it for inner reasons, not because someone is keeping score or because you will be punished if you don't."
-JON KABAT-ZINN

Several years ago while I was speaking about this aspect of confidence, a seminar attendee said, "Could you be a little more specific? What's an example of how to set a good example?"

That was a timely question, as our family had just been given an opportunity to put our principles in action (which is what setting a good example is all about).

A month earlier, our son Tom had received second-degree burns when a waiter had dropped a boiling pot of coffee on him. Fortunately, Tom recovered fully and without scars; however, we had a decision to make. Several acquaintances (one of whom was a lawyer) were urging us to sue. "This was clearly negligence," they said. "The restaurant should pay." "There's Tom's college fund," said another. "He's lucky it wasn't more serious. They should compensate him for his suffering."

We had to decide if we were going to take advantage of the waiter's mistake. The waiter had been truly apologetic about what had happened and the restaurant had volunteered to pay the medical bills. Were we going to take people's advice and make a lucrative deposit in Tom's bank account, or were we going to practice what we preach?

What we believe and preach is that overzealous litigation has hurt our society in many ways. Kids can't go on field trips anymore, several of our favorite adventure outing companies have been forced to go out of business because of impossibly high liability insurance, and doctor friends have retired early because of frivolous lawsuits.

For Example

------ ◉ ------

"Everyone thinks of changing the world. No one thinks of changing himself."

—LEO TOLSTOY

We decided the only way our sons would understand that values don't get abandoned when there's a chance to get rich was to choose not to sue. By setting this example, we hope they will understand that principles aren't for sale. They will see that ethics aren't situational, to be adhered to only when convenient.

Some people couldn't believe we were passing up this financial windfall. They thought we were naive or stupid for passing up an excellent chance to secure Tom's financial future. Our response was "We've got to start somewhere. If we don't have the courage of our convictions, how can we ask our sons to?" How can we expect Tom and Andrew to project compassion to their fellow human beings if we don't? Our decision was based on our belief that it's important to set an ethical example even when there is easy money to be made. How could we with integrity complain when others jumped on the lawsuit band-wagon if we did exactly the same thing when opportunity presented itself? The principle is the point.

It's the Principle of the Thing
◎

"People seem not to see that their opinion of the world is also a confession of character."

—ANONYMOUS

Og Mandino, author of *The Greatest Little Secret in the World*, died while I was writing this chapter. Og influenced thousands of people with his life-changing message that we are here to love and serve each other. In the days following his passing, many people expressed their gratitude in an impromptu e-mail memorial service. Person after person spoke of how he had touched them. Over and over people eulogized this fine man with "I never heard Og say anything bad about anyone." I thought to myself, "That was the measure of the man."

Perhaps we can learn from Og's example. Vow to yourself that from this day forward, you are not going to disparage anyone. I believe this is one of the practical ways we can act with integrity on a daily basis. In workshops on leadership I ask participants, "Who is someone you know who acts with integrity? What is it about them that makes them models of integrity?" The answer to the second part of the question is often "They don't bad-mouth or gossip." Who is someone you know who acts with integrity? Is one of their admirable characteristics that they choose not to malign other people?

It's an issue of trust. If we bad-mouth someone, the person

listening may agree with what we're saying, and may indeed be thinking the same thing. At some level, though, they will never trust us again. They will be wondering, "If she's saying this about him, what's she's saying about me?" In my workshops we suggest that whenever you're tempted to say something negative about another person you ask yourself, "Will it help or will it hurt?" If your observation won't help and it could hurt, have the confidence and the presence of mind to zip your lip. We call this Tongue Glue! Believe me, you won't regret *not* saying anything, but boy, will you regret saying something you wish you hadn't.

Joseph Joubert said, "Children have more need of models than of critics." We all do. Resolve today that you are going to be a model of integrity that is beyond criticism.

Sample Starting Today Assignment

"Greatness is not found in possessions, power, position, or prestige. It is discovered in goodness, humility, service, and character."

—WILLIAM WARD

TODAY'S ASSIGNMENT IS TO DESIGN a mission statement to guide your daily actions. Write a motto that captures your principles so it is easier to put them into practice. If you don't know where to begin, you might want to scan through this book. *Concrete Confidence* features over three hundred inspiring quotes that can also serve as philosophies. Be sure to post your motto where you'll see it frequently. You've heard the saying "Out of sight, out of mind?" Keep your motto "in sight, in mind" so it serves as a constant reminder of your commitment to set an example of integrity, even when you're being tempted to act otherwise. ◉

Action Plan for Setting an Example

Louis works in an organization where it's common to bad-mouth the boss. None of the employees like the curmudgeon, one of the nicer nicknames the owner is called. Louis doesn't feel it's right to gossip about the guy who gives him his paycheck, but so far he hasn't had the confidence to say so.

BLOCKERS	BUILDERS
Immoral *"Everyone else 'talks stink' about him. Why shouldn't I?"*	Moral *"Just because other people are doing it doesn't make it right."*
Confused values *"I might as well. He's never going to find out what I said."*	Clear values *"I want to act with integrity, and gossiping isn't acting with integrity."*
What conviction? *"It's okay just to do it with my buddies. They feel the same way."*	Courage of our conviction *"If what I'm going to say isn't going to help, it doesn't deserve to be said."*
Push principles aside when tempted *"You think that's bad. You should hear what he did to me last week."*	Practice our principles even when tempted *"Instead of complaining about it, why don't we approach him with what we would like?"*
What philosophy? *"He is such a jerk. I can't believe he was promoted into that position."*	Pick and post a philosophy *"I'm going to put my motto up where I can see it every day."*

MY PERSONAL STARTING TODAY ASSIGNMENT

Starting today I'm going to _____

_____

Signed _____ Date _____

Be an Encourager

"When you carry out acts of kindness you get a wonderful feeling inside. It is as though something inside your body responds and says, Yes, this is how I ought to feel."

— RABBI HAROLD KUSHNER

hat is a compliment you've received recently? When was the last time you heard an encouraging word?

After hearing this question one woman said, "I've worked for a federal agency for fifteen years. I can't think of the last time someone paid me a compliment."

Are you overdue for some praise? That's almost a rhetorical question, isn't it? We all are. William James said, "The deepest desire in human nature is the craving to be appreciated." Instead of waiting to receive overdue appreciation, why not start giving it? Instead of passively hoping someone else will give us the recognition we deserve, why don't we start giving other people the recognition they deserve? Craving means "to yearn for persistently, wistfully, and sadly." Appreciation is indeed a persistent need. The need for appreciation doesn't disappear after one compliment. Compliments need to keep coming or we feel no one cares. We feel our efforts don't count if they go unnoticed.

Give Gratitude
━━━━━━◉━━━━━━

"Gratitude is not only the greatest of all the virtues, but the parent
of all the others."
–CICERO

Gratitude, being appreciative of benefits received, is a key to confidence. Confident people like their lives, and a big part of liking your life comes from noting all that's right in your world. It's not enough to feel grateful, we must express it. We need to tell others how much we've enjoyed the benefits they've produced for us and others. People can't read our minds. If we don't voice our appreciation, they may not know it exists.

This was never better demonstrated to me than at a fiftieth wedding anniversary celebration I attended. Relatives and friends had gathered from around the country to celebrate the couple's five decades of marriage. The festivities included music, dancing, a video featuring highlights of their lives together, and many testimonials as people stood and told their favorite story of the patriarch and matriarch. At the end of all the tributes, the wife turned to her husband and said, "This has been the most wonderful day of my life. But I still haven't received the one thing I want most."

"What's that?" he asked. "You haven't told me you loved me," she said. Her husband of fifty years looked at her and kidded, "I married you, didn't I?" When his wife's face fell, he realized that this was no joking matter. He caught himself, gave her a heartfelt hug, and said, "I love you, Rose." After fifty years of marriage, she still wanted to hear the words.

Is there someone in your life who is waiting for the words? Many times we think our actions speak for themselves. They don't. George Eliot said, "I like not only to be loved, but to be told I am loved." Our loved ones want to hear us say, "I appreciate you." "I need you." Who in your life would love to hear what he or she means to you?

Be a Blessing to Someone

"Make yourself a blessing to someone. Your kind smile or pat on the back just might pull someone back from the edge."
— CARMELIA ELLIOTT

One participant said, "Sam, I'm just not comfortable giving compliments." He'd brought up a good point. Paying a compliment is a skill, and some of us have never learned how to express and accept "blessings." In fact Kin Hubbard said, "Some people pay a compliment as if they expect a receipt." Here are six short steps to gracious compliments so you never again need to be tongue-tied when trying to give someone a verbal pat on the back.

1. *Make it specific.* Sweeping statements like "That's the prettiest dress I've ever seen" invite skepticism. Overblown compliments such as "That's the best meeting I ever attended" elicit suspicion. If you note exactly what was done well, the recipient believes you're telling the truth and knows the compliment is genuine. Specific observations such as "I really like your dress. It's feminine and professional at the same time" or "Thanks for keeping us focused on the issues instead of letting the discussion deteriorate into a gripe session" are perceived as being sincere.

2. *Make it immediate.* If someone puts in a seventy-hour workweek, she deserves to hear about it now, not six months later in a performance evaluation. In the interim, her attitude may have soured because she concluded no one noticed or cared enough to say anything. As Ralph Waldo Emerson said, "You cannot do a kindness too soon because you never know how soon it will be too late."

3. *Evaluate whether it's better to give the praise in public or in private.* Dr. Haim Ginott said, "If you want children to improve, let them hear the nice things you say about them to others." Some people blossom when complimented in front of others; some wilt. It might not be appropriate to praise an employee in front of co-workers if they'll resent you for singling him out and playing favorites. On the other hand, it can be beneficial to give kudos publicly if someone has achieved something extraordinary and deserves to be lauded for their contributions. Assess your group's mood, the individual's style, and the anticipated reaction; and then make a judgment call about whether to say something to and about the employee when others are present or when it's just the two of you.

4. *Address their suspicion.* If you rarely praise anyone, you must explain why you are doing so now, so the recipient doesn't wonder if you have an ulterior motive. You may even want to say, "You might be wondering why I'm complimenting you now after months of not saying anything. It's just that I realized how much time and effort you've been pouring into this project, and you deserve to hear how much it's appreciated."

5. *Follow with a question.* People often don't know what to say following a compliment, so they end up denigrating it. "Oh, it's nothing." "You don't have to make such a big deal about it." Instead of stopping with "That was a great meeting," follow your compliment with a question: "Where did you learn to keep everyone on track?" You can avoid that awkward silence when no one knows what to say if you segue into asking for information.

6. *Be sure to use the word* and, *rather than the word* but, *and don't include any criticism.* If you follow a compliment with any qualification, you are wiping out your good effect. You've probably heard of the sandwich technique of performance appraisal, in which you're supposed to place a compliment in the middle of two criticisms to make critiques more palatable. It doesn't work. As Henry Ward Beecher said, "The meanest, most contemptible kind of praise is that which first speaks well of a man, and then qualifies it with a 'but.' " If you say, "You did a good job getting those brochures mailed out, but you forgot to put in the sales flyer," the employee will hear only that she didn't do what she was supposed to.

What About Me?
─────── ◉ ───────

"Words of comfort, skillfully administered, are the oldest therapy known to man."
─LOUIS NIZER

"I compliment other people all the time," a woman said plaintively, "now I wish someone would do it for me. I work for a hypercritical boss. I can do a hundred things well, and he doesn't say anything. Let me do one thing wrong, and boy, do I hear about it! Last week I gave a sales presentation to a prospective client. We won the account and their representative said it was due largely to my proposal. Did my boss compliment me? No. He said, 'Next time, put more time into your visuals so they don't look so amateurish.' "

I first empathized with the woman and then suggested, "Stop waiting for your boss to say something nice. It may never happen. Instead of simmering in silence because of his insensitivity, train him to give more balanced feedback. From now on, don't let yourself become discouraged by his disparaging remarks. If what he's saying is basically true, agree: 'You're right, slides would be more professional than a flip chart. Next time I'll ask our graphics department to help me prepare the AV part of my proposal.' Then don't stop there. Ask, 'What did you like about my presentation?'" Ask him to point out something you did effectively, instead of letting him point out only what you did poorly.

Do you have a chronic naysayer in your life? Comedian Richard Lewis cracks, "My mom always calls and asks, 'Is everything all wrong?' " If you have someone in your life who undermines your confidence by noticing only what's wrong, make it a point to ask him what you did well. Hold him accountable for giving you both positive and negative feedback so his constant fault-finding doesn't erode your esteem. Do this for yourself and for anyone around you whose efforts deserve to be recognized and rewarded.

Do Good
─●─

"If you do a good job for others, you heal yourself at the same time, because a dose of joy is a spiritual cure."
-ED SULLIVAN

A while ago, our son brought home his midyear report card. He received all As and Bs, yet in the "Comments" column there was only one sentence: "Tom is very disorganized." That's it. Those four words summed up an entire semester's work. Now I knew that Tom had come in second in the geography contest for his school. Was that mentioned? No. I knew that Tom loved books, and that he was reading several grades above his grade level. Was that mentioned? No.

From that day forward, whenever school personnel looked over his records, their entire perception of this child was going to be determined by the letter grades and the one cryptic comment his teacher had chosen to write. I realize that teachers are overworked, underpaid, and underappreciated. I also know that taking an extra thirty seconds to write one positive or encouraging observation about each child can make a big difference in how that child feels about himself.

I requested a parent-teacher conference. In our meeting, we discussed ways Tom could better organize his schoolwork, and then I asked "What does Tom do well?" The teacher said he was a joy to have in class: he always had something to add to the discussion, and was curious and eager to learn. I asked if she would put a couple of her compliments on his report card so that he would know his good points had been appreciated and future teachers would know he *had* good points.

That experience taught me not to stand by silently when

someone deserves some encouraging words. If you're overdue
for some recognition, have the confidence to ask for it. Say, "I
put a lot of time and effort in on this, and it'd mean a lot to
me to hear that it matters." If someone else is overdue for some
appreciation, give it.

Just Say, "Thank You"

────────── ◎ ──────────

*"The compliment that helps us on our way is not the one that is
shut up in the mind, but the one that is spoken out."*

-MARK TWAIN

And if someone does give you a compliment? Believe it or not,
our level of confidence affects our ability to receive compliments
graciously. People without confidence find it difficult to accept
praise because it doesn't mesh with their image of themselves.
They may even argue with well-intended individuals who are just
trying to be courteous. Vow from now on that if people are
thoughtful enough to say something nice, you won't make them
sorry they spoke up. Be polite and use these three steps for
accepting compliments graciously.

1. *Just say, "Thank you."* Do not in any way counter what
they've just said. If someone says, "I like your new haircut,"
and you reply, "I hate it. I asked her for a trim and she
chopped it all off," she will feel insulted. Instead, simply say
"Thank you." If someone compliments you on a meal you just
prepared, and you feel it wasn't up to your normal standards,
don't respond with, "Actually the lasagna was a little burned
on the bottom." Just say, "Thank you."

2. *Tell them how the compliment makes you feel.* Say,
"Thanks for saying something. I was feeling a little self-
conscious about it, so I'm happy to hear someone likes it" or
"I'm glad you enjoy my cooking. I get a lot of pleasure out of it
and it's nice to know someone else does, too." In other words,

compliment the complimenters. Let them know you appreciate them taking the time to pass on their positive feedback.

3. *Ask them a related question.* Move the conversation forward by throwing the conversational ball back to them. "Where do you get your hair cut? I really like the way your hair is styled" or "Do you enjoy cooking?"

You Can Do It
◉
"Nothing will strengthen a man more than the confidence shown in him."
— JOHANN WOLFGANG VON GOETHE

Sometimes we give encouragement in words. Sometimes we give it in opportunities. While living in Washington, D.C., in the late seventies, I decided to start a running group for women. Running had become an important part of my life, and I wanted to share its benefits with others. I advertised my program in the Open University catalog, and over a hundred women showed up on the steps of the National Capitol Building for our first meeting. I explained our format. We would meet twice a week and train together at some of D.C.'s most scenic spots. Runners of all abilities and sizes were welcome. Our goal was to finish a ten-kilometer race at the end of our six-week program.

To this day, I remember the wonderful feeling in that group. In that first session, we had women who could not run half a mile, much less six miles. We had women who had sworn off running because they had ventured out on a run with a boyfriend or husband and had given up, exhausted, after trying to keep up with his killer pace. We had self-described klutzes who claimed they had never done anything athletic in their lives. The difference was our group was completely supportive, with no competition or pressure. We didn't care if you ran a seven-minute mile or a seventeen-minute mile. We didn't care if you were 110 pounds or 210 pounds. We gathered together to (literally and figuratively) stretch ourselves, jog, talk, and enjoy the vistas of that spectacular city.

Run for It
─ ◎ ─

"The only reason I would take up jogging is so I could hear heavy breathing again."
-ERMA BOMBECK

At the beginning, there was some skepticism and more than a few shared Erma's philosophy. "You're telling me I can run six miles after six weeks? Get out of here!" I was resolute in my belief in them. I had done it and knew they could, too. In our training runs, I made a point of joining up with everyone at least once to offer some encouraging words. "You're doing great." "Looking good." "That's two miles tonight!"

On the morning of the race, we all showed up in our bright pink T-shirts. Everyone had pre-race jitters, but they were also loving every minute and determined to do their best. Do you know what? Every single one of those ladies crossed the finish line, many of them with hands raised jubilantly in the air. Many of them came up afterward to say the reason they had been able to complete the race was because someone had believed in them.

Build Others Up with Belief
─ ◎ ─

"I was successful because you believed in me."
-ULYSSES S. GRANT

Who is successful because you believed in them? It's easy to be a naysayer. It's far more valuable to give people the encouragement they need to help them do something they're not quite sure they're capable of. They may not trust themselves enough to try something new. Someone else saying, "You can do it!" could be just the catalyst they need to take that first step.

I'm frequently approached by aspiring writers who want to know how they can get published. I could be realistic and discourage them by telling them about the enormous odds against ever getting an agent, much less an advance or a contract. I could tell them the industry is increasingly celebrity-driven, and if you're not a name you stand little chance of bestsellerdom. These statements are true, but they're also tactless. I would rather be optimistic and encourage people by telling them about the lasting satisfaction they'll experience by putting their thoughts to paper. I would rather be supportive and tell them to proceed because they'll have a tangible legacy that will outlast them. I would rather tell them I have never met any authors who were sorry they wrote their book: I have only met authors who were sorry they didn't write their book *sooner*.

Are you an encourager or a discourager? Which do you think people would rather hear, predictions of faith or failure?

Who believes in you? Who has told you, "You can do it"? Can you remember how their certainty transferred to you so you were able to succeed? Who could *you* do that for? Look around. Is someone tentatively stretching her wings? Can you be the one to give her the strength she needs to turn her insecurity into assurance? Encourage means "to inspire with courage, spirit, or hope." Can you be the one to give people the courage, hope, or spirit they need to stretch themselves?

The Circle of Compassion
⊙

"Kindness in words creates confidence. Kindness in thinking creates profoundness. Kindness in giving creates love."
-LAO-TZU

Nathaniel Branden observed, "There is overwhelming evidence that the higher the level of self-esteem, the more likely one will treat others with respect, kindness, and generosity." The obverse is also true. The more kindly you treat others, the better you feel about yourself, which in turn inspires you to be more considerate, and so on. I call this process the Circle of Compassion. You've heard the saying "It's better to give than receive." I think it's better to give *and* receive.

A gruff foreman took exception to this idea. He harrumphed, "It's just not my style to give praise. I don't think I should have to go around giving people pats on the back. They're getting paid to produce. That ought to be enough."

I confronted this manager about his unwillingness to give employees what they needed most just because it wasn't his style. I noted, "You're not getting paid to do only what's comfortable for you. You're getting paid to get desired results through your people, and that means creating an environment in which they feel their efforts are appreciated. It's not fair to let employees operate in a feedback vacuum where they never know if what they're doing is valued."

He begrudgingly agreed to start paying more compliments and reported back with a great story. He laughed, "I went up to my secretary of twelve years and said, 'You're the best damn secretary in the whole world.' She dropped what she was doing, turned to me, and asked suspiciously, 'Ralph, are you sick?' I reassured her I wasn't on my deathbed, and that I just felt she deserved to hear how much I appreciated her." When Ralph told us this story, he added that from then on he planned to address his employees' understandable skepticism so they would know he didn't have anything up his sleeve, he was just passing along some overdue recognition.

Human Kind
────⊙────

"A compliment is the applause that refreshes."
-JOHN WIERLEIN

A county manager protested that he didn't feel appreciation would make much of a difference for employees who worked for the government. Claude said, "How are we supposed to motivate employees when we're shackled by a bureaucratic system? I have one employee who does more work than the other three people in the office combined, but she pulls the same salary. I've got two staff members who have 'retired on the job,' but I can't do anything about it because they're protected by their union."

I agreed with Claude that it can be a challenge to keep morale high when our hands are tied by red tape, but a survey given to thousands of managers and workers demonstrated that it *is* possible. Workers were asked to rank the following ten criteria in the order most important to their job satisfaction. Managers were asked to rank the factors in the order they thought their employees would place them. Before you read about the results, please take the test yourself and rank the criteria from 1 to 10 (with 1 being the most important factor in determining job satisfaction and 10 being least important) the way you think *other* people would.

Good wages _____
Job security _____
Promotion and growth
   with company _____
Good working
   conditions _____
Interesting work _____

Management loyalty to
   workers _____
Tactful disciplining _____
Appreciated for work _____
Sympathetic to whole
   person _____
Feeling in on things _____

Claude ranked the factors the way many other managers do. He scored good wages as 1, job security as 2, and promotion and growth as 3. The irony is that he had ranked lowest the three factors employees often rank highest. Most employees say the most important factors in their job satisfaction are first, being appreciated for good work, second, feeling like they're treated as a whole person instead of just a number, and third, feeling informed, involved, and updated as to what's going on around them.

No wonder some managers have a hard time keeping their employees motivated. They have a complete misconception about what determines morale. They think if employees are well paid, have opportunities for advancement, and know they have a secure job, that should be enough to keep them happy. Wrong. Employees want to be treated like human beings first. That's what inspires them to give 100 percent.

I told Claude this survey is good news because it means he can influence the three criteria most important to employees. He may be handcuffed by the hierarchy and unable to control salaries, promotions, and job security. He *can* make a difference, even in the midst of a less-than-perfect system, by choosing to give individuals the recognition they need so they feel appreciated and valued.

Ralph Waldo Emerson noted, "Whenever you are sincerely pleased, you are nourished." Claude may not be able to pay his employees the dollars they deserve, but he can pay them in praise and nourish their spirits, if not their pocketbooks.

A German proverb is "One only has to die to be praised." Don't let that be true for the people around you.

Sample Starting Today Assignment

*"When someone does something good, applaud!
You will make two people happy."*
—SAMUEL GOLDWYN

YOUR STARTING TODAY ASSIGNMENT IS to think of someone who deserves some *spoken* applause. Maybe it's the person at work who never causes any trouble and gets taken for granted in the process. Maybe it's the waitress at the coffee shop who is always so friendly. Maybe it's the family member who never hears (and may be doubting) how much he or she means to you. John Updike believed that "ancient religion and modern science agree: We are here to give praise. Or, to slightly tip the expression, to pay attention." Make it a point today to pay at least two people the attention they deserve so that they know someone cares. Use the steps to give blessings graciously so the recipient knows your compliment is sincere. Give people some encouraging words so they will know their efforts are noticed and that they do matter. ◉

Action Plan for Being an Encourager

Cindy is moving to a city that is not known for its courtesy. She's heard so many stories about its rude people, she's worried about what it might be like to live there. She decided she would have the courage and the confidence to be pleasant to everyone she met, in the hopes they would choose to treat her "in kind."

BLOCKERS	BUILDERS
Discourage *"I was waiting in line for almost an hour. You should hire more help."*	Encourage *"You've sure been handling these people graciously."*
Assuming they know how we feel *"You'd think someone would make an effort to welcome a newcomer."*	Telling them how we feel *"Hi. I'm Cindy. I just moved into the apartment next door. Do you have suggestions about local markets?"*
Too shy to give compliments *"That saleslady really knows how to apply makeup. She probably already knows that, though."*	Gracious when giving compliments *"You are an artist with makeup. Could you please give me a few pointers?"*
React to other people's behavior and make them pay for mistreatment *"I can't believe what a jerk this taxi driver is. He's not getting any tip from me."*	Build up others with belief and start the Circle of Compassion *"Have you lived here long? What are some of your favorite places in the city?"*

MY PERSONAL STARTING TODAY ASSIGNMENT

Starting today I'm going to _____

_____

_____

Signed _____ Date _____

Stand for Excellence

"We are all looking for someone who will make us do what we can."

- RALPH WALDO EMERSON

W ho is someone who held you accountable for excellence? Who is someone who wouldn't let you slide, who demanded that you perform up to your potential? This taskmaster may not have been popular with you at the time, but you feel indebted to him or her now for pushing you to a level of accomplishment you might not otherwise have achieved.

When I ask this question in classes, someone will often say, "I can't believe I'm saying this because I couldn't stand this guy . . . ," and then he or she grudgingly admits gratitude to this individual for "making me do what I could."

A teenager told me he hated his high school swim coach. "He was a real slave driver. Every workout was torture. He would drive us to the breaking point with nonstop sprints, long-distance training swims, and all-out relays. At the end of every practice, we had to do twenty starts in ten minutes. Diving flat out and hauling ourselves out of the pool in that short time was exhausting. Most of the time I was so tired that as soon as I got home I fell into bed and was sound asleep a minute later.

"All that hard work paid off, though. Our team was undefeated that year and we won our conference championship for the first time in the history of our school. We dedicated our trophy to Coach because we knew his persistence on our behalf had made it all possible."

Don't Let Them Be Lazy
———————⊙———————

"This is what is hardest: to close the open hand because one loves."
—FRIEDRICH NIETZSCHE

A woman in a session said she mentally thanks her parents every time she sits down to play the piano. "I hated lessons. My mom had an all-out war every afternoon just trying to get me to practice. I begged them to let me quit, but they thought I had a gift and refused to let me throw it away.

"I now earn my living making music. I play during the dinner hour at a local country club, and earn more money in twenty hours a week than I would if I had gone to college and earned an MBA. My early-evening gig lets me be home with my children during the day. I'm so grateful my folks cared enough to endure my flak and did not let me walk away from something they knew would be good for me in the long run."

Be a Tough Taskmaster
———————⊙———————

"One of the toughest things to learn is the ability to make yourself do the thing you have to do, when it ought to be done, whether you like it or not."
—THOMAS HENRY HUXLEY

As this pianist's parents found out, one of the toughest things is to learn how to motivate other people to do the things they have to do, when they ought to be done, whether they like it or not. We all like to be liked. Unfortunately, most of the times we hold people accountable for doing the things they ought to do, we will *not* be liked. That's why we must believe in the importance of this so we can remain strong in the face of battle.

If people give us a hard time, we've got to be convinced that what we're doing is worthwhile or else we'll lose our confidence and cave in under their verbal battering. If we give in and allow people to escape from their duties, we've just taught them that if they put up a big enough stink, we'll back down.

This is especially important with children. Imagine it's bedtime. If we yell at the kids to turn off the TV and get ready for bed, what do you think will happen? Not much. Instead, take the two minutes to get up and go to where they're watching TV. Say, "Kids, give me your eyes." People's attention is where their eyes are pointed. If our kids aren't looking at us, they're not listening to us. If they don't turn away from the TV and look at you, walk in front of them and turn off the TV so you have their full attention. Then tell them, "I'll say this once. TV off in five minutes. Okay, what's our agreement?" They'll probably mumble back, "TV off in five minutes."

So does the TV get turned off in five minutes? Probably not. At that point, you go back to the room. Don't repeat yourself. Instead of scolding, "I thought I told you to turn off the TV. Weren't you listening? Why don't you ever obey me?" simply say, "Kids, what was our agreement?" They'll probably protest, "But, Mom, this is our favorite program. Please, can't we stay up a little longer?"

At this point, don't explain your decision. If you say, "It's a school night, you've got to get up early in the morning," they'll quickly say, "We promise to get up on time tomorrow." If we explain an order, recipients immediately think of all the reasons our explanations aren't valid. They learn if they're clever enough to refute our rationale, we're left with nothing to do except to concede, "Okay, you can watch the rest of the program, but you better keep your promise." We've just taught our kids to counter our every command, to debate every directive.

Instead, raise your eyebrows, not your voice. Put your hand up (it's a visual signal that stops arguments and wards off debates) and say, "I'll say it one last time. What was our agreement?" and then stop talking. Your kids will reluctantly trudge off to bed and will respect you for being consistent. You are not doing them a disservice by holding them accountable; you are doing them a service by teaching them to do what they're supposed to do when they're supposed to do it, whether they like it or not. They won't think you're being mean, they'll just think you mean what you say.

Gut It Out
——◉——

"Tell a man he is brave, and you help him to become so."
-THOMAS CARLYLE

A woman said her physical therapist was the person who had positively influenced her. "I had both my legs crushed in a freak accident. I was walking between two parked cars and the driver in front backed up without looking and pinned me against the other car. I was in and out of the hospital for months and had several surgeries. The doctor warned me he wasn't sure how much mobility I would regain, and prescribed extensive physical therapy.

"I'd like to be able to say I was a model patient, but I wasn't. I was mad at the world and took it out on the medical staff. I was filled with rage. The driver walked away without a scratch; I was the one who ended up in a wheelchair. I was assigned a physical therapist who gave me no slack. I guess Natalie thought I was feeling so sorry for myself, I didn't need anyone else feeling sorry for me.

"Every day she pushed me past my point of endurance. In the beginning, the pain and frustration of trying to move my legs even an inch was almost more than I could bear. I begged her to leave me alone, but she wouldn't. I'm glad she didn't, because six months after I was wheeled into the rehab clinic, I walked out under my own power. I'm indebted to her because I couldn't have done it on my own."

No Slackers
————— ◉ —————

"I'm not lazy. I'm just motivationally impaired."
-POPULAR T-SHIRT SAYING

Are you wondering, "HOW do we hold someone accountable?" Use the Seven Steps to Stop Slacking Off to motivate people to do what they're supposed to do, when they're supposed to do it.

1. *Ask yourself, "Was the expectation or standard outlined and agreed to in the beginning?"* Maybe you're upset because an employee has been reporting to work late. Ask yourself, "Was this employee informed when she was hired or transferred to your department that being on time was an important criterion of employment? Or was it assumed that she knew everyone was supposed to be on site and ready to produce by eight A.M.?"

2. *Ask yourself, "Has the expectation or standard been consistently enforced?"* If the employee wasn't disciplined when she arrived late, she may have concluded that it wasn't a big deal. If she broke the rules and nothing happened to her, she may have concluded that this rule doesn't apply to her and/ or it doesn't really matter that much.

At this point, she may feel entitled to come in a little late. (After all, you've been "letting" her get away with it.) If you try to discipline her at this juncture, she'll feel you're being unfair. She's likely to object, "I've been late before and didn't get in trouble. Why now?"

3. *If the standard wasn't outlined at the outset or enforced consistently, admit mea culpa* (Latin for "my fault"). Say, "It was my fault for not addressing this earlier." Or say, "You're right. I should have said something the first time you were late so you knew how strongly we feel about this issue."

4. *Say, "Starting as of ____," and state a specific target date with a built-in transition time.* It's not reasonable to expect someone to comply with a new requirement immediately. She may have legitimate logistical difficulties that are contributing to her tardiness. By building in some leeway, you leave her an opportunity to make changes in car-pool arrangements, day-care drop-offs, or whatever, so she can comply with the expectation by the deadline.

5. *Specify measurable, positively phrased expectations and outline the exact consequences if she chooses not to comply.* Saying "You better not be late again" accomplishes little. State the desired rather than the dreaded behavior and attach numbers to it so it can't be misinterpreted. Say, "Starting September 15, you need to be in the building and at your desk by eight A.M. ready to take phone calls and help customers. If you are more than five minutes late, you will receive a verbal warning. If you are late again within the same month, you will receive a disciplinary letter in your personnel file. If you are late three times in one month, you will have a day off without pay, and if you are late four times, that will be cause for dismissal."

At this point, you may mention if there's a reward for consistently coming in on time. Some companies feel promptness is a requirement of employment; others feel it deserves to be rewarded. Your organization's policy may be to offer a mental health day for every six months of on-time performance.

6. *Ask, "What is your understanding of our agreement?"* Do *not* ask, "Do you understand?" If you do, the person will probably nod reluctantly, which does not constitute an agreement. By having to say out loud exactly what is expected of her and the consequences for not complying, she has agreed to a verbal contract.

7. *Schedule a follow-up appointment.* It's important that people know you mean what you say. By saying, "We're going to get together on October 1 at nine A.M. to review your time cards," you let the person know this isn't going to disappear; she will be held accountable for her action or inaction.

Mind Your Manners
─────── ◎ ───────

"Manners easily and rapidly mature into morals."
—HORACE MANN

Sometimes the best thing we can do for loved ones is to make them answerable for their treatment of others. A slight modification of Mann's observation is "Good manners mature into good citizenship." If we teach youngsters common decency, they turn into decent human beings. If we hold them accountable for being sensitive to the rights of others, they learn to think of someone other than themselves.

A single mother in a session said she had attended the workshop to improve her own confidence, and was pleasantly surprised to hear some tips that were going to help her deal with her twenty-four-year-old live-at-home son. "I love him, but it's time for him to get a life! You've helped me see that the best thing I can do for him is to stop doing things for him. Why should he go out and get his own apartment and car as long as he can use mine? Why should he get a job when he's got free bed and board? Why should he pick up after himself if I do it for him?

"I've realized I'm not doing him any favors by condoning his freeloading. He can't respect himself for living off his mother. It's time for him to support himself, instead of me supporting him. I know this isn't going to go over very well with him, but I guess parenting isn't supposed to be a popularity contest. It's time to do what's best, and that means kicking him out of the nest."

Sample Starting Today Assignment

"What if, right at this very moment, I am living up to my full potential?"
—LILY TOMLIN AND JANE WAGNER

Nɴᴏᴛ ᴍᴜᴄʜ ᴄʜᴀɴᴄᴇ ᴏf ᴛʜᴀᴛ. Very few people feel their life is everything it should be. Whom can you make a difference for by holding them accountable for their actions instead of overlooking their digressions? Today's assignment is to identify someone at work or at home who is not living up to his potential. Use the Seven Steps to Stop Slacking Off to persuade him to keep his agreements and behave in ways of which he can be proud. Resolve to help people do what they're supposed to do, when they're supposed to do it, whether they like it or not. It may not put you at the top of their popularity list, but down the road, they may thank you for helping them be all they can be. ◎

Action Plan for Standing for Excellence

Stacy is the adviser of a high school cheerleading squad. The girls want to participate in a regional competition. If they win, they get to go to the national finals in Florida. This is the first time they've ever prepared for this level of competition, and they didn't know it would take so much work. Stacy is getting a lot of flak and needs to keep her confidence in the face of the girls' griping.

BLOCKERS	BUILDERS
Let them be lazy *"Well, there were a few mistakes, but it was close enough."*	Hold them accountable *"Girls, we've got to do it again until we can run through the routine without a mistake."*

Let them quit	Don't let them give up
"I know it's hot. We'll stop early today."	*"Girls, it's going to be hot at the contest, too. We've got to get used to it."*
Cave in to their complaints	Persevere despite their complaints
"You're making me out to be a meanie. I give up. It's not worth getting all this guff."	*"I know you don't like me right now, but you will when you climb up on that platform to get your first-place trophy."*
Slackers get away with not performing up to standard	Slackers are held accountable for performing up to standard
"Jessica came late to practice again. I won't say anything because I don't want to hear more of her excuses."	*"Jessica, can I talk to you in private, please? Did you want to continue to be on this squad? If so, you need to be here five minutes early from now on."*

MY PERSONAL STARTING TODAY ASSIGNMENT

Starting today I'm going to _____

_____

_____

Signed _____ Date _____

Serve by Educating

"Teachers affect eternity; who knows where their influence will end?"
- HENRY BROOKS ADAMS

Do you have a favorite teacher? Someone who transferred his or her passion for a topic to you? Someone who triggered your interest in a vocation that resulted in a rewarding career? Maybe this teacher didn't give you a skill or knowledge, but an attitude. Maybe he or she taught you how to be yourself in the midst of peer pressure or tickled your intellect and made you feel it was okay to be smart.

Appreciate in Kind
———— ◉ ————

"One can never pay in gratitude; one can only pay 'in kind' somewhere else in life."
-ANNE MORROW LINDBERGH

I think we can pay in gratitude *and* in kind. Have you taken the time to thank the special teachers who favorably affected you? Can you imagine what it would mean to them to receive a note saying how much their contribution has meant to you? One seminar attendee said, "I feel helpless because the individual I want to thank is gone. My grandfather lived with us the last few years of his life. He used to get up every morning at dawn and practice tai chi in our backyard. I was so impressed with this gentle martial art that I asked him to teach me. Tai chi is a wonderful combination of meditation and choreographed exercise. I have so many fond memories of us greeting the day together, synchronizing our peaceful movements as the sun rose. My grandfather passed away last year while I was out of state visiting colleges. I have so many regrets because I never really told him how much our mornings meant to me. Now it's too late."

No, I told her, it's not. I suggested Kim pay her grandfather back in kind. She could volunteer to teach tai chi at a local retirement home or rec center. By doing for others what her grandfather had done for her, she could pass on his legacy and show her appreciation rather than say it. Felix Frankfurter said it best: "Gratitude is one of the least articulate of the emotions, especially when it is deep." Gratitude can sometimes be expressed better in actions than in words.

Carry On
—◉—

"The final test of a leader is that he leaves behind in other men the conviction and the will to carry on."
—WALTER LIPPMANN

With all due respect to Mr. Lippmann, I think the final test of a teacher is to leave behind in his or her students the confidence and the skill to carry on.

I'll always remember the time I was visiting my dad while on a speaking tour in California. He reentered the house after collecting the mail and started sorting through it. He opened one letter and read it silently. I noticed then that he was just sitting there quietly, a tear rolling down his cheek. "Uh-oh," I thought, "it's bad news." "What is it, Dad?" I asked.

He passed me the letter and motioned that it was okay to read it. It was from a former student. Dad was then director of vocational agriculture education for the state of California, but for many years he had served as a shop and ag teacher for a small high school in New Cuyama. The letter writer said, "You may not remember me, but I remember you. I was in your welding class fifteen years ago. All the other teachers had labeled me a troublemaker. You were the only one who gave me a chance. I took your welding class just to bide time until I could legally drop out of school on my sixteenth birthday.

"That first week, you told us our semester project was going to be a four-animal stock trailer, and that we were going to make it together from scratch. I thought you were crazy. After teaching us the basics, you put us to work. That fifty minutes in shop every day was the only time I ever enjoyed school. I'll never forget that first time we loaded some horses into the trailer and transferred them to another pasture. I remember looking in the rearview mirror and thinking, 'We built this. We built this.'

"You probably didn't know it, but the skills you taught me in that one semester have supported me, my wife, and our two children. I have my own welding business, thanks to your belief in me, and I hope to put my two kids through college with the income I've earned from welding. Just thought you'd like to hear that one of your shop students made good. Thanks."

"The great use of life," said William James, "is to spend it for something that outlasts you." My dad is gone now, but I'm sure he'd feel a lot of satisfaction in knowing that the hundreds of hours he spent on behalf of his students have outlasted him.

Teach What You've Been Taught

——————— ◉ ———————

"If you have knowledge, let others light their candles at it."
-MARGARET FULLER

What do you do well that you could share with others? A self-taught chess enthusiast started an after-school chess club at our local elementary school. He volunteers his time two afternoons a week and shares his expertise with the youngsters. I talked with him at the end of the school year chess party and tournament and asked what motivated him to start the club. He said, "My reward is when their eyes light up when they grasp a new move, or when they buckle down and really think their way through a tough spot. My parents couldn't have cared less about chess, so I had to learn on my own. I wish someone had supported my interest in chess when I was young, so it gives me a lot of satisfaction to turn around and do it for these kids."

An Indian saying is "Everything that is not given is lost." Find a skill that you can give so it is not lost.

Share Your Skills
◎

"Education is the apprenticeship of life."
-ROBERT WILLMOTT

A retired couple moved into our neighborhood a few years back. They bought an undeveloped lot and rented the house across the street to live in while they built their dream home from the ground up. I walked by one morning and complimented Verne on the progress he was making. Verne climbed down from his almost-completed roof to share this story. "When I was a junior in high school, I was sent to my grandfather's house for the summer. He was in construction, and I was expected to work alongside him. Believe me, that was not how I'd intended to spend my summer! I wanted to hang out with my pals and the gals at the lake, and there I was hammering nails and hauling around lumber instead.

"I didn't appreciate what my grandfather was doing for me then. I do now. One of the reasons I became a successful real estate developer was because I *knew* the business. I could walk the properties with the contractors and see if the workers had been cutting corners. I could personally inspect the beams, the windows, and the wiring, and know if they'd been done properly. Now I'm here building my own home with my own two hands. It's tremendously satisfying, and I am able to do it because of that summer my grandfather took me on as an apprentice and taught me a trade."

Sample Starting Today Assignment

"Knowledge exists to be imparted."
—RALPH WALDO EMERSON

YOUR ASSIGNMENT IS TO IDENTIFY a skill that has enriched your life and to figure out how you're going to teach it to others. How are you going to impart your knowledge? How are you going to take on an apprentice and teach him or her a trade? How are you going to share your enthusiasm and abilities with others so they discover for themselves the joy of that particular talent? Henry Ford said, "Anyone who keeps learning stays young." The same could be said of educating. How are you going to stay young by giving someone an education in life skills? ◎

Action Plan for Serving by Educating

Hal is a genius with cars. He and his father used to spend hours in the garage tinkering with their Chevy. They would find junkers that had been in accidents, rebuild them, and sell them for a nice profit. Hal has been wondering how he might be able to pass on this ability to others.

BLOCKERS	BUILDERS
Thank the person who taught us . . . someday	Thank the person who taught us . . . today
"Dad knows how much I enjoyed those times together."	*"I'm going to surprise Dad with a thank-you letter. He deserves to know how much I appreciate what he did."*

Keep your skills to yourself	Pass your skills on to others
"I get nervous when I have to speak in front of others. Plus, how do I know anyone is interested?"	*"I think other people might enjoy knowing how to do basic maintenance on their own car."*
I'm not a teacher	Teach what you've been taught
"You have to go to school to be a teacher. I'm not qualified."	*"If I just share what I know, people may be able to put that information to good use."*
Focus only on our nervousness	Focus on how this knowledge could benefit others
"What if I offered a basic car maintenance class at the local community college, and no one signed up? I'd be embarrassed."	*"I'll offer the class and if only two people show up, that's fine with me. We'll have a lot of fun, and I'll teach them whatever they want to know."*
Not interested in giving an education	Take on an apprentice and give an education
"Kids these days aren't interested in cars like we were."	*"Maybe my nephew would like to learn about cars. I'll call him."*

MY PERSONAL STARTING TODAY ASSIGNMENT

Starting today I'm going to _____
_____
_____

Signed _____ Date _____

PART VI

Control: Who's in Charge?

"Self-command is the main elegance."

- RALPH WALDO EMERSON

Looking for Some Body to Love

"Your body is the harp of your soul."
— KAHLIL GIBRAN

Ha! More like the tuba of my soul. Thousands of participants in my workshops have confessed they hate their body. They share comic Steven Wright's sentiment: "When I die, I'm going to leave my body to science . . . fiction." Then, of course, Phyllis Diller had to one-up Wright by reporting that she had willed her body to science . . . but science contested the will.

How do you feel about your body? Appearance is not a petty issue. We can't separate how we feel about our "package" from how we feel about ourselves. Do you like the way you look? Are you proud of your body or embarrassed by it? Does everything work the way it's supposed to, or do you have physical disabilities and health problems?

Understand that it doesn't matter how we *actually* look. What matters is how we *feel* about how we look. People may tell us we're attractive, but their perceptions don't count unless we agree with them. If we see ourselves as physically flawed (whether it's having pimples or twenty extra pounds), we find it hard to have a healthy regard for ourselves. In fact, it's almost impossible to like ourselves if we're not comfortable with the way we look.

Fat Chance
——————◎——————

"Your medical tests are in. You're short, fat, and bald."
-ZIGGY (TOM WILSON)

It's hard to feel confident if we don't feel in control of our body. My weight has yo-yoed most of my life. While visiting my sister many years ago, I glanced in the mirror one day and expressed disgust at my extra pounds. Having heard this many times before, my sister said in exasperation, "I'm sick and tired of hearing you complain about your weight, Sam. Either put up or shut up."

Her advice may not have been elegant, but it was effective. Either it was important enough for me to do something about my weight or it wasn't.

The following head-to-toe tally can help us decide once and for all how we feel about our body parts, if it's within our control to change our body parts, and if it's important enough to us to, as one student said, "take action or take it easy."

Head-to-Toe Tally
——————◎——————

"If you happen to have a wart on your nose or forehead, you cannot help imagining that no one in the world has anything else to do but stare at your wart, laugh at it, and condemn you for it, even though you have discovered America."
-FYODOR DOSTOYEVSKY

Please complete this exercise and elaborate on the parts you like and don't like. Maybe you think your hair is too curly or you don't like its color. Maybe your eyes are too close together or you have to wear glasses. Maybe your nose would give Jimmy Durante some competition. Maybe your breasts rest on your stomach. (As Gypsy Rose Lee said, "I've got everything I used to have, it's just a little lower to the ground.") Please include anything I didn't think of but that is important to you.

BODY PART OR ASPECT	LIKE?	DON'T LIKE?	CAN CHANGE?	CAN'T CHANGE
Hair				
Eyes				
Nose				
Lips, teeth, chin				
Complexion, skin				
Ears				
Shoulders				
Arms				
Chest, breasts				
Waist, stomach				
Hips, bottom				

Legs, knees

....

Feet, ankles

....

Height

....

Weight

....

Other

....

Take a Good Look
⊙

"If you don't take care of your body, where will you live?"
—POPULAR T-SHIRT SAYING

Now, take the three-step Put Up or Shut Up Test.

1. First, circle the body parts you *do* like. Take a moment to appreciate those aspects of yourself that please you.

2. Next, circle the body parts/aspects you don't like that you can't change. In *Tongue Fu!* I tell the story of a seven-foot-tall young man who finally developed a sense of humor about his height instead of being perpetually perturbed by people's smart-aleck remarks. He started wearing T-shirts that said, "No, I'm not a basketball player!" The back of the shirt asked, "Are you a jockey?" He realized since he couldn't control his height, he might as well have fun with it instead of being frustrated by it. If you can't do anything about a certain characteristic, draw a line through it and put it out of your mind. There are more important things to do with your time than gnash your teeth

over things you can't change or control. Accept it, choose to appreciate yourself (warts and all), and get on with your life.

3. Now circle the body parts/aspects you don't like that you can change. The question to ask is "Is it important enough for me to do what needs to be done to change it?" If so, do it. If not, cross it out and accept it as it is.

A man said to me after a class, "I started losing my hair when I was forty years old. I tried everything: toupees, hair transplants, and Rogaine. I even resorted to the dreaded 'comb over' hairstyle where you wrap hair from one side of your head to the other in the hopes that no one will notice. Nothing worked. I finally realized I could let this rule my every waking moment or I could live with it. I threw away my toupee and have been a free man ever since. My Fun Fu! line is, 'I'm not bald, I'm just taller than my hair!' "

A woman told me she had been called Beaver Teeth throughout her school years because of her two protruding front teeth. "My older sister teased me mercilessly. I was so self-conscious. I would never smile with my mouth open, and I often covered my mouth with my hand when I spoke. Our family didn't have money for braces, so I suffered with this terrible nickname the whole time I was growing up. I never thought I was attractive. As soon as I opened my mouth to say something, I would see people's eyebrows go up when they saw my buck teeth.

"A couple of years ago, I took my twelve-year-old daughter to see an orthodontist, and during her consultation the doctor asked if I wanted to get my teeth fixed, too. He explained that many people my age were choosing to get braces, and that, with the new clear styles, they weren't that noticeable. My first thought was that it was vain or silly for a mother of three to be wearing braces, and then I thought, 'I would rather look silly or vain for a couple of years than be self-conscious for the rest of my life.' " At this point, the woman opened her mouth to show off her braces and said, "Three more months to go!"

Flip-Flop Philosophy

◉

*"When you appreciate the beauty and uniqueness of things, you
receive energy."*

–JAMES REDFIELD

The first year my husband and I were married, my folks traveled
from California to our Washington D.C., home for Thanksgiving.
Les spent the entire day preparing an elaborate meal. I kept
going into the kitchen and saying, "Come on out, Les, and join
us. My parents want to spend some time with you." He begged
off, saying he needed to peel the potatoes or set the table. That
evening I told him I wished he had spent less time in the
kitchen and more time with my mom and dad. He looked at
me in surprise and said, "Sam, I can't believe it. Half the women
in the country would love to have a man spend all day cooking
in the kitchen so they could spend time with their parents, and
you're complaining about it. Don't you realize how rare this is?"

He helped me see the flip side of the situation. Ever since
then, if I'm unhappy with a situation, I apply the flip-flop philosophy. If you're not happy with something, ask yourself,
"What's the obverse of this situation?" Examining the opposite
makes us appreciate the original.

What's a situation that's not to your liking? Perhaps your husband spends all day Saturday taking care of his garden instead
of going shopping with you. Well, at least he's home doing
something useful. Imagine your kids are yammering for you to
go in the pool with them and all you want is to be left alone to
read your book. Ask yourself, "What's the opposite of this situation?" Would you rather they didn't crave your attention or
want you to play with them? What if you resent having to commute on the freeway to your workplace every day? Could you
flip-flop the situation and realize that at least you have a
good-paying job to commute to, which in this day and age is
not a sure thing?

Hip Hip Hooray!

————————◉————————

"God made the human body, and it is the most exquisite and wonderful organization which has come to us from the divine hand. It is a study for one's whole life. If an undevout astronomer is mad, an undevout physiologist is even madder."

—HENRY WARD BEECHER

If you're wondering what this has to do with body image, it's just that, after forty-five years, I've done a flip-flop with my body. Instead of denouncing it, I started thinking about all it's done for me. It has run half marathons. It plays a decent game of tennis. It doesn't have aches and pains. It gets up every morning and functions the way it's supposed to. It thinks, feels, smells, sees, moves, hears, and talks. All in all, it has served me very well. More than very well—it's been a joy and a blessing.

How do I reward it? I abuse it, ignore it, and obsess over the parts I don't like. I sometimes even hate it for its size and shape. What did it ever do to deserve this? It's an innocent victim. It's been trudging along all these years, doing the best it could, and not only have I not appreciated it, I've heaped scorn upon it.

It deserves better. My body has been my constant companion for over four decades, and I've finally come to feel affection for it. "Thank you for that walk." "Thank you for going to sleep within seconds." "Thank you for waking up refreshed and energetic." "Thank you for carrying me up these stairs." "Thank you, mind, for these thoughts that are flowing." "Thank you, fingers, for allowing me to type these words."

I don't think mean things about my body anymore. I thank it all the time. Because I've realized my body doesn't have to be healthy. It could be different. I want to appreciate what my body's got, instead of bemoaning what it's not.

Could you apply the flip-flop philosophy to your body? Could you come to see it as a faithful servant and give it the affection it deserves? Instead of becoming upset because you have to wear bifocals, could you be glad that you can still see? Instead of obsessing about your wrinkles, could you appreciate that you're growing older and remember that it beats the alternative? Instead of complaining because you can't get up the stairs as quickly as you used to, could you be grateful you can get up them at all?

If kindness begins at home, could we be a little kinder to this physical home that is doing the best it can on our behalf? It's important to follow the advice given in the Desiderata: "Beyond a wholesome discipline, be gentle with yourself." Instead of verbally or physically abusing your "homebody," could you treat it a little more gently, a little more lovingly?

Unconditional Confidence
◎
"I'm not into working out. My philosophy is, No pain, no pain."
– CAROL LIEFER

I thought about leaving this next story out of the book, because I don't want to send the message that the only way people can feel confident is if they're thin. A lot of us already buy into that belief, and I don't want to support or perpetuate it. What I believe is what I've just said. The body is an amazing mechanism and it's important to love and appreciate it as the miracle it is, instead of thinking it has to look a certain way or else we're unhappy with it.

The key to confidence is liking ourselves. That includes our bodies. If we like our body only as long as it looks good, but hate it as soon as it gains a pound, starts to sag, grows a few wrinkles, or loses some hair, then we've just rendered our confidence conditional. We need to be grateful to our body regardless of how it looks. It's still serving us. It's still getting us around, pumping blood, breathing oxygen, registering ideas, and sensing our environment.

I think it's admirable to have a fit body and to have the discipline to keep it looking good and operating optimally. That's healthy. What's not healthy is having a specific image of the ideal body, and if our body doesn't look like that, we don't like ourselves.

Health = Hope
———◎———

"He who has health, has hope; and he who has hope, has everything."
—ARABIAN PROVERB

I decided to include Sarah's story because the changes she made to her body served as a catalyst for positive changes in other areas of her life. I ran into Sarah, an attorney, several years after she took my course, and she shared this story. "When I took your seminar, my confidence was at an all-time low. I had realized that despite my lawyering skills, I was being written off because I didn't look the part. In law school, I had immersed myself in my studies, staying up until all hours of the night, often getting only three or four hours' sleep. The only exercise I ever got was walking from class to class on campus. I had really packed on the pounds, and I just continued those bad habits when I joined the firm. I thought of my body (if I thought of it at all) as something in which to carry around my mind. I guess I'd always thought, 'Judge me by my wits, not by my waist.'

"I finally realized that I was sabotaging my effectiveness by neglecting my appearance. You told us that Dorothy Parker quote: 'I shall stay the way I am, because I do not give a damn.' I decided I *did* give a damn and I didn't want to stay the way I was. I resolved to work at improving my physical side as diligently as I had my intellectual side. I set up appointments with a personal trainer three times a week so I wouldn't duck out of my commitment. I subscribed to one of those food services that prepares and delivers a week's worth of meals, so all you have to do is zap it in the microwave and you have an instant dinner.

"I've lost sixty-five pounds in the last year, and I've gone from a size 18 to a size 8. I've received many compliments, and I've never felt better. In an ideal world, I wouldn't be judged by my looks, but this isn't an ideal world. I started this health regime for professional reasons, but it's turned out to be one of the best things I've ever done for myself personally, too."

What is the best thing you could do for yourself personally? Maybe you've wrestled with your weight, too, but for whatever reason, you don't have the discipline at this point in your life to drop those extra pounds and keep them off. If that's the case, use the "put up or shut up" philosophy and stop giving yourself a hard time about how you look. Leo Rosten said, "If you're going to do something wrong, you might as well enjoy it." Employ the flip-flop philosophy and appreciate all the things your body is, instead of this one thing it isn't. Your body isn't awful, it's awesome.

Sample Starting Today Assignment

"I take care of me, I am the only one I've got."
—GROUCHO MARX

ARE YOU TAKING CARE OF you? Today's assignment is to decide once and for all what you can change and what you can't, and whether you care enough to take appropriate action. Perhaps most important, cherish your body as the loyal servant it is and thank it for the many ways it supports you in all that you do.

Calvin Coolidge believed, "We cannot do everything at once, but we can do something at once." We can't obtain an ideal body all at once. We can take steps to having a healthier body at once. What is one thing you are going to do today to take better care of your physical self? ◉

Action Plan for Looking for Some Body to Love

Victoria suffers from psoriasis. Her skin often breaks out and is sometimes covered with weepy sores. She covers her arms in long sleeves and her legs in pants. She can't stand to see herself in mirrors and avoids them. She's not confident because she doesn't think anyone could be attracted to someone who looks the way she does.

BLOCKERS	BUILDERS
Body is an albatross we hate *"I think my body is ugly."*	Body is an asset we appreciate *"I'm grateful for all the other aspects of my body that work perfectly."*
Embarrassed by our appearance *"I want to go to a gym, but I'm not about to let anyone see me in shorts or a leotard."*	Evaluate our appearance *"Can I do anything about my skin? Yes. The doctor says this medicated ointment will help."*
Can't shut up about our looks *"I can hardly bear to look at myself. Why does this have to happen to me?"*	Put up or shut up *"Is it important enough to me to take that self-hypnosis class to try to reduce my stress?"*
Sedentary and don't like to exercise *"I don't feel like exercising. Sweating just makes me itch more."*	Exercise so we'll get in better shape *"I'm going to start walking to work. It's a mile each way. It'll be an energetic start and end to the day."*
Don't accept our body because it doesn't look the way we want it to *"If only I could get rid of this rash. Then I'd get a date."*	Appreciate our body because it serves us well *"Thanks, body, for getting me around all these years."*

MY PERSONAL STARTING TODAY ASSIGNMENT

Starting today I'm going to _____

_____

_____

Signed _____ Date _____

Say Bye-Bye to Butterflies

"We always experience anxiety whenever we confront the potential of our own development."
— SØREN KIERKEGAARD

Do you feel anxious in new situations? Would you like to know how to kiss those butterflies good-bye? Or as book editor Jennifer Enderlin says, "Would you like to learn how to fly with your butterflies?" so you can transform uneasiness into excitement?

Musicians, dancers, singers, and athletes have all mastered the ability to control their jitters so they can give their best performance. You too can learn how to collect yourself before important events so you can, as Raquel Welch once said, "be yourself on purpose."

Stress Rehearsal
◉

"One important key to success is self-confidence. An important key to self-confidence is preparation."
— ARTHUR ASHE, JR.

I was coaching a women's tennis team for an upcoming match and told them we were going to have a stress rehearsal. "A stress rehearsal?" one of the players said incredulously. "I'm stressed out enough without rehearsing it!"

I assured her that this was a *mental* dress rehearsal and that it would alleviate her stress, not add to it! If you've ever played a sport and had an awful day ("I couldn't hit the broad side of a barn today"; "I'm making one mistake after another"), you probably didn't prepare a game plan.

I suggested the players maximize their physical performance with mental preparation. You too can be the picture of confidence—if you use these ideas to get your head ready before a situation in which you want to do your best. I'll give a sports example first, and then explain how we can speak confidently in front of a group, which is the number one fear of many people.

Five Steps to Being the Picture of Confidence
⊙

"We are what we think. All that we are arises with our thoughts."
—THE BUDDHA

All that we *do* also arises with our thoughts. Use this five-step method to make sure your thoughts are working for rather than against you so you can operate optimally.

1. *Conduct a mental dress rehearsal.* Tennis players could picture warming up and hitting easy, smooth strokes cleanly over the net. They could imagine gliding around the court agilely, getting to their shots in plenty of time to hit sweet returns. They could visualize their first serves, going in and rushing to the net with plenty of time to put away a crisp volley.

2. *Picture the bad stuff and plan how you can handle your worst nightmare with poise.* Imagine your opponents making some questionable line calls, and you electing to keep your cool and win the next point. Envision the other team trying to psych you out by stalling between points, and you choosing to maintain your composure. See yourself not becoming exhausted, but calling on your energy reserves and playing enthusiastically at the end of the match.

3. *Use the drive time to the event wisely.* Instead of chatting with the other person in the car or idly listening to the radio, select a specific assignment: "I'm going to get 70 percent of my first serves in," or "I'm going to hit the ball at least three feet over the net so it lands deep in the court." Please notice these orders are phrased *positively*! If you say to yourself, "Don't double-fault," or "I'm not going to attempt low-percentage shots today," you'll probably end up doing the very thing you don't want to do. You must imprint what you want to do ("Swing slowly and smoothly") instead of what you don't want to do ("I'm not going to kill the ball every time it comes near me"). Rather than worrying about letting the team down, motivate yourself with "I'm going to play sweet tennis and enjoy every minute."

4. *Create a one- or two-word command to clear out mental clutter.* Create a quick, positive order you can give your mind so it has something constructive to obey at the moment of truth. Break down the essence of each stroke into a pivotal part. For your serve, maybe it's keeping your head up. Think "Eyes up" just before you serve. For a backhand, maybe it's "shoulder to net." For a forehand, maybe it's "racquet back." The purpose of these words is to direct your behavior in positive ways at crucial moments.

5. *Control your thoughts during downtime with rituals.* Choking happens when you allow doubts (e.g., "I'm already down a break. If I lose this game, I'll never be able to come back") to creep into your brain. If you fill your mind with a positively phrased mantra, there won't be any room for destructive distractions. Championship players often bury their heads in their towels during changeovers, and they stare at and adjust their racquet strings between points. Why? They know if they look around, they're going to notice the players squabbling on the next court; they're going to hear (and perhaps get annoyed at) the planes flying overhead; they're going to notice the photographers taking pictures just behind the court. If you allow your mind to go blank when play is halted, it will fill up with observations about your surroundings. Instead, fill your mind with mental pictures of what you intend to do next.

Turn Anxiety into Eagerness
————————— ◎ —————————

"People use words like 'anxiety attack' as if anxiety is out there and attacks you."
—WAYNE W. DYER

A young man reported he was able to use these five steps to become the "toast of the party." He said, "My best friend Rob asked me to be the best man at his wedding. At first I was flattered, but then I realized I'd have to give a toast at the reception. That may not seem like a big deal to you, but I'm terrified of getting up and speaking in front of a group. Just the thought of it was enough to send me into an anxiety attack. I decided to take your workshop to see if it could help me overcome my nervousness about making that toast.

"Those five steps made a big difference. For two weeks before the ceremony, I mentally rehearsed what I wanted to say. Then I pictured the bad stuff. I saw myself standing up, opening my mouth, and nothing coming out. I imagined my voice cracking and everyone laughing at me. I imagined stumbling over my words and making a fool out of myself. As you suggested, I came up with clever comebacks so I could keep my poise in case any of that happened. To overcome my fears, I reminded myself that the toast was about *Rob*, not about me. I wasn't there to impress people, I was there to honor my best friend.

"On the way to the reception after the wedding, I turned off the radio and practiced my speech in my mind. I focused on what I planned to say (what a great guy he is and how glad I am he's found his perfect match in Wendy) instead of worrying about forgetting my speech in front of God and everyone. A couple of minutes before the tributes started, I excused myself for one last rehearsal and reviewed my reminder notes. I had put down three words to trigger the points I wanted to make, and I had written in large block letters DO IT FOR ROB.

When it was time, I stood tall, squared my shoulders, and clinked my glass to get everyone's attention. Then, I turned to Rob and Wendy, looked right at them, and spoke from my heart. Thanks to those ideas, I overcame my dread and did a decent job.''

What if It Goes Wrong?
———————— ◉ ————————

"Calamity is the test of integrity."
-**RICHARDSON**

You may be thinking, "Great, everything went well for him. But what if it hadn't? How are you supposed to respond if the real-life event doesn't go as you've scripted it?" If your worst-case scenario does materialize, follow Elizabeth Lindsey's elegant example.

An hour and a half before the conclusion of the 1996 Maui Writers Conference, we had a brainstorm. "Wouldn't it be great to close the conference with a hula done by Elizabeth, an actress and former Miss Hawaii?" After words, words, words for four days straight, a hula from the heart seemed the quintessential way to honor our aina (host land and location) and bid our audience a fond farewell.

We quickly found Elizabeth, who was attending the conference to screen her PBS documentary *And Then There Were None*, and pitched our idea. Luckily for us, she had a CD of her favorite music with her and graciously agreed to our plan. She dashed up to her room to change and prepare for her impromptu performance—now less than an hour away.

The awards ceremony ended and it was Elizabeth's turn to take the stage. Two thousand eyes focused on her as she shared a Hawaiian blessing and signaled for the music to begin.

It was the wrong song. This is when Elizabeth showed everyone in the room that calamity is the test of character. She calmly and courteously said, "It's song number fourteen." There were a couple of moments of silent scrambling by the sound crew and the music started again. It was *still* the wrong song.

At this point, Elizabeth could have done several things. She could have become frustrated and let her annoyance show. She could have reprimanded the tech crew, "That's not it! It's 'Ka-ena,' number fourteen!" She could have let out an exasperated sigh. She did none of these.

Maintaining her composure, she stood tall and graciously, silently waited for the correct music. After an interminable pause and one more incorrect selection, the crew finally located the right song. The beautiful strains filtered out from the sound system and Elizabeth began to dance. She moved to the music with complete, loving concentration. She *became* the hula; every movement was done with utmost care and meaning. The crowd knew they were witnessing something special. The hula ended with Elizabeth in a final pose, arms extended in a loving embrace. The audience rose as one to applaud her amazing performance.

Everyone there was so impressed with Elizabeth's choice to transcend those temporary difficulties and give her gift to the group. She demonstrated that it's possible to maintain your poise, no matter what. When it was all over, what will people remember? The glitches? No. They will remember a woman who personified grace under pressure.

Benjamin Disraeli said, "There is no education like adversity." Elizabeth taught us all a lesson that day: it's not what happens to us, it's how we handle it that counts. We can transcend adversity and turn trials into triumphs if we resolve to act with character in times of crises.

Never Be Nervous Again

—————◎—————

"I'd be more brave if I wasn't so scared."

-HAWKEYE PIERCE, *M*A*S*H*

Are you thinking, "Well, it was easy for her to be brave in that situation. She's a professional actress who's appeared in public many times." Good point. Elizabeth has learned how to act confident even when she doesn't feel confident, and you can, too. Actors know they can project an emotion just by positioning their body in a certain way. If they want to appear sad, all they have to do is drop their chin, pull down the corners of their mouth, cast their eyes down, let their shoulders slope and their body sag. The audience will see them as being sad, and lo and behold, the actors will start feeling sad.

Actors can also project sadness by thinking back to a sad experience and reliving it. Remembering the sorrowful experience revives that emotion, and their body language begins to reflect what they're feeling on the inside.

Either way, whether you act yourself into feeling sad or feel yourself into acting sad, you can transform yourself into the mental and physical state of sadness within seconds. If you can do this with sadness, why not do it with confidence?

What's an important event coming up in which you would like to walk in with confidence? Give yourself five minutes of privacy beforehand so you can prepare yourself mentally. To make yourself feel confident, recall an experience where you were at your best. Perhaps you won an award at school, your friends threw you a birthday party, or you accomplished a long-time goal. Remember that on-top-of-the-world feeling? Do you find yourself breaking into a smile as you re-experience the glory of that moment? Hang on to that feeling.

Next, act yourself into feeling confident by standing tall. Pick your shoulders up and roll them back. Keep them there and don't let them slump forward. Lift your head and animate your face. Some of us get a hangdog look when we're tense or nervous; our facial features become set in a dark, gloomy expression. Fellow speaker Terry Paulson asks, "Are you enjoying yourself? Why don't you let your face know it?" Let your face show confidence by lifting your eyebrows and the corners of your mouth. It's almost impossible to be gloomy when you do this because you are literally and figuratively lifting your spirits and brightening your outlook.

William James said, "Believe that life is worth living, and your belief will help create the fact." Believe you are confident, act as if you were confident, and you will help create the fact. I know some people call this attitude "Fake it till you make it." Many of us have an aversion to the word *fake* because it has negative connotations. I don't believe this is faking it. This is understanding that if we wait around until we feel an emotion, it may never happen. We can increase our ability to project confidence by mentally and physically preparing ourselves, by adopting the emotions and actions that will enhance rather than undermine our performance.

The Made-up Mind
— ◎ —

"Strength is a matter of the made-up mind."
—JOHN BEECHER

We've probably all heard the phrase *mind over matter*. Have you also heard the variation of that phrase: "If you don't mind, it doesn't matter"? This is literally true. If we don't pay attention to doubts, they lose their power to drain our strength.

I was given an opportunity several years ago to put the mind-over-matter philosophy into practice. My doctor delivered the not-too-welcome news that I needed an MRI, a procedure that involves your being slid inside a large cylindrical tube. Although the tube is open at both ends, the inside compartment is quite cramped so you feel totally enclosed.

The first words out of the nurse's mouth as she was writing up the request slip were "Are you claustrophobic?" I assured her I wasn't and asked why she wanted to know. She proceeded to describe the apparatus and told me horror stories of patients who had panicked because they felt trapped. The first fears crept into my mind.

The clerk who handled the paperwork for my flight to Oahu glanced at the trip request form and said, "Oh, you're having an MRI. You're not claustrophobic, are you?" I told her small spaces didn't bother me, but by then I was starting to worry.

Two days before the procedure, the technician called to confirm the appointment. Guess what his first question was? "Are you claustrophobic?" I felt like screaming, "Well, if I wasn't before, I sure am now!" He warned, "If you're claustrophobic, you've got to tell me now, because this is the last chance to order a tranquilizer." He also shared a story about a patient who had lost it inside and repeated that I wouldn't have another chance to request a sedative. By now, the butterflies were in full flight. How could I not be nervous with all these doomsday predictions?

Thankfully, the day before the appointment, a friend found an article in a science magazine about "Miracle MRIs." The author pointed out what an advantage it is for doctors to be able to use this painless space-age diagnostic tool to find out what is wrong with patients instead of having to resort to exploratory surgery.

Remember the flip-flop philosophy that was introduced in "Looking for Some Body to Love"? That article allowed me to do a flip-flop with the MRI. Instead of approaching that procedure with apprehension, I was able to approach it with appreciation. Instead of letting people talk me into a state of claustrophobia, I resolved to talk myself into a state of calm confidence.

I placed one of my son's shirts over my eyes with the hope that what we can't see can't hurt us (right?) and to keep me from focusing on the chamber ceiling—all of two inches away from my nose. I listened to the beautiful sounds of the Brothers Cazimero on the CD headset and filled my mind with how lucky I was to be able to have this painless procedure instead of having to go under the knife. I was able to turn my stress into serenity, and you can do the same.

From this day forward, when preparing for a scary event, re-fuse to focus on your fears. Choose instead to focus on positive projections. Dwell on how you want to behave and mentally rehearse your ideal performance. I'm not saying your real-life performance will go exactly as you've scripted it in your mind, I am saying it will go better. Practice doesn't make perfect, it makes better.

Transcend Timidity
————————◎————————

*"Doubts and mistrust are the mere panic of timid imagination,
which the steadfast heart will conquer, and the large
mind transcend."*

-HELEN KELLER

What if other people are doing you a disservice by offering dire warnings? Perhaps you're going to get married and people keep asking, "Are you getting nervous?" Reply, "I'm looking forward to the wedding. I've got friends coming from all over the country, and I can't wait to see them." If you're preparing for an important test and someone says, "Are you worried?" say, "No, I've studied hard for this test and I know I'm going to do well." What if you'll be competing in a tournament and a teammate says, "Are you scared?" Say, "I'm glad to have made it to the finals, and I'm going to play the best I can." If you're pregnant, your due date is fast arriving, and an insensitive stranger warns, "Labor is going to hurt!" say, "Probably, and I'm going to focus on how much we want this baby and how glad I am to welcome her into the world."

From now on, choose to talk yourself into performing well instead of out of performing well. Get those butterflies flying in formation. Put your anxiety to good purpose by using that en-ergy to generate your best-case scenario.

Sample Starting Today Assignment

"Become so wrapped in something that you forget to be afraid."
—LADY BIRD JOHNSON

THE ASSIGNMENT IS TO THINK of a situation coming up, one in which you would like to walk in with confidence. How are you going to use these techniques to turn your dread into determination so the experience turns out the way you want it to? Use the flip-flop philosophy to focus on why you do want to do this, rather than on why you don't. Promise yourself you are going to mentally rehearse that event (instead of worry about it) so you fill your mind with positive (rather than pessimistic) predictions. Decide in detail how you want the event to unfold, and then fill your mind with those thoughts so there's no room for doubts. Instead of trying to eliminate anxiety, embrace it as a source of abundant energy that can be used to your advantage. Use that energy to create your optimal experience. ◉

Action Plan for Saying Bye-Bye to Butterflies

Annette has joined a group to improve her speaking ability. She is scheduled to give her first talk the next day, and she's terrified. She knows the group is supportive, but she is still worried about having to get up in front of everyone.

BLOCKERS	BUILDERS
Buy into butterflies	Say bye-bye to butterflies
"What if I get up there and go blank? I hate it when everyone's looking at me."	*"I'm glad I'm taking this step to build up my speaking skills. Good for me for having the courage to do this."*

Stress rehearsal
"Remember what happened to Mitzi last week? She dissolved into tears when she lost her train of thought."

Mental dress rehearsal
"I am going to stand tall. I am going to make eye contact with everyone in the room at least once, and I'm going to speak with conviction."

Add to stress
"They're going to be judging me, too. They're even going to count my uhs."

Alleviate stress
"I am going to focus on getting my message across so everyone in the room learns something of value."

Panic
"Oh no, it's my turn next. Let me out of here."

Poise
"Good, I'm up next. I can't wait to share this story that means so much to me."

Dread
"Here goes nothing."

Determination
"Here I come."

MY PERSONAL STARTING TODAY ASSIGNMENT

Starting today I'm going to _____

_____

_____

Signed _____ Date _____

Just Do It

*"My parents told me I wouldn't amount to anything because I
procrastinated so much. I told them, 'Just wait.'"*
— COMEDIAN JUDY TENUTA

Is your motto "Procrastinate
now?" Is tomorrow the busiest day of your week? Johann Wolfgang von Goethe said, "The most important thing is to learn to
rule oneself." Yet many of us find ourselves ruled by unhealthy
habits. We're full of well-meaning intentions to change . . . next
Monday.

Nathaniel Branden observed, "We are the one species that is
able to form a judgment about what is best for us to do—and
then proceed to do the opposite." Why do we do this? More
important, how do we stop doing this?

A big part of confidence is feeling we're in control of life. It's
hard to have self-respect if we are knowingly harming ourselves
by doing the exact opposite of what we're supposed to be doing. The purpose of this chapter is to take a look at our habits
to evaluate whether they're helping or hurting us. If they're
aiding us, great. If they're hampering us, let's do something
about it.

Hateful Habits

─────── ◉ ───────

"It seems, in fact, as though the second half of a man's life is made up of nothing but the habits he accumulated during the first half."

—FYODOR DOSTOYEVSKY

What habits did you form in the first half of your life? A Guatemalan proverb is "Everyone is the age of their heart." I think everyone is the age of their habits. Our habits either keep us young or make us old. Are you ready to change the unhealthy habits you formed in the first half of your life? If not, why not? As Voltaire said, "Why, since we are always complaining of our ills, are we constantly employed in redoubling them?"

I recently changed my life by changing a habit that was making me ill. I had gotten in the habit of putting the boys to bed around nine or nine-thirty and then working for another couple of hours to take advantage of the quiet time. Then, since that was often the first and only time of day I had some time to myself, I would read the newspaper, watch the news, and maybe take in a late-night talk show. I usually went to bed after midnight. The next morning I would drag myself out of bed (after five or six hours of sleep) and sleepwalk through the morning until I had a good couple of cups of coffee in me. Most days I didn't know whether to drink my java or dive into it.

Then I read *The Artist's Way Journal*, in which author Julia Cameron suggests we start every day by writing for thirty minutes in what she calls Morning Pages. She believes writing is a tangible way to purge the negative thoughts that accumulate throughout the day. Expressing the mental angst that clogs our senses gets it out of our system, freeing us to be more creative.

She introduces a great metaphor as to why journaling is so valuable. She says she was watching TV and had flipped the channel to a sports station showing a Baja California off-road race. The four-wheel-drive vehicles were traversing rugged terrain and were slipping and sliding all over wet, bumpy, rutted roads. She noticed the windshield wipers thunking back and forth as they tried valiantly to scrape off the sludge being thrown up on the glass. She suddenly realized that Morning Pages serve as *spiritual* windshield wipers, clearing away the gunk we encounter so it doesn't obscure our vision and muddy our perspective.

I realized I didn't want to do Morning Pages, I wanted to do morning walks. I was already writing six to ten hours a day, so I didn't need spiritual windshield wipers. I needed *physical* windshield wipers. I didn't need to sit down at my desk and write; I was already doing that. I needed to get out from behind my desk and get my sedentary body moving. Ah, the power of the well-written word. That insight was just the catalyst I needed.

The Buddy Bonus
◉

"Motivation is what gets you started. Habit is what keeps you going."

-JIM RYUN

I'm convinced that hope is what gets us started and *buddies* are what keep us going. Ideally, I'd have the self-discipline to haul myself out of bed and take those morning walks myself. Realistically, I knew there would be days I'd be sorely tempted to turn off the alarm and go back to sleep. I knew I'd keep the commitment if a friend was joining me, so I called my friend Shannon and proposed we start going for a walk every morning from six to six-thirty. Her first words were "Did my husband put you up to this?"

I assured her that wasn't the case and then itemized all the reasons this would be the best thing we'd done for ourselves in a long time. It would get us outside to take advantage of the exquisite island mornings, it would get our mojos (metabolism) working, and it would give our bodies some much-needed toning. Doing it together would ensure that we'd show up and do our daily duty, and we'd be back home in time to get the kids off to school. Shannon knew all this was true. She half jokingly suggested I go pick on someone else, and then agreed to give it a try.

That next morning we met each other halfway (so to speak) in the neighborhood and embarked on our campaign to get physical. It has yielded benefits we couldn't have anticipated or hoped for. Not only have our morning walks energized our minds and bodies, they have put us back in charge of our lives. They have been the catalyst for our efforts to exercise (!) some control over our days. We play amateur therapist for each other, brainstorm about my books and the writers conference, and talk about our kids. We always carry pad and pencil to record the epiphanies that occur when the blood is flowing. I agree with the saying that "Angels speak to a man when he is walking." They speak to women, too. We arrive home raring to go, appreciative of our world, motivated to be kind to our families, and eager to jump into our work.

Discipline = Dignity
◉

"Self-respect is the fruit of discipline: the sense of dignity grows with the ability to say no to oneself."
-**ABRAHAM J. HERSCHEL**

With all due respect to Abraham Herschel, I think our sense of dignity grows with the ability to say *go* to oneself. Every time we kick ourselves in the bottom and get up off our duff (mixed metaphor!), we like ourselves a little better for making ourselves do what we know we should.

Rising early also prompted me to take a long hard look at how I was spending my evenings. Was it constructive to insert into my brain, moments before falling to sleep, images of plane crashes, murders, economic disasters, political backstabbing, and human tragedies? What a thoroughly depressing way to end one's day. Sweet dreams, *hah*! How much better to turn off that news, listen to some beautiful music, read a few pages of an intriguing novel, and go to sleep at a decent hour. I wake up before the alarm clock rings these days, and while I may not exactly bounce out of bed, I'm closing in on sprightly.

Catalytic Steps
————◉————

"I've decided to try to be a better person, but not right away of course. Maybe a few days from now."

—SALLY TO CHARLIE BROWN IN A *PEANUTS* CARTOON

Maybe you agree with Susan Richman, who has said, "The trouble with dawn is that it comes too early in the day." Or you're one of those people who say that if the urge to exercise comes over you, you should lie down until it passes. The habit you change doesn't have to involve getting up early in the morning, and it doesn't have to involve exercise.

The key is to take *any* catalytic step that triggers favorable results. Taking one positive step often sets off a chain of positive results. As Eleanor Roosevelt put it, "When you are genuinely interested in one thing, it will always leads to something else." When you get involved in changing one habit, it always leads to changing other habits. All of a sudden you're a lot closer to being the person you want to be. You like yourself and your life—the definition of confidence.

So, why don't we act on our good intentions if we know it's going to reap such positive results? George Santayana said, "Habit is stronger than reason." I think bad habits are the personal equivalent of treason. The very nature of a habit is that we do it by rote. We don't think about the consequences. In fact, habit is defined as "an acquired mode of behavior that has become merely or completely involuntary." You've probably heard the proverb "First we own our habits, then they own us." If we have acquired unhealthy habits, we can de-acquire them. The way to reverse automatic behaviors is to have a reason that is stronger than the habit.

Turn Yourself Around

——————⊙——————

"The difference between perseverance and obstinacy is that one often comes from a strong will, and the other from a strong won't."

—HENRY WARD BEECHER

The way to turn yourself around is to turn your *won'ts* into *wills*. Name a habit you've been trying to change but haven't been able to. Please be specific. Select something in your life that is compromising your physical health or your self-respect. "Always bear in mind," noted Abraham Lincoln, "that your own resolution to succeed is more important than any one thing." Perhaps this next suggestion can successfully motivate you to take long-delayed action.

A reporter approached Jack Nicklaus during a golf tournament and complimented his play. The reporter then added, "You're looking better than you did ten years ago. What are you doing?" Jack replied, "I'm running." The reporter wondered, "So you really like to run, huh?" Jack countered with "I hate it, but I like what it does for me." Jack knew intuitively that in order for us to act, the perceived benefits must outweigh the perceived difficulties.

What I've learned in years of talking with people about their confidence is that when we're not doing something we want to do, it's *not* that the benefits don't outweigh the difficulties, it's that we're concentrating exclusively on the difficulties. All we have to do is focus on the benefits, and we're inspired to take action.

A woman took my workshop because she was suffering from empty-nest syndrome. "My self-image has gone south. The last of my five kids just left home and I've lost my identity. I've been a mom for so long, I don't know what to do with myself."

I asked Wanda what she wanted to do. She said, "Well, I left college when I got pregnant with my first child. I've always wanted to go back and finish my degree." I asked why she hadn't, and she started listing all the obstacles. "I don't know how to track down my transcripts, I'm not sure what I want to study, parking is so hard to find, and," she concluded apprehensively, "I'd be the oldest woman on campus."

I told Wanda that dwelling on the downsides of going back to school was dooming her efforts and debilitating her confidence. I suggested she switch her focus to all the perks of returning to school. "Imagine how rewarding it would be to be back in an academic environment. Imagine how much you'd enjoy exploring different interests and meeting new friends. Imagine how satisfying it would be to walk onto that stage and receive your diploma. Imagine how your horizons will expand when you take this catalytic step to improve yourself."

Wanda is now happily and confidently taking college courses because she concentrated on the advantages of college instead of its disadvantages. She learned that the key to mobilizing yourself is to focus on the outcome instead of immobilizing yourself by focusing on the obstacles.

Decide to Decide
————— ⊙ —————

"Until one is committed, there is hesitancy, the chance to draw back, always ineffectiveness. . . . The moment one definitely commits oneself, then Providence moves, too. All sorts of things occur to help one that would never otherwise have occurred. . . . Boldness has genius, poetry, and magic in it. Begin it now."
—JOHANN WOLFGANG VON GOETHE

This is a special quote to me because my father shared it with me at a pivotal time in my life and it applies to many situations when we're trying to make up our minds and can't.

A young woman said plaintively, "I'm putting off college, too, but not because I'm focusing on the difficulties. I just can't decide what to study. I'm not procrastinating because I don't want to do it, I'm just not sure what I want to do."

That was a good point, so I described my own experience with that same dilemma. It was 1969. I was in my final year of high school, trying to figure out which college to attend and what major to pursue. So many decisions, so much confusion. Did I want to go into journalism and become a reporter? Did I want to pursue my interests in sports? Did I want to be ambitious and go for a career in law or medicine? Back and forth I went. Hours of pondering produced no progress. I vacillated between one career and another, envying those lucky souls who knew early on exactly what they wanted to be when they grew up.

Finally, Dad gifted me with Goethe's quote and helped me see that batting this complex choice back and forth in my mind would never produce the right answer. What was important was to make the best decision I could given the information I had. Once I was on my chosen path, experience would soon provide evidence as to whether it was the right one. If it wasn't, then that experience hadn't been wasted; it had helped me come closer to knowing what the right path was. The only waste of time would be to stay in the starting gate, waiting for providence to provide me with the perfect plan of action. Discovering the ideal career is often a by-product of trial and error; rarely is it obvious at the outset.

Albert Einstein confessed, "How do I work? I *grope*." How do we live? We grope. Are you not clear as to what you want to do? Are you waiting for divine intervention? Are you procrastinating, hoping the perfect course of action will appear to you in a dream? Well, that happens sometimes . . . but not often enough to count on. It's more effective to take Einstein's approach and experiment until you find what you want. Sitting around waiting for a lightning bolt of inspiration to strike is *not* a pro-active way to live your life.

Dr. Maxwell Maltz said, "Our self-image and our habits tend to go together. Change one and you change another." The final chapters in this book are all about changing habits and patterns so they serve rather than sabotage us.

Sample Starting Today Assignment

*"I don't wait for moods. You accomplish nothing if you do that.
Your mind must know it has got to get down to earth."*
—PEARL S. BUCK

THE ASSIGNMENT TODAY IS FOR you to get down to earth
and change a habit that is no longer serving you. Instead of complaining
about how it's undermined you, concentrate on how you can turn it
around. If you've been putting off a project because you couldn't decide
how to proceed or because you didn't have the discipline to proceed,
resolve to turn your inaction into action. Thomas Jefferson said, "Nothing
can stop the man with the right mental attitude from achieving his goal;
nothing on earth can help the man with the wrong mental attitude."
What's your attitude right now? Are you still saying, "*But* I'm afraid" or
"*But* I'm not sure"? Get off your *but* and do it. Remember that feeling
follows action. Decide to decide instead of waiting for the perfect moment or divine inspiration. You'll respect yourself and feel more in
charge of your life. ◎

Action Plan for Just Doing It

Ron has gotten in a habit of watching sports on TV. He started
out watching football; then it was hockey, basketball, and baseball.
Before he knew it, he was spending most weekends in his lounge
chair in front of the TV.

BLOCKERS	**BUILDERS**
Hateful habits that sabotage us	Healthy habits that serve us
"I'm an adult. I can do what I want to do. So I like sports."	*"I'm thirty years old. This is not a good way to be spending my life."*

Procrastinate on intentions *"I'll get outside when we start* *getting some spring weather."*	Proceed with intentions *"This weekend I can watch* *my two favorite teams, and* *then I need to get outside."*
Immobilized *"Where do I start? It's been so* *long since I played I probably* *won't even be able to hang on* *to the ball."*	Mobilized *"I'll just see if I can join in on* *that neighborhood flag football* *game on Saturday mornings.* *They don't take themselves too* *seriously."*
Focus on obstacles *"My cleats are so old, I'll have* *to get new ones. They cost $75* *these days."*	Focus on outcome *"It's going to be fun to be out* *there throwing the old ball* *around again."*
Can't get started, can't decide *"I've always been a procrasti-* *nator. I'll turn over a new* *leaf, after New Year's."*	Catalytic steps, decide to de- cide *"I'll call Mark and see if he* *wants to get together for a* *scrimmage with some friends."*

MY PERSONAL STARTING TODAY ASSIGNMENT

Starting today I'm going to _____

_____

_____

Signed _____ Date _____

Know What You Stand For (And What You Won't Stand For)

"Art, like morality, consists of drawing the line somewhere."
— G. K. CHESTERTON

onfidence also results from drawing the line somewhere. It's said the test of good manners is to be patient with bad ones. Not too patient, though.

Do you believe you have inalienable rights and that it's okay to speak up for them? Do you demand fair treatment, or do you often feel taken advantage of? Do you keep the balance of needs being met, or do you often back down and give in to what other people want? Do you find yourself saying yes when you really want to say no?

In my years of speaking on Tongue Fu! and confidence, I've learned how important it is to speak up for ourselves when we're being stepped on. The more we relent (give in to other people), the more we resent (feel ill will). The more we go along to get along, the less we like other people and the less we like ourselves. A better course of action is to ASSERT and avert. Remember, people can't walk all over us unless we lie down.

Assertiveness vs. Aggressiveness
————————————— ◎ —————————————

"I'd like to buy a book on chutzpah and I'd like you to pay for it."
-CARTOONIST GOND

You may be thinking, "Is there a way to be assertive without being aggressive? I'm tired of being pushed around by bullies, but I don't want to become one myself."

Good point. What is the difference between assertiveness and aggressiveness? Aggressiveness, as illustrated in the line from Gond, is "a forceful action intended to dominate or master . . . a hostile, injurious, or destructive behavior or outlook." That is *not* what I'm advocating! Confidence is not acting in selfish ways, going after what we want, mindless of the consequences to others.

Confidence is being assertive, which is "to state or declare positively . . . to demonstrate the existence of . . . to compel recognition especially of one's rights." I love that definition because that is exactly what we're trying to achieve. We're saying, "I exist. I have rights." When we don't assert ourselves, it's as if we cease to exist, we have no say in our own lives. Asserting ourselves is the means by which we cause other people to recognize what we need and how we feel. If we remain silent, people may never know they're trampling us.

The Three Types of Tramplers
————————————— ◎ —————————————

"Silence is the door of consent."
-BERBER PROVERB

What I've learned over the years is that people who trample our rights usually fall into one of three categories.

1. *They don't know.* If we tell these people, "What you said yesterday really bothered me," they might reply, "Oh my gosh, did I say that? I'm sorry, I was so wrapped up in what happened I didn't realize I was taking it out on you." These people are genuinely unaware that what they said or did was unfair, unkind, or inappropriate.

I'll never forget the time a man showed up early for a Tongue Fu! workshop. He strode up, got right in my face, and said, "My boss is making me take this course." "Oh really?" I said noncommittally. "Yes," he said, "He thinks I'm too intense. Do *you* think I'm too intense?"

I might have laughed out loud if I hadn't intuited that this man was 100 percent serious. He was a perfect example of someone who was intimidating without meaning to be. As I got to know him that morning, it was obvious that Earl had a brilliant intellect and just didn't understand that his high-wattage energy was a wee bit overwhelming.

2. *They know, and think it's our responsibility to speak up about it.* These tramplers know that what they're doing is not right, but think if it really bothers us, we'll say something about it. If we approach them with what's troubling us, they're likely to retort, "Well, if you didn't like it, why didn't you say something before?" They think silence is the same as approval.

I learned about this type the hard way. Early in my work life, I joined a company and agreed to a big salary cut because I believed in what they were doing and was excited about the type of work. I was a gung-ho employee. I went in early and stayed late. After six months of zealous effort, I was waiting for a call into the head office to hear a "Job well done," a "Here's a bonus," or a "You deserve a raise." Nothing.

Another six months went by with me producing impressive revenue for the business. I continued to think, "Any day now, I'm going to get that financial pat on the back, that overdue thank you, a promotion, *something*." Nothing. At that point, my attitude started to suffer. "I don't seem to be appreciated here. Why am I bending over backward for a business that doesn't see fit to notice or reward my contributions?" I started wondering if it was worth staying.

Finally, after another three months went by, I considered quitting because I wasn't going to tolerate this unfair situation anymore. I decided before making that brash move, I would let the boss know how I felt. I marched into his office, and said, "I think I deserve a raise." He looked at me calmly and said, "You're right, you do. I was wondering when you were going to have the courage to come in and ask for it."

He taught me a valuable lesson. We can't wait for someone else to give us what we want, need, and deserve. If we're in a situation where we're not getting what we deserve, we can't expect the other person to do the right thing and act on our behalf.

A woman in a seminar was rather shocked when I shared this particular idea. She said, "Sam, this doesn't sound like you. This is such a cynical viewpoint." I don't think it's cynical. I think it's realistic. I'm not saying there aren't generous, considerate individuals out there who look out for our best interests; there are. We just can't expect or wait for these benevolent beings to rescue us by rectifying situations that aren't fair.

3. *They know, and they don't care.* These tramplers know very well that what they're doing is not right, fair, or kind, and it doesn't bother them a bit. In fact, one woman put her hand up in a session and added, "You don't know my boss. It's not that she doesn't care that she steamrolls over other people. She *enjoys* it. She does it on purpose. She takes an almost perverse pride in running roughshod over everyone in the office. It's part of her persona. If I told her I thought she was being unfair, she'd say, 'Tough,' or 'That's your problem.' "

Unfortunately, there are people who knowingly and willingly verbally abuse others because they think it gets results, and they don't care what it costs. They want what they want when they want it, and if someone gets hurt in the process, "Too bad."

Speak Up, or Forever Hold Your Peace
⊙

"My wife and I have a perfect understanding. I don't try to run her life . . . and I don't try to run mine."
—ROBERT ORBEN

What type of trampler would you guess your person is? Guess what? It doesn't matter! Do you notice a trend? The trend is, if we don't speak up, the situation will stay the same! Tramplers who try to run (or ruin) our lives either don't know that what they're doing or saying is bothering us, or they know and think if it's important enough we'll say something about it, or they flat out don't care.

From now on, if we don't like what's happening to us, but we're not making an effort to correct it, we can't lay the blame totally at the feet of the instigator. If we're not taking action to improve unfair situations, we are partially responsible. Confidence is understanding that if we don't like how we're being treated, we must take the responsibility for rectifying it.

I believe in birthdays. The way I figure it, it's the one day a year you can do exactly as you please. I was really looking forward to my big 4-0, especially since someone had offered to throw a party for me. As the day grew closer, I hadn't overheard any of the telltale clues that often give away a surprise celebration, but I reassured myself that the planner had just been extra clever at keeping the details a secret. The big day came . . . and went. The planner took me out to dinner the next evening and apologetically explained that he had been so busy he hadn't had time to put something together.

I learned a valuable lesson. If you care strongly about something, *say so*! Think enough of yourself to speak up and say, "This is important to me." Confident people don't play the martyr about issues that matter to them.

What's important to you that you've been silently wishing someone would notice and/or provide? Confident people don't sit back and passively hope their fondest desire will be realized.

Confidence is also not letting it go by and misrepresenting your true feelings by shrugging off something you care about and saying, "It's okay, really, it's no big deal. It's just a birthday." From now on, don't passively wait for someone to bring you flowers. Ask for them, or get them yourself.

Don't Be Meek, Speak
━━━━━━◉━━━━━━

"The meek shall inherit the earth, if that's okay with you."
-GRAFFITI

The meek don't inherit much of anything. Those who speak are the ones who get what they want out of life. The challenge is, how do we stand up for our rights without stepping on those of others? How do we handle difficult people without becoming difficult ourselves? We ASSERT.

A = Assess the situation objectively vs. emotionally. Use the journalist's tools (Who? What? Why? Where? When?) to make sure we're considering just the facts. We sometimes catastrophize events by using extreme words ("He *always* points out what I do wrong"; "she *never* considers how I feel"). Describe what's happened specifically rather than subjectively to make sure our feelings are justified, not knee-jerk.

S = See both sides. Almost any time we're frustrated, we're seeing things from our point of view only. Instead of giving in to the urge to lash back and put other people in their place, we need to put ourselves in their place. Why are they acting this way? Is there a legitimate reason for their conduct? Uncovering the reasons behind someone's unpleasant behavior can help us understand it. And as Confucius once said, "The more a man knows, the more he forgives."

S = Study the consequences. Just because we don't like what someone is doing doesn't mean it's smart to confront him about it. In today's world of hair-trigger tempers and physical assaults, "it is sometimes better to ignore an insult than to avenge it," as Seneca once said. If someone wheels into the parking space you've been waiting for and arrogantly flips you the solitary salute, ask whether giving that individual a piece of your mind might put you in jeopardy. Perhaps it would be better to give yourself peace of mind by putting the whole thing in perspective. Someone stealing your parking place isn't on a par with world peace, and isn't worth risking life and limb.

E = Express what you want, not what you don't want. If you decide this issue is worth pursuing, remember to request the desired behavior. Complaining about what you don't like makes you a problem reporter. Requesting what you would like turns you into a problem solver. Instead of "Stop interrupting," say, "Please wait until I'm finished" or "Please hear me out." Instead of "Quit telling me how to run my life," say, "I know you're saying this because you love me and want what's best for me. And please let me make my own decisions and learn my own lessons."

R = Responsibility rests with you. The statement "There are no victims without volunteers" certainly has exceptions. It also has a lot of truth. Confident people don't moan and groan when they're treated unfairly; they ask for what they want. From now on, don't volunteer to be a victim by simply hoping people will do the right thing and be more sensitive to your needs.

T = Take action. "Knowledge is not enough, we must apply," observed Goethe. "Willing is not enough, we must do." It's unreasonable to expect people to be able to read our minds. They won't know how we feel unless we tell them. Insensitive people may not even realize they're trampling on our toes. The next time someone tries to take advantage of you (whether innocently or intentionally), ASSERT yourself, and you may be able to avert a conflict.

Don't Simmer in Silence, Speak Up

————————— ⊙ —————————

"Calm self-confidence is as far from conceit as the desire to earn a decent living is remote from greed."

–CHANNING POLLOCK

A secretary said, "I'm really frustrated about something that's happening at work, but I'm not comfortable complaining about it. It's just not like me to be a bitch." (Her word.) I hastened to correct her, saying, that's *not* what confidence is. To modify what Channing Pollock said, assertiveness is as far from bitchiness as the desire to eat a decent meal is from gluttony. The goal is to actualize our rights without alienating others.

I asked what was bothering her and she explained, "Every day right before closing time my boss dumps all his accumulated tasks on my desk. I really resent having to stay late to finish this work he gives me at the end of the workday. He waltzes out of there at five o'clock and I end up staying until six or seven. I'm thinking about quitting because I'm not going to stand for it anymore."

I asked, "Have you said something to him about it?" "Well, no." I recommended she brainstorm a solution and give her manager a chance to correct things before she took the drastic step of walking off the job. After assessing the situation, she came up with a plan that was a win for both of them. Ann proposed to her boss that he drop off his accumulated paperwork and phone messages an hour before lunch and then again an hour before closing. That way she could process the more urgent items in a timely manner the same day and still leave at a reasonable hour.

Her supervisor readily agreed to the suggestion and complimented her for coming up with such a clever idea. When she told him she had almost quit over this issue, he asked, "What issue?" When Ann explained about staying late to finish his del-egated-at-the-last-minute tasks, he said in amazement, "I had no idea!" How could he have known? He was out of there early and had no way of knowing she was staying behind a couple of hours after he left. Ann couldn't believe she had almost submitted her resignation over an issue her manager hadn't even been aware of, one relatively simple to resolve.

Take a Stand
———————⊙———————

"They cannot take away our self-respect unless we give it to them."
—MAHATMA GANDHI

A former student came up to me at a grocery store and said, "I have to thank you for that 'relented/resented, asserted/averted' idea. My husband was downsized last year and has been unable to find work. I understood that this was quite a blow to his ego, but it had gotten to the point where I resented him lying around the house all day while I handled all the chores. What really bothered me was when he slept in while I made breakfast, and then left his dirty dishes in the sink, as if I was his maid or something. When he finally did roll out of the sack, he never even took two minutes to make the bed. I'd go upstairs later in the day, and the pillows would be spread all over the place.

"I hadn't spoken up because I didn't want to start a fight. Your class made me realize that by relenting, I was definitely resenting, and that it was time for me to assert and avert. As you suggested, instead of complaining about what I didn't like, I requested what I *would* like. Saying, 'I think it's unfair for you to make me do all the work while you sit around and mope' would have started a fight for sure. Instead I said, 'Bill, could we have a policy that the last one out of bed makes it? And that if you eat off it, you put it in the dishwasher?'

"Do you know, that's all it took? He said, 'Sure,' and that was the end of it. If I hadn't said anything, that bed *still* would not be getting made, those dirty dishes would still be sitting in the sink, and we would have been building toward a major blowup."

ASSERT and Avert

———————————⊙———————————

"I understand you have trouble making decisions. Is that true?"
"Well, yes and no."

-ANONYMOUS

A woman in one of my sessions was brought up in a household where you never expressed your beliefs if they conflicted with what others thought. Akiko said, "In my culture, females were supposed to submit to the beliefs of men and elders. I worked in my parents' store because that was expected of me. I married a man my parents picked out for me. I moved to a city I hated because it was my husband's hometown and that's where he wanted to live.

"When you said that relenting leads to resenting, I thought, 'That's the story of my life!' I've been yielding to my parents' and my husband's demands for years. I had no self-esteem. Your class convinced me that it's not wrong to stand up for my rights, and that rights don't have to be an either/or situation. It's not fair for my husband to get what he wants all the time, and I just have to go along with it. And it's not fair for me to insist on doing things my way all the time. It's fair to keep a balance between what he wants and what I want. Several times a day I use the ASSERT steps to help me think through difficult situations and decide what a fair course of action is."

From now on, when you're not happy with what's happening, ASSERT. That decision-making process can help you decide to speak or to forever hold your peace.

Sample Starting Today Assignment

"Being kind doesn't mean one has to be a mat."
—MAYA ANGELOU

BEING ASSERTIVE DOESN'T MEAN ONE has to be a jerk. It can mean diplomatically speaking up and getting justice for yourself and others. Your assignment today is to think of a situation with which you're unhappy. Is someone treating you in an unfair or unkind way? Are you not getting what you want, need, and deserve? Resolve that you are no longer going to suffer in silence and volunteer to be a victim. Assess the situation objectively; see both sides; study the consequences; express what you want; assume responsibility; and take action. As a result, your confidence will soar because you will be taking control of your life rather than passively letting other people or circumstances control you. ◉

Action Plan for Knowing What You Stand For (And What You Won't Stand For)

Gail doesn't like action flicks, and those are the only ones her husband will see. She'd rather not watch "rock 'em, sock 'em" pictures, but going out to the movies on Friday night is about the only date they ever have. If she suggests a movie, he disparages it as a "woman's movie—all talk and no action"—and refuses to go.

BLOCKERS	BUILDERS
Dictator or doormat	Dictates fair treatment
"I haven't seen a movie I want to see for years."	*"It's fair for him to see what he wants to see, and fair for me to see what I want to see."*

Relent and resent
*"Another martial arts movie.
Okay, if it's supposed to be a
good one, I'll go see it with
you."*

Assert and avert
*"Bruce, why don't you see if
one of your buddies wants to
see it with you? You can have
a boys' night out."*

Chutzpah
*"I've had enough. Do you re-
alize what a jerk you've been
insisting that I go to these
movies with you? I've hated
every single one of them, and
I'm not doing it anymore, and
that's final."*

Harmony
*"Why don't we go to the four-
plex together? You can go to
your movie and I'll go to
mine. We'll meet afterward
and swap stories over a bottle
of wine."*

Aggressive
*"I don't care if you don't like
it. That's the way it's going to
be."*

Assertive
*"Bruce, this is a win-win situ-
ation that's fair to us both."*

MY PERSONAL STARTING TODAY ASSIGNMENT

Starting today I'm going to _____
_____
_____

Signed _____ Date _____

PART VII

Courage: Go for the Bold

"Life expands or contracts in proportion to one's courage."

— ANAÏS NIN

Take Life by the Lapel

*"Life loves to be taken by the lapel and told: 'I am with you, kid.
Let's go.'"*
— **MAYA ANGELOU**

Who's steering your life? Do you have both hands on the wheel or are you wandering all over the road? Are you in the driver's seat or the backseat of your life?

I've noticed an interesting trend in my years of giving seminars. Invariably, as people file in to take their seats, a few immediately move forward and claim a chair in the front. Others head toward the rear of the room and grab a seat in the last row. The students in the first couple of rows usually exude a bright-eyed eagerness to learn. They take responsibility for getting value, believing they will benefit if they just pay attention. The people with a front-row attitude almost always fulfill their own positive expectations and have a profitable encounter.

The ones in back enter with their mental arms crossed, a show-me skepticism. They put the responsibility for their experience in the hands of the presenter. If the speaker delivers an outstanding program, they grudgingly declare it worthwhile. If he or she doesn't, they write the experience off as a waste of time. They don't seem to understand or accept that the quality of that experience depends as much on them as it does on the instructor.

Joan Didion suggested that "the willingness to accept responsibility for one's own life is the source from which self-respect springs." Do you have a "front row" or a "back row" mentality? You've heard the phrase "Life is 50 percent how you take it, and 50 percent what you make it?" Confident people don't wait for life to prove its value to them. They are determined to take value from every experience and to make the most of every day, no matter what.

Are You Running Your Life, or Is It Running You?

━━━━━⊙━━━━━

"Nowadays, most men lead lives of noisy desperation."

-JAMES THURBER

Is your life your own? Or do you feel, as John Lennon did, "Life is what happens to you while you're making other plans"? A government employee who took one of my seminars snorted when he heard this question. "You've got to be kidding. My life is *nothing* like I thought it would be. It's everyone's but my own. I get a steady paycheck, but that's about all you can say for it. Many of the people around me have retired on the job. Their goal is to get through the day while doing as little as possible. The problem is, I'm stuck. It's the old golden-handcuffs syndrome. Where else am I going to earn enough money to feed a family of five? I feel like I've sold out, but I'm not about to walk away from this position and throw away thirty years of seniority."

I told Neil I understood he felt he'd "souled out," but that didn't mean he had to condemn himself to a meaningless life. All he has to do is get actively involved in one meaningful activity that feeds his soul. He doesn't have to do anything radical like quit his job. He can respect himself, even if a large part of his life isn't to his liking, as long as he has something to look forward to, one personally satisfying pursuit that compensates for his disheartening work life.

Put Your Heart and Soul into It
————————— ◉ —————————

"The amount of satisfaction you get from life depends largely on your own ingenuity, self-sufficiency, and resourcefulness. People who wait around for life to supply their satisfaction usually find boredom instead."
–WILLIAM MENNINGER

I asked Neil what he liked to do. He had to think about it for a while, but finally he said, "Well, I used to like to sing. My father and uncle were in a barbershop chorus and I used to tag along to their sing-alongs." I suggested he contact his local chapter and get reinvolved with an activity that held fond memories for him.

Neil took another of my seminars a year later and reported, "I had thought of myself as being locked into a dead-end job, but your workshop helped me realize I still had six hours of freedom every day, plus weekends, to fill as I pleased. I joined the community chorus and started my own quartet with three other guys. We have more enthusiasm than skill, but we all love to sing. Our quartet puts on performances at rest homes, birthday parties, shopping malls, you name it. And, in December, I participated in a production of Handel's *Messiah* at the concert hall. We had over a 150 voices in the choir backed by a full symphony. It was one of the most moving experiences of my life. I still get 'chicken skin' [Hawaiian phrase for goose bumps] just thinking about belting out the Hallelujah chorus at the top of my lungs while surrounded by the sound of that magnificent choir and orchestra. I haven't enjoyed myself that much in years. And you know what? I do feel like I'm back in charge of my life instead of just getting through the day."

"God respects me when I work" states a Thai proverb, "but he loves me when I sing." What makes your heart sing? How can you honor your obligations and your soul's need to be engaged in something meaningful? Oliver Wendell Holmes said, "Most people go to their graves with their songs still unsung."

Vow not to leave your songs unsung. What are you going to bring into your life that will cause you to wake up in the morning with anticipation rather than apathy?

What a Wonder-Full World
◎

"He who can no longer pause to wonder and stand rapt in awe, is as good as dead; his eyes are closed."
-ALBERT EINSTEIN

Another way to feel more satisfied with our lives is to be in a constant state of appreciation. We may not be able to control all the events in our lives, but we can control how we experience life's events. Instead of wondering why we don't have what we want, we can be in wonder about what we have. No matter what our current situation is, there's probably more right with it than wrong. Or, as G. K. Chesterton said, "The world will never starve for want of wonders, but for want of wonder."

When I'm speaking on the mainland, I'm often asked, "Is everyone in Maui happy?" Residents in the other forty-nine states assume that people who live in paradise must be in a constant state of bliss. If only that were so. Unfortunately, many of us overlook how lucky we are to live here. Our conversations turn to the high price of gas, gripes about the UH football team, traffic jams, and other such petty grievances. How is it that we often take the gift of user-friendly beaches, tropical breezes, and ever-present sunshine for granted? Why is it we often overlook how fortunate we are to be alive and healthy?

Maslow's hierarchy of needs has the answer. Abraham Maslow postulated that human beings have a pyramid of needs, starting at the bottom with the primary need to have food, water, safety, and shelter. If we don't have anything to eat or drink and we don't have a safe place to stay, survival needs drive our every waking moment. That's all we can think about. Only after we have the basic needs of bed and board taken care of are we free to concern ourselves with the needs above these in the pyramid: finding a partner, having children, joining a community. Only after those needs for connection are satisfied can we move on to self-actualization needs. Maslow concluded that a fulfilled need is no longer a motivator. Once a need has been met, it no longer dominates our thoughts, and we often end up taking it for granted.

For many of us, our safe, healthy, free lives have become fulfilled needs. Since most of us wake up every morning free of pain and with enough to eat; since most of us have friends and family; since most of us have jobs and the financial wherewithal to purchase most of what we need, we take all these things for granted. We overlook how truly fortunate we are to have these blessings. Instead of appreciating that we have the freedom to do what we want on a weekend, we gripe about having nothing to do. Many of us can walk into a grocery store and buy pretty much what catches our fancy, but instead we complain that nothing catches our fancy. In Hawaii, many of us have the freedom to go outside any day of the year in our shirtsleeves, yet many of us moan and groan if the trade winds are a little late.

The good news is we can *override* Maslow's hierarchy of needs. We can consciously reverse the tendency to take things for granted. All we have to do is reawaken ourselves to the wonder of the world around us. All we have to do is, as Joe Knapp suggested, "Wake up with a smile and go after life. . . . Live it, enjoy it, taste it, smell it, feel it."

Own Your Life
━━━ ◉ ━━━

"You have got to own your days and live them, each one of them, every one of them, or else the years go right by and none of them belong to you."
— HERB GARDNER

My friend Dorothy Douthit started a habit years ago that helps her own each and every one of her days. As the principal of a private school, she finds her days are sometimes filled with misbehaving students, squabbling teachers, unhappy parents, unrealistic curriculum requirements, and other assorted challenges. There are, of course, many rewards to her job, among them being affectionately called Doctor D by thousands of grateful grads. She still wanted to find a way to counteract the stress of her demanding job.

Dorothy decided to start off every morning with an ocean swim at Ala Moana Beach Park. Since making that decision more than seventeen years ago, Dorothy has risen at dawn every day, with no exceptions. Dorothy swims if it's raining. Dorothy swims if she stayed up late the night before. Dorothy swims when it's cold, and when she's got a cold. Dorothy swims even if she's got a seven A.M. business meeting. (She just gets up earlier and swims in the dark. She says it's like swimming in black velvet.) She has bumped into sea turtles, watched countless sunrises over Diamond Head, and befriended other early risers who take advantage of the placid waters and the white sand beach.

Dorothy literally and figuratively reawakens herself to the wonder-filled world every morning. Those ocean dips start her day off on a positive note and bring her back into tune with nature. That ritual helps her stay centered despite the various crises she encounters on a daily basis. She may not be able to control what the day brings, but she *can* control how she brings in the day.

How can you exercise more control over your life? How can you start taking responsibility for the quality of your days instead of letting them happen to you?

Count Your Blessings
◉

"The unthankful heart discovers no mercies; but let the thankful heart sweep through the day and, as the magnet finds the iron, so it will find, in every hour, some heavenly blessings!"
-HENRY WARD BEECHER

In *Tongue Fu!* I recommended that we hang a Calendar of Comments in a highly visible spot and take fifteen seconds a day to record something that went well. It could be an unexpected phone call from a long-lost friend, a client kind enough to say thank you, a belly laugh at a funny one-liner from Jay Leno, an enthusiastic welcome home from the dog, a project completed, an impromptu picnic. The power of this calendar is that it serves as a visible reminder of all that's right with our world.

A friend with three teenagers said she is so grateful she did this. "If we didn't have that calendar posted where we can all see it, our family would have forgotten we ever got along together. These teen years have been hell," she reported. "My two sweet little girls went from 'Mom, could you help fix my hair?' to 'Mom, can't you do something about your hair?' If we didn't have that calendar as evidence that we've actually had good times together, none of us would believe it."

Remember in Part II of this book when we discussed the importance of counting our personal blessings so that we increased our awareness of our good qualities? It was suggested that you make more deposits than withdrawals from your Confidence Account so you maintain a healthy balance of self-regard. You can do the same thing with the blessings around you. By choosing to have a thankful heart, you will experience life as George Bernard Shaw described it: "an accumulation of treasures rather than a series of trials and tribulations."

Sample Starting Today Assignment

"Each day is a gift. Unwrap it."
—SAM HORN

YOUR ASSIGNMENT TODAY IS TO move into the front row of your life. What is one specific thing you're going to do to take life by the lapel and say, "Let's go!" If you're locked into a dissatisfying job or relationship, how are you going to compensate for it by getting involved in a meaningful activity? What are you going to do to reintroduce yourself to the wonders of the world? Are you going to post a calendar and take the time to count your blessings? Are you going to consciously overcome Maslow's hierarchy of needs and appreciate what you've got, instead of bemoaning what you "don't got"? For today, instead of taking things for granted, take them as gifts and unwrap them. ⊙

Action Plan for Taking Life by the Lapel

Ruby's children have bought her a home in a retirement community. She isn't particularly happy with the move, but her two daughters live out of state and they say they feel better knowing she is in a safe neighborhood that has nearby medical care and a variety of recreational activities.

BLOCKERS	BUILDERS
Back-row "show me" mentality *"Hah, the golden years. Everyone looks like an old fogie to me."*	Front-row mentality *"I'm going to take advantage of those bus trips."*
Life takes you by the lapel *"I never thought I'd be living alone, hundreds of miles from my grandchildren."*	You take life by the lapel *"They've got an orientation for new residents. I'm going to go."*
We wonder what it's all about *"How'd I ever end up this way? Howard and I were supposed to retire together."*	What it's all about fills us with wonder *"At least I've still got my health. I'm going to go for a swim in their big pool."*
The days own you *"Nothing ever happens on these soap operas. What a waste of time."*	You own your days *"I'm going to call Becky and see if she and the rest of the gals want to come over for some bridge."*

Take everything for granted	Appreciate everything
"That was heartless of my kids to stick me here. They just wanted me out of the way."	*"I'm fortunate to have kids who would pay for me to live in this beautiful community."*

MY PERSONAL STARTING TODAY ASSIGNMENT

Starting today I'm going to _____

_____

_____

Signed _____ Date _____

Face and Erase Your Fears

"Men are not prisoners of fate, but only prisoners of their own minds."

— FRANKLIN D. ROOSEVELT

Prisoners of their own fears is more like it. Do you have fears that are holding you back? What is making you reluctant to risk?

Avoid a Fear, Keep a Fear

"There are always two voices sounding in our ears—the voice of fear and the voice of confidence. One is the clamor of the senses, the other is the whispering of the higher self."

—CHARLES B. NEWCOMB

I love Newcomb's quote because it captures the essence of risk taking. We can give in to the clamor of the senses, or we can listen instead to the whispering of the higher self and take those steps onto the path of confidence.

This idea was dramatically demonstrated to me in an outing I took with my friend Leslie years ago on New Year's Day. We ventured out to the North Shore of Oahu to tackle the waves at Hawaii's famous Waimea Bay. The winter surf was booming in at a good eight feet. Leslie and I stood on the sand with our boogie boards, wondering, "Should we go in; shouldn't we go in?" If we did, we might get tumbled around and turned inside out and upside down. On the other hand, we could experience the thrill of a lifetime in those big-time waves.

Twenty minutes later, we were *still* standing on the beach, wondering, "Should we go in; shouldn't we go in?" After another few minutes of debate, we finally agreed to take the risk and go in. I remember to this day paddling out past the surf line, hanging on to our boogie boards, and gazing at the horizon with a mixture of horror and excitement as a huge set rolled in. We looked at each other with fear and anticipation as we tried to decide whether to catch it. We knew that once we committed, there would be no turning back. You can't tell an eight-foot wave "Sorry, I changed my mind." We decided to go for it. We kicked as hard as we could to match the speed of the wave and caught it. The swell lifted us up and shot us forward, down the front of the wave. *Whoosh!*

Aaahh, the exhilaration of sliding down the face of that breaker, cutting back and forth as we rode it all the way in until we scraped our bellies on the beach. We looked at each other in exultation, nodded in agreement, and went back out for another set, another shot of adrenaline, and another exciting ride. It was one of the most intense and electrifying experiences of my life.

On the drive home, Leslie and I agreed that we never would have experienced those joyous few hours if we'd given in to the voice of fear and stayed on the beach.

Regrets or Results?
──────◎──────

"Change and growth take place when a person has risked himself and dares to become involved with experimenting with his own life."

-HERBERT OTTO

What are you aching to try? What do you dream of doing? Do you want to start your own business? Do you want to get your solo pilot's license? Do you want to ask someone out? Are your fears immobilizing you? Are you standing paralyzed on the sand, wondering, "Should I, shouldn't I? Should I, shouldn't I?" You'll never know standing on the beach. As Hue Wheldon said, "The crime is not to avoid failure. The crime is not to give triumph a chance." Your assignment is to give triumph a chance by going in!

Jawaharlal Nehru said, "The policy of being too cautious is the greatest risk of all." Are you being too cautious? Are you focusing on your fears instead of fast-forwarding to your final outcome? Are you thinking of all the things that could go wrong instead of focusing on what could go right?

Now, I'm not talking about tackling twenty-foot surf. Remember earlier when we talked about reasonable goals being significantly challenging, yet achievable? That's the type of risk we want to take as well. Twenty-foot surf would have chewed us up and spit us out. Eight-foot waves were certainly challenging, but we thought we could handle them without risking life and limb. It was a wise, not a rash, risk.

So what is it that you want to do? Write a book? Have an exhibit of your own artwork? Travel somewhere by yourself? Are you standing on the beach and listening to that voice of fear list all the reasons you shouldn't take this risk? Are those doubts serving your higher self? I don't think so. They are serving your lower self. A crusty female admiral said, "A ship is safe in port— but that's not where it's meant to be." Are your dreams in port? It's time to venture out.

Leap of Faith
— ◉ —

"It is only by risking our person from one hour to another that we live at all. And often enough, our faith beforehand in an uncertified result is the only thing that makes the result come true."
—WILLIAM JAMES

I was fortunate to be at the National Horse Show outside of Washington, D.C., the night a show jumper set a world record in the puissance. This is an amazing event in which a horse and rider compete on a course that culminates with an extremely high obstacle, often over six feet tall. This particular evening, all the other horses had been eliminated except this one. The rider could have settled for the first-place trophy and called it quits. He must have felt his horse was at its best, because he asked for the wall to be raised to a world record height and elected to have another go-round.

What's important to understand is that the horse couldn't even see over this towering seven-foot obstacle. It's completely unnatural for an animal to jump over something when it does not know what's on the other side. What would prompt this horse to launch himself over this almost impossibly high barrier? He trusted his rider. There's a saying in equestrian circles that if a rider "throws his heart over the fence," the horse will follow. That is what happened.

The rider guided his mount over a couple of easy warm-up jumps and then galloped his horse toward the massive wall. The horse's ears first fixed forward on what lay ahead, and then flitted back to await the signal from its rider. The rider's entire body language spoke determination and a powerful will. There was no room for fear. A second of doubt or hesitation ("Can we make it?") would rob them both of the 100 percent confidence needed to attempt this feat. In the last few paces, the spectators could almost see the rider mentally gather up the horse and propel their energy up and over the wall. The horse responded with a mighty leap of faith. They cleared the jump with not an inch to spare.

The crowd rose as one in a thundering ovation. The jubilant combo cantered around the arena in a victory lap, the rider waving to the crowd. It was one of the most magnificent athletic achievements I've ever witnessed, and it happened because the rider believed it was possible.

Confidence Continuum
————————◉————————

"The important thing is this: to be able at any moment to sacrifice what we are for what we could become."
—CHARLES DU BOIS

If you want your dream to come true, you too need to throw your heart over the obstacles in your path. Overcome your fears by making a leap of faith. Are you wondering how to do that? You talk yourself into doing something that scares you by understanding the Confidence Continuum, and by understanding that every time we make a decision, we move ourselves either forward or backward on the continuum. Our goal is to always move forward out of our comfort zone instead of moving back into it. We want to take steps that build our confidence rather than block it.

Dozens of times throughout the day, we are faced with decisions that cause us to either advance or retreat. Our dilemmas can be as simple as whether to ask someone to lunch and as complicated as whether to ask someone to marry us. Our decision can be as straightforward as whether we should go back to sleep or as complex as whether we should go back to school. When we stand at the crossroads wondering which way to go, our goal is to build confidence by taking the path of progress that adds value and makes us grow.

The chart that follows can help us visualize this decision process so we can see more clearly which options will move us forward and which will move us backward.

The Confidence Continuum

Trying to decide whether to take a risk? Want to try something that's a little intimidating? Not sure whether to accept or refuse someone's request?

Picture yourself standing at the center of the Confidence Continuum and ask yourself (1) if taking this action will move you forward on a path of growth and/or (2) if turning it down will cause you to retreat back into your comfort zone. In other words, will acting produce more benefits than not acting?

As long as it's a wise and not rash risk, take the option that leads to progress. It will be a vote of confidence in yourself.

< C O N F I D E N C E   C O N T I N U U M >

←───→

<Retreat into comfort zone?	Move forward on path of growth?>
Stick with what's comfortable *"Me? Sing karaoke? Not in this lifetime!"*	Strive for what's creative *"Okay. I'll try karaoke once. I'll never know unless I try."*
Repeat what's known *"I'm going to have lunch at my desk again, as always."*	Reach out to what's new *"I'm going to ask Donna if she'll have a picnic in the park with me."*
Safe *"You've got to be kidding. There's no way I'm going to try rafting."*	Scary *"I'm going to sign up for the raft trip this weekend. I've heard it's fun."*
Familiar *"I'm going to turn down that job offer. I'd have to move to a different town and I wouldn't know anyone."*	Frightening *"I'm going to accept that job offer. It will be a chance to stretch myself and meet new friends."*

This summer I stayed on Governors Island, which is across the bay from Manhattan by the Statue of Liberty. One morning I needed to ferry over by five-thirty A.M. to get myself uptown to a TV station to be interviewed on *Good Day New York,* then get myself downtown to meet with my editor and publisher, and finally get myself midtown to give a seminar for the Learning Annex. I had a choice. I could be courageous and drive (*Eeeek!*) or I could take the safe but expensive route and pay for taxis.

Now, I don't know how you feel about driving in big cities, but I'm used to commuting on two-lane roads through sugar-cane fields here on Maui. The very thought of trying to drive through unfamiliar streets in an unfamiliar van with six lanes of weaving, honking, speeding cars, trucks, and bicycles was enough to make me say, "No way." I know that thousands of people do it every day. I'm just not one of them and didn't want to be.

I asked myself, "What's the path of growth?" If I gave in and took a cab, then the next time I was in New York, I'd be faced with this same dilemma all over again. I wouldn't make any progress by giving in to my trepidation, I would only perpetuate the problem. The only way to get rid of my fears was to work through them. Sure, it scared me to drive in New York. But if I did it and survived, then this fear would no longer have the power to limit my life.

Suffice it to say, I took the van and arrived home late that evening in one piece. Yes, it was nerve-racking. Yes, there were close calls. Yes, I rode my brakes a lot and many New York drivers felt obliged to tell me exactly what they thought of my slowpoke driving. But I did it. And the next time I'm in New York, I'll do it again. Freedom has replaced that fear.

Bold Rush
━━━◉━━━

"Avoiding danger is no safer in the long run than outright exposure. The fearful are caught as often as the bold."
—HELEN KELLER

Are you thinking, "But what if you had taken that leap of faith and it *hadn't* turned out well?" This was one woman's fear. Adrienne said, "I've always wanted to have my own business, but what if I risk everything and end up bankrupt? What if my venture doesn't work out and I can't find another job? How can you take a risk confidently when you can't be sure how it's going to turn out?"

Good question. First, I asked Adrienne the type of business

she was interested in and what her qualifications were. "I'm a graphic artist," she explained. "At least that's what pays the bills. My hobby is calligraphy. I want to be an entrepreneur and make personalized invitations and announcements." Intrigued, I asked her if she had ever sold any. "Oh yes," she replied. "The first Saturday of every month, I have a booth at the swap meet. I usually sell all my stock of handmade stationery and note cards. I just don't know if I can make a living out of it."

Wise or Rash?
————◉————

"An individual dies . . . when, instead of taking risks and hurling himself toward being, he cowers within, and takes refuge there."
—E. M. CIORAN

I told Adrienne she was smart to evaluate risks *before* taking them. It's wise to examine fears to find out if they're well-founded. If we discover our misgivings are indeed justified, then hurling ourselves headfirst into the situation would be fool-hardy. If we discover that our fears are simply the natural discomfort we feel whenever we attempt something new, different, or a little beyond our current capabilities, then it's wise to face that fear instead of fleeing from it. Although we can never know for sure how things will work out, we can minimize the risk we are taking and maximize the likelihood that our leap of faith will land us on solid ground. We can influence the risk-reward ratio in our favor with the following five RISKS steps:

R = Research. Check to see if the precedents are positive. Has what you want to do been done before? If so, who did it, where, and how? Why reinvent the wheel? Learn from the experiences of others. Adrienne could check out the competition and the climate for the type of business she's planning. Is the market already saturated? Is there a need for her type of service? Is her industry likely to grow or decline?

I = Incubate. You can improve the odds of success by incubating the idea. Incubate means "to maintain . . . under conditions favorable for . . . development." That means to construct a viable backup plan. Could Adrienne continue with her current job for another year so she could build a nest egg to tide her over that first tough year in business?

S = Support group. Network with peers to obtain that all-important emotional support. Get involved with like-minded souls who can share your concerns, anxieties, hopes, and dreams. Could Adrienne get involved with a social club or professional association and surround herself with people who share her interests? Could she start making contacts within the crafts community so she had people to turn to in time of need?

K = Knowledge. Build your expertise and learn as much as you can about the skill, activity, or place. Could Adrienne take a Small Business Administration course and develop a sound business plan while learning about financial, legal, and personnel issues? Could she attend crafts seminars sponsored by successful artists to learn specific strategies for how to make it in the business?

S = See it as a done deal. Dane Rudhyar said, "Man can only become what he is able to consciously imagine, or to 'image forth.' " We move forward only when we have a clear destination in mind, and we have already imagined ourselves arriving there safe and sound. We wouldn't start our journey if we didn't know where we wanted to go and how we planned to get there. Could Adrienne post a picture of herself showing samples of her wares? Could she brainstorm a clever name for her company ("Write On!") and have a supply of business cards made up?

Chicken Soup for the Soul authors Jack Canfield and Mark Victor Hanson made a mock-up of the *New York Times* bestseller list with their book as number one a year *before* it was distributed widely. They both say they were so confident this book would succeed and they were so ready to take responsibility for making their dream come true that it didn't have a chance of doing otherwise.

No-Regret Risks
————— ◉ —————

"If you want to conquer fear, don't sit at home and think about it. Go out and get busy."

—DALE CARNEGIE

Finally, I told Adrienne, *after* she had evaluated all the risks and taken steps to minimize them, she might want to remember this story. Years ago I was asked to be the closing keynote speaker at a Women in Business conference. I will never forget the startling message of the panel that preceeded me. This panel featured five women who had all started their own business . . . and failed. Each told a heartbreaking story of pouring body, soul, and bank account into a venture, only to have it fold. Yet not *one* of them regretted starting her own business. They weren't happy they'd gone bankrupt, and they certainly wished they'd done things differently. But to a woman, they all said they weren't sorry they had taken the risk. They also agreed that they couldn't wait to open their own business again, a little more wisely this time, as a result of their experience.

Courage of Your Convictions
————— ◉ —————

"Courage is not simply one of the virtues, but the form of every virtue at the testing point."

—C. S. LEWIS

It takes courage, the "mental or moral strength to venture, persevere, and withstand danger, fear, or difficulty," to convince yourself to venture out of your comfort zone. "All adventures," noted astronaut Sally Ride, "especially into new territory, are scary." It is indeed scary to venture forth and take risks. You'll probably also find, as these entrepreneurs did, that it's worth it. From now on, when you're contemplating an adventure, picture yourself on the Confidence Continuum. Will this challenge move you forward on the path of growth? Will deciding not to do it cause you to retreat back into your comfort corner? Go for the growth.

Sample Starting Today Assignment

"To play it safe is not to play."
—ROBERT ALTMAN

To PLAY IT SAFE AND not take risks is to not live. What is a risk you're considering? Could you evaluate the RISKS to reduce the potential downsides and then take that leap of faith? What is something you want to try that's a little scary? Could you see yourself on the Confidence Continuum and ask yourself whether taking this action would move you forward or backward? Would choosing to do this build your confidence or block it? Today's assignment is to confront a fear and work through it, instead of retreating from it. Do something new, different, or a little beyond your current capabilities. Chances are, you won't regret doing it; you'll only regret *not* doing it. ◎

Action Plan for Facing and Erasing Your Fears

Lenny wants to ask a woman out, but he's afraid she'll turn him down. They work in the same building and he sees her fairly often in the halls and in the elevator. She's been friendly, but he doesn't know if she's "just being nice." He wants to build up enough confidence to ask her for a date.

BLOCKERS	BUILDERS
Avoid a fear, keep a fear *"I can't ask her out. If she said no, I couldn't face her again."*	Face a fear, erase a fear *"The only way I'll ever know if she's interested in me is to ask her out."*
Regrets *"She probably already has a boyfriend anyway. I'm just going to drop the whole thing. It was a dumb idea."*	Results *"I'll just ask her to meet me for lunch in the employee cafeteria. That's a low-risk date."*
Should I, shouldn't I? *"What could we talk about? I'd be so nervous around her I wouldn't know what to say."*	Go in *"I'll never know standing here on the beach. There she is. Go over and ask her."*
Unsure steps *"Uh, you wouldn't be interested in a date, would you?"*	Leap of faith *"Hello, I'm Lenny. I was wondering if you'd like to join me for lunch in the employee cafeteria tomorrow?"*
Rash risk *"I'll impress her and ask her to go skiing with me this weekend."*	Wise risk *"Or we could try the deli across the street if you like salads."*
Regret not taking action *"I'm such a chicken."*	No regrets because took action *"Good, I'll look forward to tomorrow."*

MY PERSONAL STARTING TODAY ASSIGNMENT

Starting today I'm going to _____
_____
_____

Signed _____ Date _____

Bring in the New

"I feel like I'm having a near-life experience."
- ZIGGY

You don't get to choose how you're going to die, or when," observed Joan Baez. "You can only decide how you're going to live now." The problem is many of us don't choose how we're going to live. We fall into routines, which become ruts, and life speeds by while we operate on automatic.

Are you in a groove or a rut? Alfred, Lord Tennyson said it best, "Come, my friends,'tis not too late to seek a newer world." The sad thing is, we rarely seek a newer world unless we have a SEE (significant emotional event). Most SEEs are traumatic: a loved one dies; our job gets eliminated; our partner asks for a divorce. These situations stop us in our tracks and force us to take stock of how we're spending our days. Our brutally honest assessment often leads to radical changes as we realize we've been leading a life that will lead to regrets.

Don't Wait for Regrets
◎

"It gets late early out there."
-YOGI BERRA

Why wait for a SEE? Let's not wait for a crisis to trigger our wake-up call. It's said, "We tend to waste what we don't value." Are you valuing your time, health, and loved ones, or are you wasting them? Are you acting as if you have all the time in the world? What if you don't? Andy Rooney noted, "Death is just a distant rumor to the young." Not just to the young. Time's a-wasting.

B-O-R-I-N-G
──── ◉ ────

"Someone's boring me. I think it's me."
-DYLAN THOMAS

A couple attended my course. They laughed out loud when I quoted author Alan Cohen's tongue-in-cheek question: "What I want to know is . . . is there life *before* death?" The husband commented, "We've been married for twenty-five years. We've become very comfortable together, perhaps too comfortable. Our idea of an evening out is moving the TV onto the patio." They realized they would like themselves and their marriage more if they kept their relationship fresh with new activities. Whether it was trying a new restaurant or exploring country roads, they vowed to do at least one thing "different" every week instead of doing the same thing month after month, year after year.

Tom Wilson's cartoon character Ziggy said, "Dawn! A brand-new day! This could be the start of something average." If you feel a lot of your days are the start of something average, it's time to do something out of the ordinary.

Routines or Ruts?
──── ◉ ────

"Variety is the mother of enjoyment."
-BENJAMIN DISRAELI

Most of us didn't intend to live ordinary lives. It's just that once we fall into routines, it's hard to climb out of them. It's time to evaluate whether our routines are adding to our quality of life or undermining it.

My friend Mary LoVerde tells a wonderful story about a young woman who felt locked into a ritual she hated. This woman lived in Hawaii and had promised her parents on the mainland that she would call every Saturday morning at nine A.M. She did this faithfully for months and had grown to resent this obligation. She couldn't go to the beach on a beautiful Saturday morning because she had to make that call. She couldn't sleep in because she had to phone them.

Mary suggested the woman summon up the courage to ask her folks if they would mind terribly if she called late Saturday afternoon instead. Mind? They preferred it! They admitted the ritual had constrained them as well and laughed ruefully about the months they had spent honoring an out-of-date tradition.

What activities do you do over and over? When was the last time you checked to see if they're serving any good purpose? How long has it been since you asked yourself if that time could be better spent elsewhere?

Change Up
◉

"Progress is a nice word, and change is its motivator."
-ROBERT KENNEDY

The importance of examining your arrangements to see if they still make sense was brought home to me years ago by my son Tom. A couple of weeks after starting first grade, Tom begged me to fix him a bag lunch. After hearing his descriptions of cafeteria cuisine (Meat Surprise!), I agreed. Those sack lunches turned into quite a chore. I was traveling constantly then, and many a night I'd get off a plane and find myself in the kitchen after midnight, after a long day on my feet, slapping ham on wheat bread. Some nights I even made late-night runs to the store to stock up on fruits and vegetables so my sons could have healthy lunches while I was away.

Imagine my shock when Tom approached me rather tentatively sometime later while I was making sandwiches for the umpteenth time. He said hesitantly, "Mom, I don't want to hurt your feelings, but could we *please* have cafeteria lunch?" Astonished, I said, "But, Tom, I thought you hated their food." "That was *last* year," he informed me. "We have a new cook this year and she's pretty good."

What obligations have you been keeping that are outdated? What agreements did you make years ago that may no longer be valid? If you check them out, you may be able to toss them out. If you discover behaviors that are no longer serving a useful purpose, have the confidence to speak up so you can move meaningless routines out of your life and make room for more meaningful ones.

Same Old, Same Old
◎

"Even if you're on the right track, you'll still get run over if you just sit there."

-MARK TWAIN

Twain's observation is so true. You may be thinking, "Everything in my life is running just fine. Why should I feel compelled to do anything differently?" Why, indeed? After all, didn't the great coach Vince Lombardi say, "Always change a losing game, never change a winning one?" If you already have a winning life, why change it?

My friend Colleen Butler, a personal trainer, informed me she and her boyfriend had decided to move. I asked, "Don't you like living in Kihei?" She said, "There's nothing wrong with Kihei, we're just ready for a change." That change ended up being a catalyst for several wonderful developments in their lives. Their new neighbors turned out to be a delightful couple with whom they've become good friends. Colleen discovered a gym a couple of blocks from her new home. On a whim she walked in, introduced herself, and asked if they needed someone to offer fitness consulting to their clients. The owner liked her style and hired her on the spot. That meant less commuting and more money for Colleen. None of these unanticipated delights would have happened if they'd stayed put.

How long have you stayed put? Are you ready for a change,

even if you don't know it? Robert South noted, "Novelty is the parent of pleasure." What unexpected pleasures could you discover simply by changing your scenery?

Open Yourself to Opportunity
◉

"Too many people are thinking of security instead of opportunity."
−JAMES F. BYRNES

Security is "freedom from fear or anxiety," while opportunity is defined as "a good chance for advancement or progress." Do these words appear mutually exclusive? I don't think they have to be. Confident people seek both security *and* opportunity in their lives. The key is to have a balance between the two.

If you've had an unstable lifestyle, perhaps the last thing you want right now is *more* anxiety. You crave security and plan to pass on opportunities to grow for a while. This was the situation for a woman named Martha. "I understand that for most people, a change of scenery is a good idea. But I was married to a career diplomat for thirty years. During that time we lived in eighteen different cities and countries. For me, staying put in one place is sheer bliss."

Good for her. Martha was a good example of "to each her own." Part of confidence is knowing what's right for you.

Sometimes, though, too much security constitutes boredom. Years ago, my husband Les and I started what we called Surprise Date Nights. One of us takes the responsibility for thinking up a fun activity. The organizer makes all the plans and just tells the other one when and where to be ready. We have gone horseback riding, sailed on an America's Cup yacht, rented a beach cottage, seen jazz vocalist Joe Williams at the Blue Note, and flown a private plane to the island of Lanai.

One of our favorite adventures was the time Les rung me down to the lobby of the Waikiki apartment building in which we were living at the time. I emerged from the elevator to find Les, grinning from ear to ear and sitting in an antique Packard convertible. The top was down and our best friends were en-

sconced in the rumble seat, a huge picnic basket resting between them. Off we went for a day of touring the island. A rain
shower that soaked us only added to the fun.

Could you institute Surprise Date Days with your partner,
kids, or friends? Rotate the responsibility so everyone gets a
chance to be in charge. You don't have to do anything radical,
just take a mini-sabbatical.

No More Monotony
⊙

"Monotony is the awful reward of the careful."
-A. G. BUCKHAM

Monotony is also the reward of the unimaginative. All it takes is
a little investment of imagination to make life eminently more
likable. Since confidence is liking yourself and your life, any effort you put into enlivening your days will pay off directly in
increased self-esteem.

A young participant reported back to me. "My friend and I
had really gotten into a rut. Every Friday and Saturday night we
went to a mall and/or a movie. That was it. That was the extent
of our big nights out on the town. After your workshop, I talked
with her about being more creative. We live in a large city, so
there's tons of stuff for us to do; we just weren't taking advantage of any of it. We decided that every Friday we would look
through the weekend section of the newspaper and force ourselves to try something different. We've been to a couple of neat
dances, tried a country-western nightclub, gone to several con-
certs, attended some college football games, and seen the Ice
Capades. We've done more fun things in the last three months
than we have in the last three years. Now a lot of our friends
are asking if they can come along on our adventures."

G. K. Chesterton observed poetically, "Adventure is the
champagne of life." Drink up.

Sample Starting Today Assignment

"Is not life a hundred times too short for us to bore ourselves?"
—FRIEDRICH NIETZSCHE

WE CAN REST OR WE can rust, it's up to us. Not many of us have too much rest on our hands, but we may have too much rust. Leo Tolstoy said, "Boredom is the desire for desires." What do you desire? How can you refresh your life? What is something different you can do that would "bring in the new"? Reevaluate your routines to see if they could be updated. Discard old rituals and develop new, more meaningful ones. Replace boredom with a brand-new outlook, and see if you don't have a healthier regard for yourself and your powers . . . for the *rest* of your days. ◎

Action Plan for Bringing in the New

Clara and her family always went to their cabin by the lake for summer vacation. Her parents had taken her and her sisters to the cabin every July, and it had been a Smith family tradition for years. They had a good time, but Clara is wondering if maybe they couldn't spend two of their four weeks differently.

BLOCKERS	BUILDERS
Put off changes until you have a SEE	Pretend to have a SEE so you can make some changes
"We've been going to the cabin every summer for thirty years. Why change now?"	*"If I only had a couple more months to live, would I really want to spend it at the same old place?"*

Bored
"I know it's not very exciting, but it's cheap."

Bold
"I'm going to start saving money, and we'll go somewhere we've never been before."

Meaningless ruts
"We drive over to the old mining camp every year whether we want to or not."

Meaningful rituals
"Why don't we take a video camera this year and record all the Smith family stories?"

Doing something radical
"I'm going to call Mom and Dad and tell them we're not coming this year."

Taking a mini-sabbatical
"I'll call Mom and Dad and let them know we'll just be there for a couple of weeks this year instead of four."

Eliminate something old
"We're never going back there again. Enough already."

Initiate something new
"We'll go to the cabin and try a new activity or place every summer."

MY PERSONAL STARTING TODAY ASSIGNMENT

Starting today I'm going to _____

_____

_____

Signed _____ Date _____

Dare to Dream

"Stories were full of hearts broken by love, but what really broke a heart was taking away its dream—
whatever that dream might be."
–PEARL S. BUCK

Have you had a dream that has been taken away? Confidence is a by-product of actualizing our dreams instead of abandoning them. Is your lifestyle congruent with what you imagined for yourself?

In one workshop, a man said cynically, "My dreams have turned into nightmares. My life is not even close to what I wanted it to be." Cynicism does not serve us. What does serve us is understanding that while we may not have everything we want, we can keep from being heartbroken as long as we have at least one thing we want. We can continue to feel alive as long as we keep one of our dreams alive.

One woman asked plaintively, "That's the $64,000 question. How can you figure out what that one thing is?" Good question. You can identify your long-buried dreams by taking a few minutes to answer these thought-provoking questions. They can help uncover and clarify what you really care about. Promise yourself you'll answer these questions honestly, even if the answers aren't "politically correct." The point is to find out what you want to do, not what you think you should want, and not what others think you should want.

Three Questions to Determine Your Dreams

—◎—

"To dare is to lose one's footing momentarily. To not dare is to lose one's soul."

—SØREN KIERKEGAARD

1. Pretend you've been to the doctor and he's given you the bad news that you have less than a month to live. What are two things you'd want to do if you only had a month left? Please understand I'm not trying to be morbid. It's just that, as I've said before, many of us don't face our mortality unless we have a crisis. I want you to use this question as a *painless* SEE (significant emotional event) so you can get the benefit of the wake-up call without the cost.

2. What one thing would you love to achieve in the next three years? What is something you've always wanted to do? Accomplishing this would cause you to look back and say to yourself, "That was time well spent."

3. Think back five years ago. What were you doing then? Where were you living? Where were you working? What kind of relationships were you in? Have you made progress since then? Are you satisfied with the progress, or in your heart, do you know you'd rather be doing something else?

Have Your Dreams Been Derailed?

───────◎───────

"We don't want to get to the top of the ladder and find out it's against the wrong wall."

–POPULAR T-SHIRT SAYING

Answering these questions can help you identify your heart priorities as opposed to your head priorities. Our heart priorities are how we'd like to spend our time. Our head priorities are how we think we ought to spend our time.

If our life consists only of head priorities, we are leading a life that will lead to regrets. It's not reasonable or responsible to think we can abandon all our "have to" obligations. What we *can* and *must* do is actively pursue at least one of our "want to" priorities to compensate for the parts of our lives that aren't to our liking.

A Dream Come True

───────◎───────

"A poem is never finished—only abandoned."

–PAUL VALÉRY

A participant in a workshop was definitely suffering from "ladder against the wrong wall" syndrome. This woman had been accepted to the well-respected UCLA film school, but had been forced to drop out. "When I first received that confirmation letter from UCLA, it was like a dream come true. I loved every minute of every class. I wanted to make documentaries, and the professors were very encouraging of my projects. The problem was, my parents missed me. I'm an only child and we've always been very close. My mom and dad started getting health problems. Every time they called, something else was wrong. They didn't want to put pressure on me, but I didn't feel right being so far away when they weren't well. I quit college after that first year and returned home."

The young woman continued with her story. "I needed to make some money to help pay bills, and the first good job I could find was with the post office. I'm taking this class because I've lost every shred of my self-esteem. I'm not very good at sorting mail, and I don't fit in at work. Most of my co-workers have been there for years, and they've been giving me a really hard time. I've never been this unhappy before, and I don't know what to do."

I told her, "Just because you couldn't finish film school doesn't mean you have to abandon your dream. It's important to think of your parents, and it's also important to think of yourself. It may not be an option for you to move back to the mainland and return to school, and with today's tough job market it's unrealistic to expect to land your ideal job. You can at least compensate for the creative void in your life by getting involved with the local movie industry. Maybe you can help out with the international film festival and surround yourself with kindred souls who share your interests. Perhaps you could call the local public broadcasting station, and ask if there are any local filmmakers who need help editing their work. Maybe you could make a video documentary of your folk's life. It's not selfish of you to pursue a heart priority, it's smart."

Someday . . .
━━━━━◉━━━━━

"We are always getting ready to live but never living."
-RALPH WALDO EMERSON

Perhaps you're clear about what you want to do, but you're putting it off because of some "I'll do it when's." For example, "I'll travel when I retire." "I'll spend more time with the kids when it's not so busy at work." "I'll start my own business when the economy's not so bad."

What if those "I'll do it when's" never happen? Confident people don't wait for ideal circumstances. They understand there will never be a perfect time—they've got to make time *now* for the important things in their lives.

One of my favorite success stories concerns a woman whose dream was to have her own home, but her "I'll do it when" was she'd have it when she got married. When she reached forty-five, she finally admitted she might not ever get married. She confessed, "At first this realization filled me with despair. I had always wanted a family and a house filled with kids. I just kept waiting for the right man, but he never showed up. I decided since meeting the man of my dreams wasn't in my control, I'd better take action on the dreams I could control.

"I bought a parcel of land (this was back when you could afford real estate in Hawaii) and designed my ideal house with the help of an architect. I oversaw every aspect of the entire construction project. Now every day when I come home and pull into my driveway (that I helped pour!), I have concrete proof of my power to make my life what I want it to be." That's confidence!

Hope Is a Risk We Must Run
◎

"Everything that is done in the world is done by hope."
—MARTIN LUTHER

What do you hope for? Victor Hugo suggested, "There is nothing like a dream to create the future." My friend John Tullius had dreamed of creating a world-class writers conference in Maui that would be to the publishing industry what Cannes is to the movie industry. Everyone told him it couldn't be done. Naysayers came up with dozens of reasons it wouldn't work. John persisted. He was clear in his vision and determined not to give up hope.

Two months after he articulated his idea, it became reality. Pulitzer Prize–winning poet W. S. Merwin was the opening keynote speaker at that first conference, and a 150 people attended. As I write this, we've just wrapped up our fourth annual conference. This event is now held at a five-diamond resort and attracts over a thousand people from around the globe. Headliners have included *Ransom* and *Apollo 13* director Ron Howard, *Rain Man* screenwriter Ron Bass, best-selling novelists John Saul, Sue Grafton, Ann Rule, and Terry Brooks, *Peaceful Warrior* Dan Millman, president of Doubleday Arlene Friedman, Random House executive vice-president Bob Loomis, and dozens of other respected agents, editors, authors, poets, and journalists.

Better yet, dozens of wannabe writers have become published authors because of the advice they received and the contacts they made at this four-day meeting. Many aspiring writers have connected with fellow scribes who share their passion for the written word. Many would-be novelists have learned valuable tips about their craft. All because one man had a dream and wouldn't give up hope.

Tom Bodett said, "They say a person needs just three things to be truly happy in this world. Someone to love, something to do, and something to hope for." What is your dream? What good could you achieve for yourself and others if you refused to give up hope?

Sample Starting Today Assignment

"Destiny is not a mater of chance, it is a matter of choice; it is not a thing to be waited for, it is a thing to be achieved."
—WILLIAM JENNINGS BRYAN

DON'T ABANDON YOUR DREAMS, ACTUALIZE them. Your assignment is to take a dream off the shelf and set about making it a reality. Identify a heart priority and set about achieving it. Don't wait for chance or an "I'll do it when." Commit to designing your destiny now, not someday. What specific steps are you going to use to put your hope into action? Resolve to keep the faith so you can soar over obstacles instead of run into them. John Barrymore said, "A man is not old until regrets take the place of dreams." Dare to dream, and you won't regret it. ◉

Action Plan for Daring to Dream

Dennis had always wanted to be a pilot. He had joined the Air Force hoping to be a jet jockey, but his eyesight wasn't good enough to pass the qualifying exam. He's always told himself he would pursue his license when the last kid was out of the house and he had the extra time and money to spend. He just packed the last kid off to college and is faced with decision time.

BLOCKERS	BUILDERS
Dull *"I'm forty-five years old, and I'm locked into a $120,000 mortgage."*	Dream *"I've always wanted to take flying lessons. Why not do it now while I still can?"*
Leading a life that will lead to regrets *"I'll do it when it slows down at work."*	Leading a life that will lead to results *"I'm going to call the general aviation field today, and see who their best instructor is."*
A life of desperation *"All I ever do is commute, work, come home, and pay bills."*	A life of deliberation *"I'm going to do this one thing for myself. I deserve it."*
Delay or defer our destiny *"Sundays are the only days this instructor has free time. That's usually when I do the yard. I'll call again in a couple of months."*	Design our destiny *"Please sign me up for the ten-lesson program starting Sunday at three P.M."*

MY PERSONAL STARTING TODAY ASSIGNMENT

Starting today I'm going to _____

_____

_____

Signed _____ Date _____

PART VIII

From Start to Finish

*"All the beautiful sentiments in the world weigh
less than a single lovely action."*

- JAMES RUSSELL LOWELL

Ready, Set, Grow!

"What a wonderful life I've had! I only wish I'd realized it sooner."
— C O L E T T E

Realize what a wonderful life you can have *right now*, if you just follow up and practice these skills until they produce tangible results.

I hope you've enjoyed the book and, more important, followed up and put these ideas into action. As Ben Franklin said, "Well *done* is better than well *said*." The following summary gives you an opportunity to set your priorities and plan your action steps.

To Sum It All Up
⊙

"Great thoughts reduced to practice become great acts."
— W I L L I A M   H A Z L I T T

C = Coach your mistakes and set up a success spiral.
O = Open your mind and heart to the wonder of your life.
N = Needs in balance. Speak up for your rights. Be appropriately assertive.
F = Face your fears. Take wise risks and bring in the new.
I = Initiate. Don't wait for friends or recognition to come to you.
D = Dare to dream. Actualize a meaningful goal.

E = Example and Excellence. Behave with integrity and hold yourself accountable.

N = No comparing. Admire or aspire instead.

C = Cultivate friendships with gracious social skills.

E = Encourage and educate. Be kind to others and pass on your knowledge.

Don't Wait
⊙

"I shall tell you a great secret, my friend. Do not wait for the last judgment, it takes place every day."
–ALBERT CAMUS

John Ciardi noted that "The day will happen whether you get up or not." Your life will happen whether you appreciate it or not. How much better though to take full advantage of this blessing we've been given—to fill our days with hope rather than despair, to spend our time wisely and playfully, and to engage in meaningful service instead of selfish consumption.

Are you thinking, "These ideas might work for other people, but not for me?" Tell that to the widower who ended up cruising around the world *free* because he had the courage to apply to be a ship's "eligible bachelor." Russ said, "When I first heard about this escort program, all my old doubts crept in. I worried that I wasn't sophisticated or good-looking enough, and told myself that there were probably thousands of other candidates and I'd never get chosen.

"I looked through my notes from your class and realized I was doing all the things I told myself I wouldn't do anymore. I filled out my application and mailed it that day. Lo and behold, two weeks later they called to see if I was available to sail on a cruise through the Panama Canal and up the coast of Mexico. Was I! That was just the first of several voyages I've made as a gentleman host, and I owe it all to having the guts to GO IN!"

Oscar Levant said, "It's not what you are, it's what you don't become that hurts." The tools for becoming more confident, for leading the life you were meant to lead, are here, laid out for you. Pick them up. Use them. Become what you're capable of being.

The High Road to Confidence
---⊙---

"Everything we do and say contributes to what we become. We might not be able to identify any specific source because there are a multitude of facts. Every kindness done to others, every prejudice overcome, every difficulty subdued, every temptation trampled underfoot, every step forward in the cause of what is good is a step nearer to the goal of being the person we have the potential to be."
—DEAN STANLEY

I hope, under the umbrella topic of confidence, you've learned dozens of ways to improve the quality of your everyday life. You've learned how to be more poised, polished, and powerful. The rest is up to you.

Keep this book where you continue to see it. Please don't put it away on a high shelf. Keep it handy. Every once in a while, serendipitously open it up to a page and read the message that's waiting for you there. It might be just what you needed to hear to keep you on the high road to confidence.

A team of readers edited the first draft of this manuscript. It was a tremendously rewarding experience, not only because they made content suggestions and caught grammatical errors, but because they volunteered encouraging words on how the ideas had already benefited them. One reader said, "Sam, you asked us not to share this information with anyone until it was published, but I couldn't help myself. I started taking a chapter with me every morning when I walked with my friend. We had the most fascinating conversations as a result. We answered the questions, discussed how particular aspects affected us, and completed the action plans.

"At the end of each walk, we both came up with our own Starting Today Assignment and then reported what happened the next morning. An indication of how much we enjoyed your manuscript is that we finished it together on Friday . . . and we're starting it all over again on Monday!"

What gratifying feedback. Perhaps you can share *Concrete Confidence* with someone, too. It would give both of you an opportunity to review and reinforce the information. The chance to swap perspectives, insights, and experiences with a friend could double your pleasure, double your fun.

The End Is the Beginning
───────── ◎ ─────────

"When you finally allow yourself to trust joy and embrace it, you will find you dance with everything."

-EMMANUAL

The quest for confidence is never really finished; however, it is my hope that reading this has helped you start your quest for concrete confidence and that you choose to continue it so you can maximize your effectiveness and enjoyment at work, home, school, and in sports and social situations. Continuing to take these steps is the key to acquiring and maintaining an unshakable self-assurance that allows you to trust and embrace yourself. As a result, you will dance with life.

Reverend David Stier said, "Let us always be open to the miracle of the second chance." May *Concrete Confidence* be your second chance at a first-class life.

POSTSCRIPT

Receiving feedback from readers is one of the most rewarding aspects of being an author. It means a lot when someone says, "The ideas in your book really work!"

I hope *Concrete Confidence* has inspired you to make some changes that have resulted in tangible benefits. Would you please take a few minutes to let me know how it impacted you? Did a particular suggestion or story touch you in some way and/or motivate you to take action? Do you have an anecdote you'd like to share? Would you like to contribute some of your own "lessons-learned" about how to become more confident?

There are several ways to contact us: snail mail, phone, fax, or e-mail. You are also welcome to check out our ACTION SEMINARS Web site. We frequently update it with news of media appearances, magazine articles, and sample chapters. Want to stay in touch? Request our free quarterly newsletter that features how-to columns, a public workshop schedule, and an order form for my other books and tapes.

I travel frequently on the mainland and would be glad to talk with you about presenting a seminar for your organization. Both *Tongue Fu!* and *Concrete Confidence* are delivered in a fun, fast-paced style that focuses on real-life information your employees and convention participants can use on and off the job. Call to discuss availability, your group's needs and fees, and/or to request a comprehensive information packet.

I look forward to hearing from you. Mahalo.

Hawaii Office	U.S. Mainland Office
Sam Horn	Cheri Grimm
P.O. Box 99	P.O. Box 6810
Kihei, HI 96753	Los Osos, CA 93412
808-879-5661 Fax 808-879-0441	805-528-4351 Fax 805-528-2581
e-mail: sam@samhorn.com	infor@samhorn.com

Web site: http://www.bookfair.com/welcome/tonguefu/book

SAM HORN, president of Action Seminars, has presented her real-life workshops to more than 400,000 people since 1981. Her impressive client list includes the Young Presidents Organization, the National Governors Association, Hewlett-Packard, Four Seasons Resort, the *Fortune 500* Forum, the US Navy, and the IRS. She was the top-rated speaker at both the 1996 and 1998 International Platform Association conventions in Washington, D.C., and is the emcee of the world-renowned Maui Writers Conference. She is also the author of *Tongue Fu!*® and *Conzentrate*. Her work has been featured in *Reader's Digest, The Washington Post*, the *Chicago Tribune, Cosmopolitan, Family Circle, Bottom Line Personal,* and *Executive Female,* to name a few. She lives with her sons Tom and Andrew in Maui, Hawaii.